Inequality, Polarization and Poverty

ECONOMIC STUDIES IN INEQUALITY, SOCIAL EXCLUSION AND WELL-BEING

This series will publish volumes that go beyond the traditional concepts of consumption, income or wealth and will offer a broad, inclusive view of inequality and well-being. Specific areas of interest will include Capabilities and Inequalities, Discrimination and Segregation in the Labor Market, Equality of Opportunities, Globalization and Inequality, Human Development and the Quality of Life, Income and Social Mobility, Inequality and Development, Inequality and Happiness, Inequality and Malnutrition, Inequality in Consumption and Time Use, Inequalities in Health and Education, Multidimensional Inequality and Poverty Measurement, Polarization among Children and Elderly People, Social Policy and the Welfare State, and Wealth Distribution.

Volume 1
De Janvry, Alain and Kanbur, Ravi
Poverty, Inequality and Development: Essays in Honor of Erik Thorbecke

Volume 2
Duclos, Jean-Yves and Araar, Abdelkrim
Poverty and Equity: Measurement, Policy and Estimation with DAD

Volume 3
Lemmi, Achille and Betti, Gianni
Fuzzy Set Approach to Multidimensional Poverty Measurement

Volume 4
Wagle, Udaya
Multidimensional Poverty Measurement: Concepts and Applications

Volume 5
Chotikapanich, Duangkamon
Modeling Income Distributions and Lorenz Curves

Volume 6
Chakravarty, Satya
Inequality, Polarization and Poverty: Advances in Distributional Analysis

Inequality, Polarization and Poverty

Advances in Distributional Analysis

Satya R. Chakravarty
Indian Statistical Institute
Economic Research Unit
203 B.T. Road
Kolkata
India

Springer

Satya R. Chakravarty
Indian Statistical Institute
Economic Research Unit
203 B.T. Road
Kolkata-700108
India
Email: satya@isical.ac.in

Series Editor

Jacques Silber
Bar-Ilan University
Ramat Gan
Israel

ISBN: 978-1-4419-2716-3 e-ISBN: 978-0-387-79253-8

DOI: 10.1007/978-0-387-79253-8

Softcover reprint of the hardcover 1st edition 2009

Printed on acid-free paper

springer.com

In memory of
Professor Prabhat Sarbadhikari,
a great teacher of Quantitative Economics

Preface

This book provides a synthesis of some recent issues and an up-to-date treatment of some of the major important issues in distributional analysis that I have covered in my previous book *Ethical Social Index Numbers*, which was widely accepted by students, teachers, researchers and practitioners in the area. Wide coverage of on-going and advanced topics and their analytical, articulate and authoritative presentation make the book theoretically and methodologically quite contemporary and inclusive, and highly responsive to the practical problems of recent concern.

Since many countries of the world are still characterized by high levels of income inequality, Chap. 1 analyzes the problems of income inequality measurement in detail. Poverty alleviation is an overriding goal of development and social policy. To formulate antipoverty policies, research on poverty has mostly focused on income-based indices. In view of this, a substantive analysis of income-based poverty has been presented in Chap. 2.

The subject of Chap. 3 is people's perception about income inequality in terms of deprivation. Since polarization is of current concern to analysts and social decision-makers, a discussion on polarization is presented in Chap. 4.

A very important development of inequality and poverty research in recent years is the shift of emphasis from a single dimension to a multidimensional structure. The reason for this is that the well-being of a population and hence its inequality and poverty depend on many dimensions of human life, such as health, employment, shelter, education and life expectancy, and income is just one such dimension. In this framework, poverty is defined as a human condition that reflects failures in these types of dimensions. Multidimensional inequality and poverty are analyzed respectively in Chaps. 5 and 6. The *Extended Bibliography* goes someway towards guiding the readers in more details.

Since the publication of *Ethical Social Index Numbers* in 1990, I have worked jointly in this expanding area with Walter Bossert, Francois Bourguignon, Nachiketa Chattopadhyay, Conchita D'Ambrosio, Joseph Deutsch, Wolfgang Eichhorn, Ravi Kanbur, Amita Majumder, Patrick Moyes, Diganta Mukherjee, Pietro Muliere, Ravi Ranade, Sonali Roy, Jacques Silber, Swami Tyagarupananda and Claudio Zoli. I am grateful to them for the benefit I derived from the direct interactions with them as my coauthors. During the period, I have also interacted with Sabina Alkire, Yoram Amiel, Tony Atkinson, Charles Blackorby, Frank A. Cowell, David Donaldson, Udo Ebert, Gary S. Fields, James E. Foster, Nanak C. Kakwani, Serge-Christophe Kolm, Peter J. Lambert, Amartya K. Sen, Tony Shorrocks, Kai-Yuen Tsui, John A. Weymark, Shlomo Yitzhaki and Buhong Zheng. I express my sincere gratitude to all of them.

Amita Majumder, Chiranjib Neogi and my young friends of the Computer Maintenance Corporation (CMC) Limited were always available for computer advice and help. Satyajit Malakar has drawn all the figures. It is a pleasure for me to acknowledge their support. My wife Sumita sat through some sessions of proofreading. I must thank Sumita and my son Ananyo without whose cooperation this book could not possibly have been written.

Contents

Chapter 1
The Measurement of Income Inequality

1.1 Introduction

Given the population size and the distribution of income, the two questions that arise in a person's mind are: what is the mean income and how unequally is the total income distributed among the individuals in the society? Loosely speaking, income inequality represents interpersonal income differences within a given population. Income inequality has become a growing concern for the policymakers because it has important effects on development, poverty, social outcomes, and public finance. In terms of social outcomes, inequality has impacts on several issues, including, health, education, incidence of crime, and violence (Deaton, 2001). The levels and heterogeneity of local inequality may affect tax collection and influence the decentralization of provision of public goods (Bardahan and Mookherjee, 2006). For a given mean income, high inequality generally implies high poverty. Development studies and public finance often employ indicators of inequality to evaluate a distribution of income or the distributional effects of a particular economic policy. Some of the standard questions that arise in this context are: (1) Is inequality in the country lower now than it was in the past? (2) Does region I of the country have more inequality than region II? (3) How much of total inequality arises because of variations of the mean incomes in different regions of the country?

According to Dalton (1920), measurement of inequality should involve social judgments. He argued that social judgment concerning measurement of inequality can be made explicit using a social welfare function that can rank alternative distributions of income in terms of society's preference. The modern social welfare approach to the measurement of inequality has been initiated by Kolm (1969), Atkinson (1970), and Sen (1973).[1] A discussion on welfare theoretic approaches to the measurement of inequality necessitates an investigation of welfare evaluation of

[1] See also Blackorby and Donaldson (1978, 1980a), Weymark (1981), Ebert (1987, 1988a), Shorrocks (1988), Chakravarty (1990, 2008a), Foster and Sen (1997), Blackorby et al. (1999, 2005) and Lambert (2001).

S.R. Chakravarty, *Inequality, Polarization and Poverty: Advances in Distributional Analysis,* Economic Studies in Inequality, Social Exclusion and Well-Being 6,
DOI: 10.1007/978-0-387-79253-8_1,

income distributions. This in turn requires a discussion on the use of the stochastic dominance approach to the assessment of inequality and welfare.

Often we may be interested in determining the significance of income variations associated with characteristics like race, occupation, region, age, etc. This requires breakdown of total inequality into its between- and within-group components for the partitioning of the population using the characteristic under consideration. It is likely that households will differ in size, composition, and needs. These attributes will determine the types of the households. In such a case, inequality and welfare evaluation of households should take into account income and type simultaneously.

The objective of this chapter is to present an extensive and analytical discussion on the measurement of income inequality. Welfare assessment of income distributions, stochastic dominance, postulates for an index of inequality and their implications, relationship between indices of inequality and welfare functions under alternative notions of inequality invariance, inequality as an ordinal concept, decomposition of inequality from alternative perspectives, and measurement of inequality when needs differ are investigated in detail.

1.2 Preliminaries

For a population of size n, a typical income distribution is a vector $x = (x_1, x_2, ..x_n)$, where $x_i \geq 0$ is the income of person i. It is assumed that no ambiguity arises with the definitions of income, income earning unit, and the reference period over which income is observed. For a fixed $n \geq 1$, the set of all income distributions is Γ^n, the nonnegative orthant of the n-dimensional Euclidean space R^n with the origin deleted. The set of all possible income distributions is $\Gamma = \bigcup_{n\in N} \Gamma^n$, where N is the set of positive integers. The positive parts of Γ^n and Γ are denoted, respectively, by Γ^n_+ and Γ_+. Let D^n be that subset of Γ^n in which all income distributions are nondecreasingly ordered or illfare-ranked, that is, for all $x \in D^n, x_1 \leq x_2 \leq .... \leq x_n$. The corresponding subsets of R^n_+, the nonnegative part of R^n, and Γ^n_+ are denoted, respectively, by $\hat{R}^n_+$ and D^n_+. We will write D, $\hat{R}_+$, and D_+, respectively, for the sets of all possible income distributions corresponding to D^n, $\hat{R}^n_+$, and D^n_+. Likewise, $R_+ = \bigcup_{n\in N} R^n_+ . 1^n$ will stand for the n-coordinated vector of ones. Unless specified, we will restrict our attention to the domains D^n and D. For any $n-$ person income distribution x, let $\lambda(x)$ (or simply λ) be the mean income. Thus, if $x \in D^n$ or D^n_+, $\lambda(x) > 0$. For any $x, y \in D^n, x \geq y$ means that $x_i \geq y_i$ for all $1 \leq i \leq n$, with $>$ for some i.

Definition 1.1. A function $H : D^n \to R^1$ is called concave if $H(tx + (1-t)y) \geq tH(x) + (1-t)H(y)$ for all $x, y \in D^n$ and for all $0 \leq t \leq 1$. For a strictly concave function $H : D^n \to R^1$, the defining inequality is $H(tx + (1-t)y) > tH(x) + (1-t)H(y)$ for all $0 < t < 1$ and for all $x, y \in D^n$, where $x \neq y$. A function $H : D^n \to R^1$ is called convex(strictly convex) if $-H : D^n \to R^1$ is concave (strictly concave).

Definition 1.2. An $n \times n$ nonnegative matrix A is called a bistochastic matrix of order n if each of its rows and columns sums to unity. If a bistochastic matrix has exactly one positive entry in each row and column, then it is called a permutation matrix.

Definition 1.3. A function $H : D^n \to R^1$ is called symmetric if $H(x\Pi) = H(x)$ for all $x \in D^n$, where Π is any permutation matrix of order n.

Symmetry is an anonymity condition. It means that the functional value of H remains unaltered under any reordering of its arguments.

Definition 1.4. A function $H : D^n \to R^1$ is called S-concave if $H(xA) \geq H(x)$ for all $x \in D^n$, where A is any bistochastic matrix of order n. For strict S-concavity of H, the weak inequality is to be replaced by a strictly inequality whenever xA is not a permutation of x. A function $H : D^n \to R^1$ is called S-convex (strictly S-convex) if $-H : D^n \to R^1$ is S-concave (strictly S-concave).

All S-concave and S-convex functions are symmetric.

Definition 1.5. For $x, y \in D^n$, we say that x is obtained from y by a rank-preserving progressive transfer, which is denoted by $x = \mathrm{RP}(y)$, if for some $i, j (i < j)$ and $\hat{c} > 0$, $x_l = y_l$ for all $l \neq i, j$; $x_i - y_i = y_j - x_j = \hat{c}$, where $\hat{c} \leq (y_j - y_i)/2$ if $j = i + 1$; $\hat{c} \leq \min\{(y_{i+1} - y_i), (y_j - y_{j-1})\}$ if $j > i + 1$.

That is, x and y are identical except for a rank-preserving positive transfer of $\hat{c}$ amount of income from the rich person j to the poor person i. The condition is equivalent to the statement that y can be obtained from x through a rank-preserving regressive transfer. Note that there can be $n!$ orderings of the population set containing n persons. We can restrict our attention to any one of them. For convenience, we have considered the natural illfare-ordering $\{1, 2, \ldots, n\}$. Since x and y belong to the same rank-preserving subset, all transfers have to be rank preserving (*see* Fields and Fei, 1978). Note that for a particular pair (i, j), rank preservation allows a maximum amount of income transfer.

In general, a progressive transfer should not change the relative positions of the donor and the recipient, that is, it should not make the donor poorer than the recipient (Dalton, 1920; Pigou, 1912). Formally, for $x, y \in \Gamma^n$, x is obtained from y by a progressive transfer, if there is a pair (i, j) such that $x_i - y_i = y_j - x_j = \hat{\eta} > 0$, $y_j - \hat{\eta} \geq y_i + \hat{\eta}$, and $x_l = y_l$ for all $l \neq i, j$. That is, there is a transfer of a positive amount of income $\hat{\eta}$ from y_j to a lower income y_i so that $x_j = y_j - \hat{\eta}$ and $x_i = y_i + \hat{\eta}$, satisfying the restriction that $y_j - \hat{\eta} \geq y_i + \hat{\eta}$. The condition $x_l = y_l$ for all $l \neq i, j$ ensures that all other incomes remain unaffected by the transfer. Although the transfer cannot make the donor (j) poorer than the recipient (i), their income positions relative to the income positions of the others may change. Note that the progressive transfer is now defined for the entire n-person income distribution space Γ^n. However, this definition coincides with Definition 1.5 when x and y belong to the set D^n (*see* Fields and Fei, 1978).

A progressive transfer can be equivalently expressed in terms of a T-transformation (Marshall and Olkin, 1979; Chap. 2). A T-transformation is a linear transformation defined by an $n \times n$ matrix T of the form

$$T = t\mathrm{IM}_n + (1-t)\Pi_{ij}, \tag{1.1}$$

for some $t \in (0,1)$ and some $i, j \in \{1,2,..,n\}$, where IM_n is the $n \times n$ identity matrix, that is, the matrix all of whose diagonal elements are one and off-diagonal elements are zero, and Π_{ij} is the $n \times n$ permutation matrix that interchanges the i and j coordinates. Letting $x = yT$, where $x, y \in \Gamma^n$, it can be verified that $x_i = ty_i + (1-t)y_j$, $x_j = (1-t)y_i + ty_j$, and $x_l = y_l$ for all $l \notin \{i, j\}$.

Definition 1.6. For $x, y \in D^n$, x is said to be obtained from y by a rank-preserving simple increment if $y_j < x_j \leq y_{j+1}$ for some j and $x_i = y_i$ for all $i \neq j$.

Since income distributions in D^n are ordered, only rank-preserving simple increments are allowed. However, if $x, y \in \Gamma^n$, then x is said to be obtained from y by a simple increment if $y_j < x_j$ for some j and $x_i = y_i$ for all $i \neq j$. Again, this definition coincides with Definition 1.6 when x and y belong to the set D^n. The following definition is taken from Fields and Fei (1978).

Definition 1.7. For $x, y \in D^n$, we say that x is obtained from y by a sequence of rank-preserving progressive transfers if $x = \mathrm{RP}_l[\ldots\mathrm{RP}_2(\mathrm{RP}_1(y))]$, where the subscripts indicate alternative stages of the rank-preserving transfers and $l \geq 1$ is an integer.

Suppose we first generate the distribution y' from y by the operation RP, that is, $y' = \mathrm{RP}(y)$. Since this is the first stage of the operation, we denote this by $y' = \mathrm{RP}_1(y)$. Next, we employ the operation RP on y' and because this is the second stage of the operation, we have $\mathrm{RP}(y') = \mathrm{RP}_2(\mathrm{RP}_1(y))$. Continuing this way, we arrive at x.

1.3 Welfare Evaluation of Income Distributions

A very useful and attractive approach to the welfare comparisons of alternative income distributions relies on the Lorenz curve. For any given income distribution x, its Lorenz curve represents the share of the total income enjoyed by the bottom $t(0 \leq t \leq 1)$ proportion of the population. Given $x \in D^n$, $\mathrm{LC}(x, j/n) = \sum_{i=1}^{j} x_i/n\lambda(x)$, the share of the total income possessed by the cumulative j/n proportion of the population gives us the ordinate of the Lorenz curve of x at the proportion j/n. The Lorenz curve of x, $\mathrm{LC}(x,t), t \in [0,1]$, is then completed by setting $\mathrm{LC}(x,0) = 0$ and defining

$$\mathrm{LC}\left(x, \frac{i+\tau}{n}\right) = (1-\tau)\mathrm{LC}\left(x, \frac{i}{n}\right) + \tau\mathrm{LC}\left(x, \frac{i+1}{n}\right), \tag{1.2}$$

where $1 \leq i \leq (n-1)$ and $0 \leq \tau \leq 1$. The convex combination of $\mathrm{LC}(x, i/n)$ and $\mathrm{LC}(x, (i+1)/n)$ considered in (1.2) defines the segments of the curve between the consecutive population proportions i/n and $(i+1)/n$ in a continuous manner. Since 0% of the population enjoys 0% of the total income and 100% of the population possesses the entire income, the curve runs from the south-west corner with coordinates $(0,0)$ of the of unit square to the diametrically opposite north-east corner with coordinates $(1,1)$. When there is perfect equality, every $t\%$ of the population enjoys $t\%$ of the total income and the curve coincides with the diagonal line of equality or egalitarian line. In all other cases, the curve falls below the line of equality. In the case of complete inequality where only one person has positive income and all other persons have zero income, the curve runs through the horizontal axis until we reach the richest person and then it rises perpendicularly. The Lorenz curve is extremely useful because it shows graphically how the actual possession of incomes differs from the hypothetical situation where everybody enjoys the same income. It can be demonstrated rigorously that the curve is increasing and strictly convex (*see* Chakravarty, 1990; Kakwani, 1980a).

In order to discuss the role of the Lorenz curve in welfare ranking of income distributions, we first define the Lorenz dominance relation. For $x, y \in D$, x is said to Lorenz dominate y, or, x dominates y by the Lorenz criterion, which is denoted by $x \geq_{\text{LC}} y$, if we have $\text{LC}(x,t) \geq \text{LC}(y,t)$ for all $0 \leq t \leq 1$, with $>$ for some $0 < t < 1$. That is, $x \geq_{\text{LC}} y$ means that the Lorenz curve of x is nowhere below and at some places (at least) above that of y. In such a case, we also say that x is Lorenz superior to y. Note that our definition of $x \geq_{\text{LC}} y$ is quite general in the sense that the population sizes associated with the distributions x and y need not be the same. The relation $\geq_{\text{LC}}$ is a quasi-ordering, that is, it is transitive but not complete. Transitivity says that for any $x^1, x^2, x^3 \in D$, if we have $x^1 \geq_{\text{LC}} x^2$ and $x^2 \geq_{\text{LC}} x^3$, then we must have $x^1 \geq_{\text{LC}} x^3$. However, if the Lorenz curves of the two distributions x and y cross, then we have neither $x \geq_{\text{LC}} y$ nor $y \geq_{\text{LC}} x$. That is, the relation $\geq_{\text{LC}}$ is not a complete relation. (In Fig. 1.1, for the three income distributions x, y, and u, we have both $y \geq_{\text{LC}} x$ and $u \geq_{\text{LC}} x$ but neither $y \geq_{\text{LC}} u$ nor $u \geq_{\text{LC}} y$.) Thus, in the case of intersection of the two curves, we have to withhold our judgments concerning

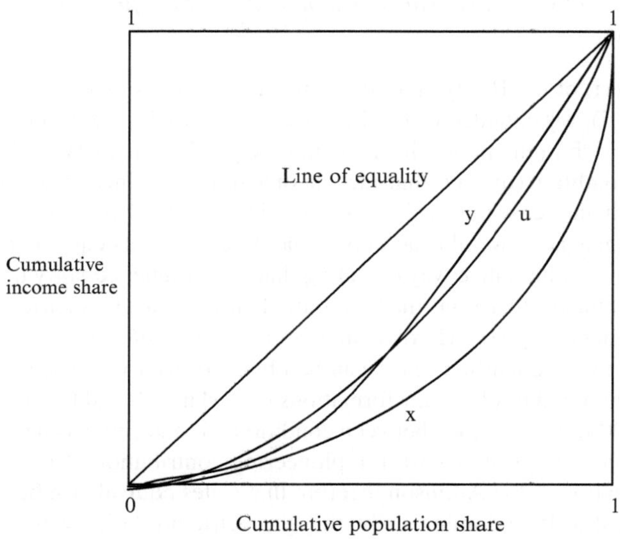

Fig. 1.1 Lorenz curve and Lorenz dominance

ranking of the underlying distributions using the relation $\geq_{LC}$. By defining appropriate preference relations on the set of Lorenz curves, Aaberge (2001) developed two alternative characterizations of Lorenz curve dominance relation.

The following remarkable equivalence theorem involving the Lorenz dominance relation was proved by Dasgupta et al. (1973):

Theorem 1.1. *Let $x, y \in D^n$, where $\lambda(x) = \lambda(y)$, be arbitrary. That is, x and y are two arbitrary distributions of the same amount of total income over a given population size n. Then the following conditions are equivalent:*

(i) x is Lorenz superior to y, that is, $x \geq_{LC} y$.
(ii) $W(x) > W(y)$ for all strictly S-concave social welfare functions $W : D^n \to R^1$.

What Dasgupta et al. theorem says is the following. For two distributions x and y of a given total over a given population size, if x is Lorenz superior to y, then x represents higher level of welfare than y for any social welfare function provided that it is strictly S-concave. Furthermore, the converse is also true. If the two curves cross, it will be possible to get two different strictly S-concave welfare functions that will rank the distributions in different directions.

The proof of Theorem 1.1 relies on the following theorem of Hardy et al. (1934):

Theorem 1.2. *For $x, y \in D^n$, where $\lambda(x) = \lambda(y)$, the following conditions are equivalent:*

(i) $\sum_{i=1}^{j} x_i \geq \sum_{i=1}^{j} y_i$ for all $1 \leq j \leq n$, with $>$ for at least one $j < n$.
(ii) x can be obtained from y by a sequence of rank-preserving progressive transfers.
(iii) If x is not a permutation of y, then there exists a bistochastic matrix A of order n such that $x = yA$.
(iv) For any strictly concave real valued individual utility function U, $\sum_{i=1}^{n} U(x_i) > \sum_{i=1}^{n} U(y_i)$.

Condition (i) of the Hrady et al. theorem simply means that $x \geq_{LC} y$. According to condition (ii), x is obtained from y by a sequence of rank-preserving income transfers from the rich to the poor. Thus, x is more equitable than y (*see also* Fields and Fei, 1978). Condition (iii) says that each income in x is obtained by a "smoothing" of incomes in y in the sense that each income in x is a weighted average of incomes in y, where the nonnegative weights add up to one. Because of its equivalence with condition (ii), it is an alternative way of stating that x has higher equality than y. Finally, condition (iv) means that x has more welfare than y by the symmetric utilitarian social welfare function $\sum U()$. Hardy et al. (1934) also demonstrated that condition (i) is equivalent to the condition that x can be obtained from y by successive applications of a finite number of T-transformations (*see* Marshall and Olkin, 1979, p.107; Muirhead, 1903). Equivalence between conditions (i) and (iv) was demonstrated independently by Atkinson (1970) in a pioneering contribution. Thus, Theorem 1.1 is a generalization of the Atkinson theorem that states equivalence between Lorenz superiority and welfare dominance by the symmetric utilitarian welfare function in the sense of sufficient weakening of the concavity and additivity assumptions.

Proof of Theorem 1.1. (i) ⇒(ii): Equivalence between conditions (i) and (ii) of Theorem 1.2 implies that x cannot be a permutation of y. By theorem 1.2, it follows from $x \geq_{\mathrm{LC}} y$ that there exists a bistochastic matrix A such that $x = yA$. Therefore, for any strictly S-concave $W : D^n \to R^1$, $W(x) = W(yA) > W(y)$.

(ii) ⇒(i): Since in Theorem 1.2, conditions (i) and (iv) are equivalent, not (i) implies not (iv). That is, if $x \geq_{\mathrm{LC}} y$ does not hold, then for some strictly concave utility function U, $\sum_{i=1}^{n} U(x_i) \leq \sum_{i=1}^{n} U(y_i)$. Given strict concavity of U, we can regard $\sum_{i=1}^{n} U(x_i)$ as a strictly S-concave function (Marshall and Olkin, 1979, p.64). Thus, if not $x \geq_{\mathrm{LC}} y$, then for some strictly S-concave social welfare function $W, W(x) \leq W(y)$. That is, not (i) implies not (ii). Hence, (ii) implies (i). □

From Theorem 1.1, it follows immediately that for $x, y \in D^n$, where $\lambda(x) = \lambda(y)$, $x \geq_{\mathrm{LC}} y$ implies that $\min_i\{x_i\} \geq \min_i\{y_i\}$. That is, x is regarded as at least as good as y by the Rawlsian (1971) maximin criterion. Since by the theorem, strict S-concavity of a social welfare means that a rank-preserving income transfer from a rich to poor increases welfare, we can regard it as an equity principle. Thus, strict S-concavity, as an egalitarian value judgment, becomes quite helpful in ranking alternative distributions of income in terms of society's preference. [*See* also Rothschild and Stiglitz (1973), for related discussion.]

Theorem 1.1 makes comparisons of welfare for distributions over a given population size. However, cross-population comparisons like intertemporal and international comparisons involve differing population sizes. For ranking distributions with the same mean where population size is a variable, we consider welfare functions that remain invariant under replications of the population. Formally, a social welfare function $W : D \to R^1$ is population replication invariant if for all $n \in N, x \in D^n, W(x) = W(y)$, where y is the l-fold replication of x, $l \geq 2$ being an arbitrary integer, that is, each x_i appears l times in y. An example of a social welfare function that satisfies this condition is the average symmetric utilitarian welfare function $\sum_{i=1}^{n} U(x_i)/n$.

We can now state the following variable population version of the Dasgupta et al. (1973) theorem:

Theorem 1.3. *Let x^1 and x^2 be two arbitrary income distributions with the same mean over the population sizes n_1 and n_2, respectively. That is, let $x^1 \in D^{n_1}$ and $x^2 \in D^{n_2}$, where $\lambda(x^1) = \lambda(x^2)$, be arbitrary. Then the following conditions are equivalent:*

(i) $x^1 \geq_{\mathrm{LC}} x^2$.
(ii) $W(x^1) > W(x^2)$ for all social welfare functions $W : D \to R^1$ that are strictly S-concave and population replication invariant.

Proof. Let x^3 and x^4, respectively, be the n_2 and n_1-fold replications of x^1 and x^2. Then $x^3, x^4 \in D^{n_1 n_2}$ and $\lambda(x^3) = \lambda(x^4)$. Since the Lorenz curve is population replication invariant, $\mathrm{LC}(x^1,t) = \mathrm{LC}(x^3,t)$ and $\mathrm{LC}(x^2,t) = \mathrm{LC}(x^4,t)$. Hence, (i) gives $x^3 \geq_{LC} x^4$. Therefore, x^3 and x^4 are two distributions of a fixed total income over a given population size and x^3 Lorenz dominates x^4. Theorem 1.1 implies that $W(x^3) > W(x^4)$ for all strictly S-concave social welfare functions W. Since W is population replication invariant, $W(x^3) = W(x^1)$ and $W(x^4) = W(x^2)$. Hence, $W(x^1) > W(x^2)$. The converse can be proved by a similar argument. □

Strictly speaking, condition (ii) in the Dasgupta et al. (1973) version of Theorem 1.3 is stated in terms of social welfare functions that fulfill the "Symmetry Axiom for Population," which demands that an l−fold replication of the population will multiply the value of the social welfare function by l. Thus, if W_{DSS} is a welfare function of this type, then $W_{\text{DSS}}(y) = lW_{\text{DSS}}(x)$, where y is the l-fold replication of $x \in D^n$. The symmetric utilitarian social welfare function $\sum_{i=1}^{n} U(x_i)$ is an example of a welfare function that meets this axiom. Then condition (ii) of the theorem will be stated as "$W_{\text{DSS}}(x^1)/n_1 > W_{\text{DSS}}(x^2)/n_2$ for all social welfare functions $W_{\text{DSS}} : D \to R^1$ that fulfill strict S-concavity and the Symmetry Axiom for Population." We, however, stated the theorem in terms of population replication invariant welfare functions since in all our future discussion we consider mostly population replication invariant indices.

Theorems 1.1 and 1.3 are restricted to the comparison of welfare using the Lorenz criterion for income distributions with the same mean. As Shorrocks (1983a) argued, for two distributions over a given population size, if one has both higher mean and higher Lorenz curve, then it has higher level of welfare as well if the welfare function is increasing under rank-preserving increments in individual incomes and strictly S-concave (*see also* Rothschild and Stiglitz, 1973). But for a clear verdict, here we need both a higher Lorenz curve and higher mean. This often may not be satisfied.

The ability of the Lorenz curve to rank income profiles with differing means improves sufficiently if we extend the concept of the Lorenz curve to the generalized Lorenz curve introduced by Shorrocks (1983a). The generalized Lorenz curve of a distribution is obtained by scaling up the Lorenz curve of the distribution by the mean income. Formally, the generalized Lorenz curve $\text{GL}(x,t)$ of the distribution $x \in D^n$ is defined as $\lambda(x)\text{LC}(x,t)$, where $\lambda(x)$ is the mean of x, $\text{LC}(x,t)$ is its Lorenz curve and $0 \leq t \leq 1$. For $x, y \in D$, x is said to generalized Lorenz dominate y, which is denoted by $x \geq_{GL} y$, if we have $\text{GL}(x,t) \geq \text{GL}(y,t)$ for all $0 \leq t \leq 1$, with $>$ for some t. Thus, generalized Lorenz dominance of x over y means that the generalized Lorenz curve of x is nowhere below and above at some places (at least) that of y.

As shown below, for welfare ranking of income distributions when mean income varies, we also need increasingness of the social welfare function. A social welfare function $W : D^n \to R^1$ is said to satisfy the Pareto Principle if for $y \in D^n$, $W(x) > W(y)$ where x is obtained from y by a rank-preserving simple increment. Strictly speaking, this is the strong form of the Pareto Principle. In contrast, the Weak Pareto Principle demands increasingness of the welfare function when rank-preserving simple increments take place for all the incomes. Throughout the text, we will use the Strong Pareto Principle and refer to it simply as the Pareto Principle.

The following theorem of Shorrocks (1983a) explains the role of the generalized Lorenz curve in ranking income distributions with different means:

Theorem 1.4. *Let x and y be two arbitrary distributions of income over a given population size n. That is, $x, y \in D^n$ are arbitrary. Then the following conditions are equivalent:*

(i) x is generalized Lorenz superior to y, that is, $x \geq_{\mathrm{GL}} y$.
(ii) $W(x) > W(y)$ for all social welfare functions $W : D^n \to R^1$ that satisfy strict S-concavity and the Pareto Principle.

Proof. The idea of the proof for the implication (i)⇒(ii) is taken from Foster and Shorrocks (1988b). Suppose $x \geq_{\mathrm{GL}} y$ holds which ensures that $\lambda(x) > \lambda(y)$. Define the distribution u as follows: $u_i = y_i$ for $1 \leq i \leq (n-1)$ and $u_n = y_n + n(\lambda(x) - \lambda(y))$. Then $\lambda(u) = \lambda(x)$. By definition, u is obtained from y by a simple increment that does not change the rank orders of the individuals. Hence, $W(u) > W(y)$. Now, $x \geq_{\mathrm{GL}} y$ implies that either $u = x$ or $u \neq x$. If the former holds, then we have $W(x) = W(u) > W(y)$. If the latter holds, then we have $x \geq_{\mathrm{LC}} u$. Hence, by strict S-concavity of W, $W(x) > W(u)$, from which we get $W(x) > W(y)$.

The proof of the converse relies on a theorem of Marshall and Olkin (1979, p.12). According to the Marshall-Olkin theorem, the statement $\sum_{i=1}^{j} x_i \geq \sum_{i=1}^{j} y_i$ for all $1 \leq j \leq n$, with $>$ for at least one j, is equivalent to the statement that $\sum_{i=1}^{n} U(x_i) > \sum_{i=1}^{n} U(y_i)$, for any increasing and strictly concave real valued individual utility function U. The former of these two statements means that we have $x \geq_{\mathrm{GL}} y$. Thus, if we have not $x \geq_{\mathrm{GL}} y$, then for some increasing, strictly concave utility function U, $\sum_{i=1}^{n} U(x_i) \leq \sum_{i=1}^{n} U(y_i)$. Given increasingness and strict concavity of U, we can say that $\sum_{i=1}^{n} U(x_i)$ is an increasing and strictly S-concave function (Marshall and Olkin, 1979, p.64). Thus, if not $x \geq_{\mathrm{GL}} y$, then for some strictly S-concave social welfare function W that satisfies the Pareto Principle, we have $W(x) \leq W(y)$. That is, not (i) implies not (ii). Hence, (ii) implies (i). □

Two simple welfare implications of the relation $\geq_{\mathrm{GL}}$ can be stated rigorously as follows. If $x \geq_{\mathrm{GL}} y$ holds then (i) x is regarded as better than y by the mean income criterion, that is, $\lambda(x) > \lambda(y)$, and (ii) x is not Rawlsian maximin inferior to y, that is,$\min_i\{x_i\} \geq \min_i\{y_i\}$. However, these two welfare functions are S-concave but not strictly so.

Theorem 1.4 shows that an unanimous ranking of two income distributions by all strictly S-concave social welfare functions satisfying the Pareto Principle is obtainable if and only their generalized Lorenz curves do not cross. Thus, the generalized Lorenz criterion takes the size of the distribution into account. Although the generalized Lorenz superiority relation extends welfare ranking to the case of variable mean, it is a quasi-ordering as well. (In Fig. 1.2, for the distributions x^4, x^5, and x^6, while $x^4 \geq_{\mathrm{GL}} x^5$ and $x^4 \geq_{\mathrm{GL}} x^6$ hold, neither $x^6 \geq_{\mathrm{GL}} x^5$ nor $x^5 \geq_{\mathrm{GL}} x^6$ holds.) However, as Shorrocks (1983a) has shown many inconclusive rankings under $\geq_{\mathrm{LC}}$ may become conclusive if we use $\geq_{\mathrm{GL}}$. To see this, suppose that the Lorenz curve of x intersects that of y once from below at a low level of cumulative income proportion and assume also that x has higher mean than y. That is, there exists a $t' \in (0,1)$ such that $\mathrm{LC}(x,t) < \mathrm{LC}(y,t)$ for all $t < t'$ and $\mathrm{LC}(x,t) > \mathrm{LC}(y,t)$ for all $t > t'$, where t' is small. Then multiplication of the Lorenz curve by the mean may be able to push

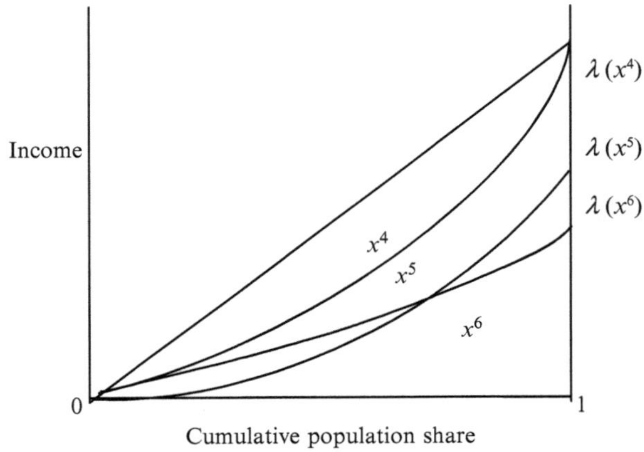

Fig. 1.2 Generalized Lorenz curve and generalized Lorenz dominance

the lower part of the curve for x up to ensure that the single crossing between the two curves does not exist and $x \geq_{GL} y$ holds. (It may be worthwhile to mention here that the Atkinson theorem which shows equivalence between conditions (i) and (iv) of Theorem 1.2 and the Shorrocks theorem were stated in Kolm, 1969. He referred to the dominance conditions in these two results as constant-sum-isophily and superisophily, respectively).

The following theorem of Shorrocks (1983a), which is the variable population counterpart to Theorem 1.4, can be proved in the same way we have proved Theorem 1.3.

Theorem 1.5. *Let x^1 and x^2 be two arbitrary income distributions over the population sizes n_1 and n_2, respectively. That is, let $x^1 \in D^{n_1}$ and $x^2 \in D^{n_2}$ be arbitrary. Then the following conditions are equivalent:*

(i) $x^1 \geq_{GL} x^2$.
(ii) $W(x^1) > W(x^2)$ for all social welfare functions $W : D \to R^1$ that are strictly S-concave, population replication invariant, and satisfy the Pareto Principle.

However, the value judgments social preferences for higher total and lower inequality may come into direct conflict in the welfare evaluation of income distributions by the generalized Lorenz criterion. For instance, an increase in the income of the richest person in the distribution y increases the total income and the resulting distribution x generalized Lorenz dominates y. Hence, x has higher welfare than y by all the welfare functions we have considered in Theorem 1.4. But this increase in the richest person's income is likely to give rise to an increase in inequality as well. In other words, preference for higher income, that is, efficiency preference, may come into conflict with the social desire for more equity. Since we have assumed that the welfare function fulfills the Pareto Principle, in this case the trade off between equity and efficiency is resolved on the side of higher efficiency. Thus, a welfare improvement in terms of generalized Lorenz superiority may be compatible with an augmentation in inequality.

An alternative efficiency preference concept that avoids the above difficulty is the requirement that welfare improves if all the incomes are increased by the same proportion. Formally, a social welfare function $W : D^n \to R^1$ satisfies the "scale improvement" condition if for all $x \in D^n$ and for all $c \geq 1$,

$$W(cx) \geq W(x). \tag{1.3}$$

A higher value of c represents a higher level of efficiency (total income) keeping the distribution of relative incomes constant, that is, keeping the ratios x_i/x_j constant. Equivalently, we say that the scale improvement condition demonstrates preferences for higher incomes under constancy of relative inequality. Clearly, this is a weaker requirement than the Pareto Principle. Note that the scale improvement condition does not alter the rank orders of the individuals. Shorrocks (1983a) proved the following theorem which shows that the welfare assessment of distributions using the scale improvement condition is equivalent to the standard practice of ranking distributions by the mean income and the Lorenz curve.

Theorem 1.6. *For $x, y \in D^n$ the following conditions are equivalent:*

(i) x weakly Lorenz dominates y, that is, $L(x,t) \geq L(y,t)$ for all $0 \leq t \leq 1$, and $\lambda(x) \geq \lambda(y)$.
(ii) $W(x) \geq W(y)$ for all social welfare functions $W : D^n \to R^1$ that satisfy S-concavity and the scale improvement condition.

Theorem 1.6 gives us the implications of replacing the Pareto Principle by the scale improvement condition in ranking distributions using the Lorenz criterion. However, efficiency increase can as well be achieved by absolute augmentation of incomes. Formally, a social welfare function $W : D^n \to R^1$ satisfies the "incremental improvement" condition if for all $x \in D^n$, for all $c \geq 0$,

$$W(x + c1^n) \geq W(x). \tag{1.4}$$

The incremental improvement condition, which preserves the rank orders of the individuals, shows preferences for higher incomes keeping the absolute income differentials $x_i - x_j$ constant. In other words, under the incremental improvement condition higher efficiency is desired under constancy of absolute inequality. A higher value of c will correspond to a higher total income. The following interesting implication of the alternative efficiency preference defined in (1.4) was demonstrated by Shorrocks (1983a):

Theorem 1.7. *For $x, y \in D^n$ the following conditions are equivalent:*

(i) $\lambda(x) \geq \lambda(y)$ and $\mathrm{GL}(x,t) - \mathrm{GL}(y,t) \geq t(\lambda(x) - \lambda(y))$ for all $0 \leq t \leq 1$.
(ii) $W(x) \geq W(y)$ for all social welfare functions $W : D^n \to R^1$ that satisfy S-concavity and the incremental improvement condition.

To make use of Theorem 1.7 in ranking distributions of income, we need to calculate the difference $\mathrm{GL}(x,t) - t\lambda(x)$ for each of the distributions and then make pairwise comparisons of these values and the mean incomes. One may note that an incremental improvement in all incomes can be achieved first by increasing the incomes proportionately and then making rank-preserving progressive transfers. Therefore, the ordering induced by the welfare functions satisfying (1.4) will be weaker than that generated by the welfare functions that fulfill (1.3).

Observe that $\mathrm{GL}(x,t) - t\lambda(x)$ is the generalized Lorenz curve $\mathrm{GL}(x - \lambda(x)1^n, t)$ of the distribution $(x - \lambda(x)1^n)$. Moyes (1987) referred to the curve $\mathrm{GL}(x - \lambda(x)1^n, t)$ as the absolute Lorenz curve $\mathrm{LA}(x,t)$ of x. The Moyes absolute Lorenz curve coincides with the horizontal axis when incomes are equally distributed. It is convex in t, decreasing in t for $0 \leq t \leq \bar{t}$, and increasing in $\bar{t} < t \leq 1$, where $\bar{t} = \bar{n}/n$ with $\bar{n}$ being such that $x_{\bar{n}} < \lambda(x) \leq x_{\bar{n}+1}$. It is easy to see that - $\mathrm{LA}(x,t)$ measures the shortfall of the total income of the bottom t proportion of the population from the corresponding total under the hypothetical distribution where everybody enjoys the mean income, as a proportion of the population size.

Tam and Zhang (1996) considered a family of alternative dominance relationships generalizing the Shorrocks approach. For any $0 < \hat{\mu} < 1$, they defined the $\hat{\mu}$ generalized curve $\hat{\mu}\mathrm{GL}(x,\hat{\mu},t)$ of $x \in D^n$ as $(\lambda(x))^{\hat{\mu}}\mathrm{LC}(x,t)$, where $0 \leq t \leq 1$. They showed that for $x, y \in D^n$ where $\lambda(x) > \lambda(y)$, $\hat{\mu}\mathrm{GL}(x,\hat{\mu},t) \geq \hat{\mu}\mathrm{GL}(y,\hat{\mu},t)$ for all $0 \leq t \leq 1$ holds if and only if $W(x) \geq W(y)$ for all social welfare functions $W : D^n \to R^1$ that satisfy S-concavity and the $\hat{\mu}$-share of income growth inequality, that is, $(\sum_{j=1}^{i} x_j)/(\sum_{j=1}^{i} y_j) \geq (\lambda(x)/\lambda(y))^{1-\hat{\mu}}$, $1 \leq i \leq n$. Essentially, the efficiency preferences considered by Shorrocks are replaced by the condition that welfare will not decrease if the income growth is shared by all the poorer sectors of the community. The result thus specifies a necessary and sufficient condition for welfare of the society not to decrease as a result of economic growth.

1.4 Stochastic Dominance

Several quasi-orderings employed in the theory of choice under uncertainty correspond closely to the ranking criteria used for welfare evaluation of income distributions. Using results from Rothschild and Stiglitz (1970), Atkinson (1970) demonstrated equivalence between Lorenz dominance and second-order stochastic dominance invoked for ranking uncertain prospects. In order to discuss this formally, we first define stochastic dominance.

We assume that the income distributions are defined on the continuum. Let $F : [0,\infty) \to [0,1]$ be the cumulative distribution function. Then $F(v)$ is the proportion of persons with income less than or equal to v. F is nondecreasing, continuously differentiable, $F(0) = 0$ and $F(v_F) = 1$ for some $v_F < \infty$. The integrals $F_2(s)$ and $F_3(s)$ of the distribution function can be defined recursively by

$$F_{r+1}(s) = \int_0^s F_r(v)\,dv \quad \text{for all } s \in [0,\infty) \tag{1.5}$$

where $r = 0,1,2,\ldots$ is an integer and $F_1(s) = F(s)$. In the case of discrete distributions with a population size of n,

$$F_{r+1}(s) = \frac{1}{r!n} \sum_{i=1}^{n(s,x)} (s - x_i)^r \quad \text{for all } s \in [0,\infty), \tag{1.6}$$

where $n(s,x) = \#\{i \in \{1,2,\ldots,n\} \,|x_i \leq s\}$ is the number of individuals having incomes less than or equal to s in the distribution $x \in D^n$ (*see* Moyes, 1999).

To illustrate the formula (1.6), let us consider the distribution $x = (1,2,6)$. Then for $s < 1$, $F_1(s) = F_2(s) = F_3(s) = 0$. Next, for $1 \leq s < 2$, $F_1(s) = 1/3$, $F_2(s) = (s-1)/3$, and $F_3(s) = (s-1)^2/6 = (s^2-2s+1)/6$. Likewise, for $2 \leq s < 6$, $F_1(s) = 2/3$, $F_2(s) = ((s-1)+(s-2))/3 = (2s-3)/3$, and $F_3(s) = ((s-1)^2+(s-2)^2)/6 = (2s^2-6s+5)/6$. Finally, for $s \geq 6$, $F_1(s) = 1$, $F_2(s) = (3s-9)/3$, and $F_3(s) = (3s^2-18s+41)/6$.

Given two income distribution functions F and G defined on the same domain $[0,\infty)$, we say that F dominates G by the $(r+1)$th degree/order stochastic dominance criterion if $F_{r+1}(v) \leq G_{r+1}(v)$ for all $v \in [0,\infty)$ with $<$ for some v, where $r \geq 0$ is an integer. If only $\leq$ holds everywhere, we say that F weakly dominates G by the $(r+1)$th degree stochastic dominance criterion. The cases $r = 0$ and 1 correspond, respectively, to the first- and second-degree stochastic dominance (*see* Hadar and Russell, 1969). The first-order stochastic dominance is also known as the rank dominance (Saposnik, 1981). The third-degree stochastic dominance is defined if we assume that $r = 2$ (*see* Whitmore, 1970).

First-order stochastic dominance of F over G is equivalent to the condition that F is preferred to G by the expected utility criterion where the utility function is increasing in its argument, that is, the marginal utility function is positive. More precisely, F first-order stochastic dominates G if and only if we have $\int_0^\infty U(v)dF(v) > \int_0^\infty U(v)dG(v)$, for all utility functions U that are increasing. That is, distribution F is preferred to distribution G by the utilitarians who approve of higher efficiency. Therefore, efficiency preference or preference for more incomes becomes the distinguishing feature of the first-order stochastic dominance. It is assumed that U is differentiable up to any desired degree.

On the other hand, second-order stochastic dominance of F over G holds if and only if we have $\int_0^\infty U(v)\,dF(v) > \int_0^\infty U(v)\,dG(v)$ for all utility functions U that are increasing and strictly concave. That is, in this case, the utilatarians have preference for both higher efficiency and higher equity. Thus, the distinguishing characteristics of second-order stochastic dominance are preferences for higher equity as well as higher efficiency. Second-order stochastic dominance of F over G is also equivalent to the condition that $F \geq_{\text{GL}} G$, that is, F generalized Lorenz dominates G. If the two distributions have a common mean, this simply reduces to the condition that F Lorenz dominates G.

Third-order stochastic dominance of F over G requires higher expected utility value under F than that under G where the marginal utility function is positive, decreasing, and strictly convex. The stochastic dominance conditions we discussed here are nested. That is, lower degree stochastic dominance implies higher degree stochastic dominance. Thus, the first-order dominance entails the one for second degree which in turn entails the third-order dominance. This means that if F first-order stochastic dominates G, then higher order dominances of F over G are ensured, the direction of ordering will remain unaltered.

Under appropriate reinterpretation of expected utility, we can interpret the stochastic dominance conditions in terms of welfare more generally (Foster and Sen, 1997). The first-order stochastic dominance turns out to be welfare dominance for all symmetric, population replication invariant welfare functions that fulfill the Pareto Principle. If we add the condition that welfare increases under a rank-preserving progressive transfer, then we get unanimity of welfare dominance with the second-order stochastic dominance. Finally, if we also desire a fixed-sized income transfer to have higher impact on welfare at lower income levels, then we identify welfare dominance as the third-order stochastic dominance.

Rather than representing an income distribution by a distribution function, we can use the inverse distribution function for the same purpose. The inverse distribution function $F^{-1}:[0,1]\to[0,\infty)$ is defined as

$$F^{-1}(t)=\inf\{v:F(v)\geq t\}\,\text{for all}\, t\in[0.1]. \tag{1.7}$$

Successive integration of the inverse function defined in (1.7) gives

$$F_{r+1}^{-1}(t)=\int_0^t F_r^{-1}(\tau)\,\mathrm{d}\tau \text{ for all}\, t\in[0.1], \tag{1.8}$$

where $F_1^{-1}(t)=F^{-1}(t)$ and r is a nonnegative integer. Letting $x_0=0$ and $n(t,x)=\min\{i\in\{1,2,\ldots,n\}|t\leq n(t,x)/n\}$, for any $x\in D^n$,

$$F_{r+1}^{-1}(t)=\frac{1}{r!}\sum_{i=1}^{n(t,x)}\left(t-\frac{i-1}{n}\right)^r(x_i-x_{i-1})\,\text{for all}\, t\in[0.1]. \tag{1.9}$$

The function $F^{-1}(t)$ represents the income of bottom t proportion of the population and is referred to as the quantile function. For example, we have considered above, $F^{-1}(t)=0,1,2,$ and 6 according as $t=0$, $0<t\leq 1/3$, $1/3<t\leq 2/3$, and $2/3<t\leq 1$. Likewise, the function $F_2^{-1}(t)$ gives the total income, expressed as a fraction of the population size n, possessed by the bottom t proportion of the population. When divided by the mean income, it gives us the Lorenz curve of the distribution x. Formally, the Lorenz curve associated with the distribution having the distribution function F and the mean $\lambda(F)=\int_0^1 F^{-1}(t)\,\mathrm{d}t$ is defined as

$$\mathrm{LC}(F,t)=\frac{1}{\lambda(F)}\int_0^t F^{-1}(\tau)\mathrm{d}\tau. \tag{1.10}$$

where $0 \leq t \leq 1$. This general definition of the Lorenz curve was suggested by Gastwirth (1971). It applies to distributions of both discrete and continuous types. This in turn shows that the generalized Lorenz curve of F is given by $\mathrm{GL}(F,t) = \int_0^t F^{-1}(\tau)\mathrm{d}\tau, 0 \leq t \leq 1$.

The Lorenz curve for the example $x = (1,2,6)$, we have considered, will then be

$$\mathrm{LC}(F,t) = \begin{cases} \frac{t}{3}, 0 \leq t < \frac{1}{3}, \\ \frac{1}{9} + \frac{2}{3}\left(t - \frac{1}{3}\right), \frac{1}{3} \leq t < \frac{2}{3}, \\ \frac{1}{9} + \frac{2}{9} + \frac{6}{3}\left(t - \frac{2}{3}\right), \frac{2}{3} \leq t \leq 1. \end{cases} \tag{1.11}$$

Ramos et al. (2000) developed a sufficient condition for weak generalized Lorenz superiority defined using F^{-1}. They showed that of two income distribution functions F and G defined on the common support $[0,\infty)$ if F crosses G once not from above and the mean of G is not higher than that of F, then F weakly generalized Lorenz dominates G. More precisely, if $\lambda(F) \geq \lambda(G)$ and there exists $v_0 \in [0,\infty)$ such that $F(v) \leq G(v)$ for all $0 \leq v \leq v_0$ and $F(v) \geq G(v)$ for all $v_0 \leq v < \infty$, then $\mathrm{GL}(F,t) \geq \mathrm{GL}(G,t)$ for all $t \in [0,1]$.

Given the inverse distribution functions F^{-1} and G^{-1} associated with the distribution functions F and G defined on the same domain, we say that F dominates G by the $(r+1)$th degree inverse stochastic dominance criterion if $F_{r+1}^{-1}(t) \geq G_{r+1}^{-1}(t)$ for all $t \in [0,1]$ with $>$ for some t, where $r \geq 0$ is an integer. The inverse stochastic dominance conditions are also nested in the sense that lower degree dominance implies higher degree dominance. The direct first-order stochastic dominance is equivalent to inverse first-order stochastic dominance. In fact, under the equality of the means, the equivalence holds for the two second-order dominances as well, which in turn are equivalent to Lorenz dominance. However, the equivalence does not continue to hold for $r \geq 2$ (*see* Muliere and Scarsini, 1989).

We conclude this section with two definitions which will be useful for our analysis in Chap. 2. For the distribution functions F and G defined on the same domain $[0,\infty)$ and any nonnegative integer r, we say that F weakly $(r+1)$th degree stochastic dominates G over an income interval $[\mu,\gamma] \subset [0,\infty)$ if $F_{r+1}(v) \leq G_{r+1}(v)$ for all $v \in [\mu,\gamma]$. If $F_{r+1}(v) \leq G_{r+1}(v)$ for all $v \in [\mu,\gamma]$ and $F_{r+1}(v) < G_{r+1}(v)$ for some $v \in (\mu,\gamma)$, then F $(r+1)$th degree stochastic dominates G over $[\mu,\gamma]$ (*see* Zheng, 1999).

1.5 Postulates for an Index of Inequality

The objective of this section is to present alternative postulates for an index of inequality and discuss their implications. We begin with a quite general definition of an inequality index that allows variability of both the population size and the mean income. Consequently, the domain of the inequality index is $D = \bigcup_{n \in N} D^n$. Note that the concept of inequality is vacuous if $n = 1$. Hence, we assume that $n \geq 2$.

An inequality index $I : D \to R^1$ is a relative or "rightist" index if equiproportionate changes in all incomes do not change the level of inequality, that is, for all $n \in N$, $x \in D^n$, it satisfies the scale invariance property

$$I(cx) = I(x), \tag{1.12}$$

where $c > 0$ is any scalar. In other words, I is homogeneous of degree zero in its arguments. In contrast, an inequality index $I : D \to R^1$ represents the concept of absolute or "leftist" inequality if it is invariant under equal absolute changes in all incomes, that is, for all $n \in N$, $x \in D^n$, it satisfies the translation invariance property

$$I(x + c1^n) = I(x), \tag{1.13}$$

where c is a scalar such that $x + c1^n \in D^n$.

Clearly, while the relative concept treats inequality in terms of income ratios, the absolute notion views inequality with respect to income differentials. A relative index has the convenient property of being invariant under changes in the currency unit of incomes, but an absolute index does not meet this property. However, as Kolm (1976a) argued if we make intertemporal comparison of inequality in a country using an absolute index, we must use real incomes. Similarly, for international comparison of absolute inequality it is necessary to use the correct exchange rate.

Research to date has not found a satisfactory solution about universal acceptability regarding the concept of inequality invariance. While relative and absolute inequality express two different notions of value judgments about inequality invariance, Kolm (1976a) pointed out that some people may prefer a centrist or compromise invariance between these extreme positions. Experimental investigations made along this line have demonstrated that an individual's attitude toward inequality equivalence need not be of relative or absolute type (*see*, e.g., Amiel and Cowell, 1992, 1994, 1999; Ballano and Ruiz-Castillo, 1993; Harrison and Siedl, 1994). Attempts have also been made to suggest alternative notions of inequality equivalence and investigations of their properties. For instance, Bossert and Pfingsten (1990) suggested an intermediate inequality concept that contains relative and absolute invariances as special cases. Further contributions along this line have been made, among others, by Kolm (1976a), Chakravarty (1988a), Bossert and Pfingsten (1990), Besley and Preston (1988), Krtscha (1994), Seidl and Pfingsten (1997), Zoli (1999a), Del Rio and Ruiz-Castillo (2000), Ebert (2004a), Yoshida (2005), Zheng (2007d), Del Rio and Alonso-Villar (2007, 2008), and Chakravarty and Tyagarupananda (2008). In this text, we will be concerned with the relative and absolute notions of inequality since many of our discussions apply to the intermediate set ups as well.

An inequality index that satisfies the relative and absolute invariance conditions jointly is a constant function (Eichhorn and Gehrig, 1982). But since a constant function does not convey any information regarding the actual level of inequality in a distribution, we consider the two conditions separately. The classes of indices satisfying the invariance conditions (1.12) and (1.13), respectively, may be quite large. Certain desirable postulates enable us to reduce the number of allowable inequality indices. The following postulates have been suggested in the literature for an arbitrary inequality index $I: D^n \rightarrow R^1$, whether relative or absolute. All properties apply for any $n \in N$.

Symmetry: For all $x \in D^n$, $I(x) = I(y)$, where y is any permutation of x.

Pigou-Dalton Transfers Principle: For all $y \in D^n$, if x is obtained from y by a rank-preserving progressive transfer, then $I(x) < I(y)$.

Dalton Population Principle: For all $x \in D^n$, $I(x) = I(y)$, where y is the l-fold replication of x, that is, each x_i appears l times in y, $l \geq 2$ being any integer.

As we have argued, Symmetry demands that inequality should be insensitive to reordering of the incomes. Thus, for a symmetric index any characteristic other than income becomes irrelevant to the measurement of inequality. Symmetry enables us to define the inequality index directly on ordered distributions (as we have done). Using this property, we can extend the function I uniquely to the space Γ^n. The Pigou (1912)-Dalton (1920) Transfers Principle, also known as the Pigou-Dalton Condition or the Principle of Transfers, demands that a rank-preserving transfer of income from a rich person to a poor person decreases inequality. Likewise, a transfer from a poor to a rich should increase inequality. As we have discussed earlier, since we have restricted attention to ordered income distributions, to maintain the ordering, we can allow only rank-preserving transfers. Thus, under Symmetry only rank-preserving, transfers are allowed (*see also* Moyes, 1999, 2007). According to the Dalton (1920) Population Principle (the Population Principle, for short), inequality remains invariant under replications of the population. Thus, if we wish to compare inequalities of two distributions with population sizes n_1 and n_2, respectively, we can replicate the former n_2 times and the latter n_1 times, so that the resulting distributions have a common population size of $n_1 n_2$. Comparison of inequalities of these two distributions with the population size $n_1 n_2$ is essentially same as comparison of inequalities of the original distributions if the inequality index satisfies the Population Principle. Thus, this postulate, which enables us to view inequality as an average concept, is helpful for cross-population comparisons of inequality. [*See* Salas (1997), for a discussion on a variant of this property.]

Clearly, we can rewrite condition (ii) of Theorem 1.1 as $I(y) > I(x)$, where $I = -W$ is strictly S-convex. Strict S-convexity implies Symmetry and reduction in inequality under rank-preserving equitable transfers. Conversely, Symmetry enables us to perform only rank-preserving progressive transfers and inequality reduction under such a transfer implies strict S-convexity. Hence, we can now state the following proposition:

Proposition 1.1. *Let $x, y \in D^n$, where $\lambda(x) = \lambda(y)$, be arbitrary. Then the following conditions are equivalent:*

(i) x is Lorenz superior to , that is, $x \geq_{LC} y$.
(ii) $I(x) < I(y)$ for all strictly S-convex inequality indices $I: D^n \rightarrow R^1$.
(iii) $I(x) < I(y)$ for all symmetric inequality indices $I: D^n \rightarrow R^1$ that fulfill the Pigou-Dalton Transfers Principle.
(iv) x second-order stochastic dominates y.

Proposition 1.1, which can be regarded as the inequality counterpart to the Hardy et al. (1934) Theorem, shows that inequality ordering of income distributions of a given total over a given population size can be implemented by the Lorenz dominance relation. Chakravarty and Eichhorn (1994) demonstrated that if there are errors in observations on income data, then all inequality indices identified in Proposition 1.1 will overestimate the extent of true inequality under certain mild assumptions about the errors.

The next three propositions, which are essentially based on Proposition 1.1, have been stated in different forms in Fields and Fei (1978), Foster (1985), Chakravarty (1990), Moyes (1999), and Chakravarty and Muliere (2003) (*see also* Eichhorn and Gehrig, 1982; Kurabayasi and Yatsuka, 1977). To state the first of these results formally, consider $x^1 \in D^{n_1}$ and $x^2 \in D^{n_2}$ such that $x^1 \geq_{\mathrm{LC}} x^2$. Let x^3 and x^4, respectively, be the n_2- and n_1-fold replications of x^1 and x^2. Thus, $x^3, x^4 \in D^{n_1 n_2}$, and $x^3 \geq_{\mathrm{LC}} x^4$. (Since the Lorenz curve is population replication invariant, $x^1 \geq_{\mathrm{LC}} x^2$ is same as $x^3 \geq_{LC} x^4$.) Define the distribution $u = (\lambda(x^3)/\lambda(x^4))x^4$. Then x^3 and u are two distributions of a fixed total income $n_1 n_2 \lambda(x^3)$ over the population size $n_1 n_2$ and $x^3 \geq_{\mathrm{LC}} u$. (Since the Lorenz curve is homogeneous of degree zero, $\mathrm{LC}(x^4,t) = \mathrm{LC}(u,t)$.) Therefore, by Proposition 1.1, we have $I(x^3) < I(u)$ for all symmetric inequality indices $I : D^{n_i n_2} \to R^1$ that reduce under a rank-preserving progressive transfer. If I is a relative index, then $I(x^4) = I(u)$ and if it is population replication invariant as well, then we have $I(x^2) = I(x^4)$. Similarly, $I(x^1) = I(x^3)$. Hence, $I(x^1) < I(x^2)$. The converse can be proved using similar arguments. This is also equivalent to the condition that $x^3/\lambda(x^3)$ second-order stochastic dominates $x^4/\lambda(x^4)$ (Moyes, 1999). By population replication invariance of the distribution function, this condition is same as the requirement that $x^1/\lambda(x^1)$ second-order stochastic dominates $x^2/\lambda(x^2)$. We are therefore now in a position to state the following:

Proposition 1.2. *Let $x^1, x^2 \in D$ be arbitrary. Then the following conditions are equivalent:*

(i) $x^1 \geq_{\mathrm{LC}} x^2$.
(ii) $I(x^1) < I(x^2)$ for all relative inequality indices $I : D \to R^1$ that fulfill Symmetry, the Pigou-Dalton Transfers Principle, and the Dalton Population Principle.
(iii) $x^1/\lambda(x^1)$ second-order stochastic dominates $x^2/\lambda(x^2)$.

Proposition 1.2 identifies the class of all inequality indices that implies and are implied by the Lorenz dominance criterion defined in the general case when both the population size and total income are not fixed. In other words, each inequality index of this type is Lorenz consistent or consistent with the Lorenz dominance relation (Foster, 1985). The corresponding result for absolute indices using the absolute Lorenz curve was proved by Moyes (1987) (*see also* Chakravarty, 1988a).

If we focus attention on fixed population size and variable mean income case, then an unanimous ranking of distributions by all inequality indices identified in Proposition 1.1, that are also relative, can be obtained by the pairwise comparison of the Lorenz curves. Formally,

Proposition 1.3. *Let $x^1, x^2 \in D^n$ be arbitrary. Then the following conditions are equivalent:*

(i) $x^1 \geq_{\mathrm{LC}} x^2$.
(ii) $I(x^1) < I(x^2)$ *for all relative inequality indices* $I : D^n \to R^1$ *that fulfill Symmetry and the Pigou-Dalton Transfers Principle.*
(iii) $x^1/\lambda(x^1)$ *second-order stochastic dominates* $x^2/\lambda(x^2)$.

We may also consider the problem of ranking distributions with a fixed mean income when the population size is allowed to vary. In this case, the domain of definition of the inequality index is $D_{\bar{\lambda}} = \{x \in D | \lambda(x) = \bar{\lambda}\}$ and the following proposition holds.

Proposition 1.4. *Let $x^1, x^2 \in D_{\bar{\lambda}}$ be arbitrary. Then the following conditions are equivalent:*

(i) $x^1 \geq_{\mathrm{LC}} x^2$.
(ii) $I(x^1) < I(x^2)$ *for all inequality indices* $I : D_{\bar{\lambda}} \to R^1$ *that fulfill Symmetry, the Pigou-Dalton Transfers Principle and the Dalton Population Principle.*

Proposition 1.4 shows that Lorenz dominance is a sufficient condition for all relative and absolute inequality indices, satisfying the postulates stated in condition (ii) of the proposition, to rank alternative distributions with a given mean in the same way.

Kolm (1976a,b) argued that greater weight should be assigned to transfers lower down the scale. With a view to making the inequality index satisfactory from this perspective he suggested the Diminishing Transfers Principle that attaches more weight to a rank-preserving progressive transfer between two persons with a given income difference, if the incomes are lower than when they are higher. Formally,

Diminishing Transfers Principle: For all $y \in D^n$, if x is obtained from y by a rank-preserving progressive transfer of income from the person with income $y_i + \hat{c}$ to the person with income y_i, then for a given $\hat{c} > 0$, the magnitude of reduction in inequality $I(y) - I(x)$ is higher the lower is y_i.

A stronger version of this is the Transfer Sensitivity Principle suggested by Shorrocks and Foster (1987) that relies on the following notion of transfer. A distribution $x \in D^n$ is said to be obtained from $y \in D^n$ by a favorable composite transfer if $y_i = x_i$ for all $i \neq j, \hat{j}, l, \hat{l}$; $y_j - x_j = x_{\hat{j}} - y_{\hat{j}} = \tilde{\alpha}_1 > 0$; $x_{\hat{l}} - y_{\hat{l}} = y_l - x_l = \tilde{\alpha}_2 > 0$; where $y_{\hat{j}} < y_j \leq y_l \leq y_{\hat{l}}$, $x_{\hat{j}} \leq x_j \leq x_l < x_{\hat{l}}$; $I_V(x) = I_V(y)$, with I_V being the variance, and α_1 and α_2 are such that the ranks of the individuals remain unaffected.

That is, rank-preserving progressive and regressive transfers of income that do not change the mean and the variance are required jointly to arrive at the distribution x from the distribution y, where the progressive transfer involves lower incomes than the regressive transfer. (The progressive transfer is from y_j to $y_{\hat{j}}$ and the regressive transfer is from y_l to $y_{\hat{l}}$). Note that the size of the progressive transfer α_1 need not be equal to the size of the regressive transfer α_2. Further, equality of the income distances between the two pairs of persons involved are also not necessary. The present definition of the transfer requires rank preservation because the domain of definition is D^n. Following Shorrocks and Foster (1987), we can now state the next postulate.

Transfer Sensitivity Principle: For all $y \in D^n$, if x is obtained from by a favorable composite transfer, then $I(x) < I(x)$.

The following interesting implication of the above postulate was demonstrated by Shorrocks and Foster (1987) (*see also* Atkinson, 2008):

Proposition 1.5. *Let $x^1, x^2 \in D_{\bar{\lambda}}$ be arbitrary. Then the following conditions are equivalent:*

(i) x^1 third-order stochastic dominates x^2.
(ii) $I(x^1) < I(x^2)$ for all inequality indices $I : D_{\bar{\lambda}} \to R^1$ that fulfill Symmetry, the Pigou-Dalton Transfers Principle, the Dalton Population Principle, and the Transfer Sensitivity Principle.

This proposition clearly demonstrates the role of third-order stochastic dominance in inequality ranking.

We have noted that the relation $\geq_{LC}$ becomes inconclusive if the Lorenz curves intersect. However, if we restrict attention to transfer sensitive inequality indices, it becomes possible to rank distributions in such a situation. To see this, we first define multiple intersections of Lorenz curves. For $x \in D^{n_1}$ and $y \in D^{n_2}$, where $n_1, n_2 \geq 3$, $\mathrm{LC}(x,t)$ is said to cross $\mathrm{LC}(y,t)$ r times and first not from below if there exist $0 = t_0 < t_1 < t_2 < \ldots < t_r < t_{r+1} = 1 (r \geq 1)$ such that

$$\mathrm{LC}(x,t) \geq \mathrm{LC}(y,t) \text{ forall } t \in [t_{j-1}, t_j) \text{ if } j \text{ is odd,} \tag{1.14}$$

$$\mathrm{LC}(x,t) \leq \mathrm{LC}(y,t) \text{ forall } t \in [t_{j-1}, t_j) \text{ if } j \text{ is even.}$$

Davies and Hoy (1995) showed that a condition involving the variance plays a crucial role in evaluation of distributions in the case of multiple crossings of the Lorenz curves. For $x, y \in D^n$, let $x^j = (x_1, x_2, \ldots\ldots, x_{n(t_j,x)-1})$, where $1 \leq j \leq r$ and $n(t_j,x) = \min\{i \in \{1,2,\ldots,n\} | t_j \leq n(t_j,x)/n\}$ (*see* Sect. 1.4). Thus, the distribution x^j is constituted by the incomes of the $n(t_j,x) - 1$ poorest persons in x. We define y^j in an analogous manner. The following proposition of Davies and Hoy (1995) can now be stated:

Proposition 1.6. *Let $x, y \in D^n$, where $\lambda(x) = \lambda(y)$, be arbitrary. Then consider the following conditions:*

(i) $\mathrm{LC}(x,t)$ crosses $\mathrm{LC}(y,t)$ r times and first not from below.
(ii) $I(x) \leq I(y)$ for all symmetric inequality indices $I : D^n \to R^1$ that are nondecreasing under rank-preserving progressive transfers and favorable composite transfers.
(iii) $I_V(x^j) \leq I_V(y^j)$ for all $j = 1, 2, .., r$.

A sufficient condition for (i) to imply (ii) is that (iii) holds.

This proposition gives us a sufficient condition for checking dominance in the case of intersection of Lorenz curves and it does not involve third-order stochastic dominance.

The Diminishing Transfers Principle suggested by Kolm (1976a,b) relies on the assumption that the income shortfall of the recipient from the donor is fixed. Mehran (1976) and Kakwani (1980b) introduced a positional version of this postulate, which demands that the proportion of population between them is given a priori. That is, a rank-preserving transfer of income from a rich to a poor will reduce inequality by a higher amount the lower the income of the donor is, given that the number of individuals between the donor and the recipient is fixed. Formally,

Positional Transfer Sensitivity Principle: For all $x \in D^n$ and for any pair of poor individuals i and j, suppose that the distribution x' (respectively, x'') is obtained from x by a rank-preserving progressive transfer of income from the $(i+l)$th (respectively, $(j+l)$th) person to the ith (respectively, jth) person where $i<j$. Then $I(x)-I(x')>I(x)-I(x'')$.

To look at normative implications of this postulate, Zoli (1999b) considered the Yaari-type welfare function (Yaari, 1987, 1988):

$$W_Y(F)=\int_0^1 F^{-1}(t)\hat{f}(t)\mathrm{d}t, \tag{1.15}$$

where $\hat{f}(t)\geq 0$ is the weight function. Mehran (1976) showed that W_Y is nondecreasing under a rank-preserving progressive transfer if and only if $\hat{f}$ is nonincreasing. Further, convexity of $\hat{f}$ is necessary and sufficient for W_Y not to reduce under such a transfer with the additional restriction that the proportion of persons between the individuals affected by the transfer is fixed. Assuming that the welfare function is of the type (1.15), Zoli (1999b) demonstrated that for two distribution functions F and G, the conditions $\lambda(F)\geq\lambda(G)$ and weak inverse third-order stochastic dominance of F over G are equivalent to nonincreasingness and convexity of $\hat{f}$. This therefore provides a normative justification of inverse third-order stochastic dominance.

Different notions of transfer we have considered so far involve only one donor and one recipient. But an equitable transfer can as well be shared by more than one recipient. One possibility in this context is that an equitable transfer from someone is equally shared by any set of worst off persons from among who are poorer than him (*see* Chakravarty, 2007, 2008a; Chateauneuf and Moyes, 2006). Since the sharing of the transfer starts from the worst off person of the society, it has a lexicographic orientation. Formally, given $y \in D^n$, we say that x is obtained from y by a lexicographically equitable transfer if

$$\begin{aligned} &x_j=y_j-c''\geq x_{j-1} \quad \text{for some } j>1, \text{ for some } c''>0,\\ &x_i=y_i+\frac{c''}{l} \quad \text{for } 1\leq i\leq l\leq j-1, \\ &x_i=y_i \quad \text{for } i\in\{1,2,\dots,n\}-\{1,2,\dots l,j\}. \end{aligned} \tag{1.16}$$

That is, a lexicographically equitable transfer involves a rank-preserving progressive transfer (of size $c''>0$) from some person (j) and it is equally shared by the set $\{1,2,\dots,l\}$ of l worst off persons from among who are poorer than the donor j. By definition, the recipients of the transfer need not be all persons who are poorer than the donor. Thus, the transfer is shared by the recipients in a lexicographic manner in the sense that if there is only one recipient then he must be the poorest person of the society. In case of more than one recipient, a person can receive his equal share of the transfer only when all persons who are poorer than him have received their shares. If the donor is the only richest person of the society, then one possibility is that the transfer is distributed equally among all the remaining persons. We can now state the following inequality postulate involving a transfer of this type.

Lexicographic Transfers Principle: For all $y \in D^n$, if x is obtained from $y \in D^n$ by a lexicographically equitable transfer then $I(x) < I(y)$.

The following proposition shows the relationship between the Lexicographic Transfers Principle and strict S-convexity (Chakravarty, 2008a).

Proposition 1.7. *A sufficient condition for* $I : D^n_{\bar{\lambda}} = \{x \in D^n : \lambda(x) = \bar{\lambda}\} \to R^1$ *to satisfy the Lexicographic Transfers Principle is that it is strictly S-convex. However, a symmetric inequality index satisfying the Lexicographic Transfers Principle need not be strictly S-convex.*

Since a lexicographically equitable transfer captures the idea of income redistribution in a very weak form, it can be regarded as a minimal condition for incorporating egalitarian bias into distributional judgments.

Often we may need to assume that the inequality index is normalized which means that the value of the inequality index is zero if the income distribution is perfectly equal.

Normalization: If $x \in D^n$ is of the form $x = c1^n$, where $c > 0$ is a scalar, then $I(x) = 0$.

Given difficulties in measuring incomes accurately, it is reasonable to assume that the inequality index varies continuously with incomes. We thus assume continuity of the inequality index.

Continuity: I is continuous on its domain.

1.6 Relative Inequality and Welfare

The objective of this section is to present alternative indices of relative inequality suggested in the literature and discuss their properties analytically in terms of welfare. The presentation is divided into several subsections.

1.6.1 The Dalton Approach

Dalton (1920) used the symmetric utilitarian social welfare function $\sum_{i=1}^{n} U(x_i)$, where $x \in D^n$, and the individual utility function U is continuous, increasing, strictly concave, and positive. Then the Dalton index of inequality is defined as

$$I_{\mathrm{D}}(x) = 1 - \frac{1}{n}\sum_{i=1}^{n}\frac{U(x_i)}{U(\lambda(x))}. \tag{1.17}$$

Since U is strictly concave, by Jensen's inequality (Marshall and Olkin, 1979, p.454), $nU(\lambda) \geq \sum_{i=1}^{n} U(x_i)$, where the equality is achieved if incomes are equal. This shows that I_{D} is bounded between zero and one, where the lower bound is obtained in the case of equality of incomes. It tells us how much welfare we can increase (in relative terms) by distributing incomes equally. Clearly, I_{D} is symmetric, population replication invariant, and decreasing under a progressive transfer. [*See* Aigner and Heins (1967) and Sen (1973), for further discussion.]

1.6.2 The Atkinson Approach

The utility numbers $U(x_i), 1 \leq i \leq n$, and $U(\lambda)$ in (1.17) are based on the cardinal utility function U. Therefore, an affine transformation of these numbers such as $\hat{U}(x_i) = \hat{e}_1 + \hat{e}_2 U(x_i)$, $1 \leq i \leq n$, and $\hat{U}(\lambda) = \hat{e}_1 + \hat{e}_2 U(\lambda)$, where $\hat{e}_2 > 0$ and $\hat{e}_1$ are constants, can as well be used. Consequently, I_D based on U should coincide with that based on $\hat{U}$. Atkinson (1970) rightly pointed out that I_D does not remain invariant under affine transformations of U. He modified the Dalton index to remedy this problem.

Atkinson (1970) also used the symmetric utilitarian social welfare function and defined what he called the "equally distributed equivalent income" x_{e} associated with a given distribution $x \in D_+^n$ of a total income as that level of income which if given to everybody will make the total welfare exactly equal to that generated by the actual distribution x. Formally,

$$\sum_{i=1}^{n} U(x_{\mathrm{e}}) = \sum_{i=1}^{n} U(x_{\mathrm{i}}). \tag{1.18}$$

He replaced the Dalton inequality by $I_{\mathrm{A}} : D_+^n \to R^1$, where

$$I_{\mathrm{A}}(x) = 1 - \frac{x_{\mathrm{e}}}{\lambda(x)}. \tag{1.19}$$

If x is unequal, by Jensen's inequality $x_{\mathrm{e}} < \lambda(x)$. Consequently, the Atkinson index I_{A} is bounded above by one. It achieves its lower bound zero whenever incomes are equally distributed. I_{A} is continuous, symmetric, and population replication invariant. It determines the fraction of aggregate income that could be saved if society distributed incomes equally without any loss of welfare. From (1.18), it follows that $x_{\mathrm{e}} = U^{-1}(\sum_{i=1}^{n} U(x_i)/n)$, where U^{-1} is the inverse of the function U. Clearly, x_e calculated using U and $\hat{U}$ are the same, which in turn implies that I_{A} remains invariant under affine transformations of U.

The following theorem of Atkinson (1970) identifies a unique functional form for I_{A} if it is desired to be a relative index.

Theorem 1.8. *The only relative inequality index of the form (1.19) is given by*

$$I_{\mathrm{A}}(x)=\begin{cases}1-\dfrac{\left(1/n\sum_{i=1}^{n}x_i^{\theta}\right)^{1/\theta}}{\lambda(x)}, & \theta<1, \quad \theta\neq 0,\\ 1-\dfrac{\prod_{i=1}^{n}(x_i)^{1/n}}{\lambda(x)}, & \theta=0.\end{cases} \tag{1.20}$$

Proof. Observe that the mean income $\lambda(x)$ is linear homogeneous, that is, $\lambda(cx)=c\lambda(x)$ for all $x\in D_{+}^{n}$ and for all positive scalars c. Given that the denominator of (1.19) is linear homogeneous, for I_{A} to be a relative index it is necessary that x_{e} is also linear homogeneous. This means that

$$U^{-1}\left(\frac{\sum_{i=1}^{n}U(cx_i)}{n}\right)=cU^{-1}\left(\frac{\sum_{i=1}^{n}U(x_i)}{n}\right), \tag{1.21}$$

where $c>0$ is a scalar. The only continuous solution to the functional equation (1.21) is given by

$$U(x_i)=\begin{cases}\hat{e}_3+\hat{e}_4\frac{x_i^{\theta}}{\theta}, \theta\neq 0,\\ \hat{e}_3+\hat{e}_4\log x_i, \theta=0,\end{cases} \tag{1.22}$$

where $\hat{e}_3$ and $\hat{e}_4$ are constants (Aczel, 1966, p.153). Increasingness and strict concavity of U demand that $\hat{e}_4>0$ and $\theta<1$. Substituting the form of x_{e} calculated using U given by (1.22) in (1.19), we get the form of I_{A} specified in (1.20). This establishes the necessity form of the theorem. The sufficiency can be verified easily[2].
□

The parameter θ in the Atkinson index I_{A} given by (1.20) represents relative sensitivity of I_{A} to transfers at different income positions. All members of I_{A} satisfy the Transfer Sensitivity Principle of Shorrocks and Foster (1987). The extent of reduction in I_{A} under a favorable composite transfer is higher the lower is the value of θ. For a given $x\in D_{+}^{n}$, I_{A} is decreasing in θ. As $\theta\to-\infty$, I_{A} approaches $1-\min_i\{x_i\}/\lambda$, the relative maximin index, which corresponds to the maximin welfare function $\min_i\{x_i\}$ of Rawls (1971). On the other hand, as $\theta\to 1$, I_{A} approaches zero, showing insensitivity to the actual distribution of income.

1.6.3 The Atkinson-Kolm-Sen and the Shorrocks Approaches

Sen (1973) argued that ethical judgments on alternative income distributions can be summarized by an ordinally significant social welfare function $W: D^n\to R^1$. It is assumed that W is continuous, strictly S-concave, and satisfies the Pareto Principle

[2] A proof of Theorem 1.8 using differentiability of U was provided in Chakravarty (1990). However, the present proof does not require differentiability.

(increasingness). We refer to these three assumptions as basic assumptions for a social welfare function.

The Atkinson (1970)-Kolm (1969)-Sen (1973) "equally distributed equivalent" or "representative" income x_f associated with $x \in D^n$ is defined as that level of income which if enjoyed by everybody will make the existing distribution socially indifferent. Formally,

$$W(x_f 1^n) = W(x). \tag{1.23}$$

Given assumptions about W, we can solve (1.23) uniquely for x_f and write it as

$$x_f = E(x), \tag{1.24}$$

where E is a specific cardinalization of W, that is, $W(x) \geq W(y) \leftrightarrow E(x) \geq E(y) \leftrightarrow x_f \geq y_f$. E possesses all the basic properties of W. The indifference surfaces of E are numbered so that $E(c1^n) = c$, where $c > 0$ is arbitrary. Given strict S-concavity of $W, x_f < \lambda(x)$.

The Atkinson-Kolm-Sen index of inequality is defined as $I_{\text{AKS}} : D^n \to R^1$, where

$$I_{\text{AKS}}(x) = 1 - \frac{E(x)}{\lambda(x)}. \tag{1.25}$$

I_{AKS} is continuous, strictly S-convex, and possesses the same boundedness property as I_{A}. It is population replication invariant if E is so. I_{AKS} gives the fraction of total income that could be saved if society distributed the remaining amount equally without any welfare loss, given that welfare evaluation is done with the appropriate social welfare function. Since contours of E are numbered, we can rewrite the denominator of (1.25) as $E(\lambda(x)1^n)$, from which it follows that I_{AKS} can be interpreted as the proportion of welfare loss due to inequality. Note that any ordinal transformation of W does not change E and hence I_{AKS}.

We explain the index I_{AKS} graphically in Fig. 1.3. In the figure, two persons share a given total income OA_2. The line A_1A_2 gives alternative distributions of this total. A_5 is the point of equal distribution and $A_5A_6 (= OA_6)$ is the mean income. SIC is the social indifference curve representing a particular level of welfare. A higher curve will represent a higher welfare. Since the social welfare function is symmetric, SIC intersects the line of total income A_1A_2 at A_4 and A_3 symmetrically around the line of equality OA_5 in the sense that A_4 and A_3 are equidistant from A_5. Consequently, either A_4 or A_3 represents the actual distribution of income. The representative income is given by $A_7A_8 (= OA_8)$. Then I_{AKS} becomes $I_{\text{AKS}} = 1 - A_7A_8/A_5A_6 = 1 - OA_8/OA_6$.

Given a functional form for I_{AKS}, we can recover E (hence W) using (1.25), (1.24), and (1.23). Thus, $E(x) = \lambda(x)(1 - I_{\text{AKS}}(x))$ shows that E is increasing in efficiency ($\lambda(x)$) and decreasing in inequality as determined by I_{AKS} (equivalently, increasing in the Atkinson-Kolm-Sen equity index $1 - I_{\text{AKS}}$). E is a particular form of the general abbreviated or reduced form welfare function $\Xi(\lambda(x), I(x))$, which is increasing in its first argument and decreasing in the second argument, where I is an arbitrary index of inequality. We refer to Ξ as abbreviated or reduced

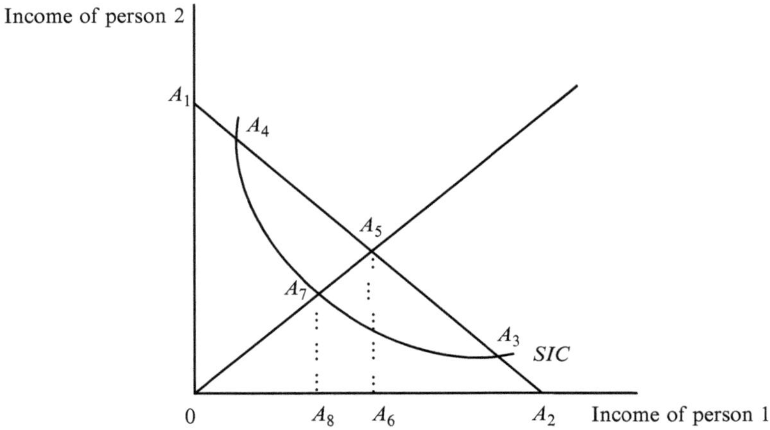

Fig. 1.3 The Atkinson-Kolm-Sen index

form welfare function because it abbreviates the entire distribution in terms of efficiency and inequality (*see* Amiel and Cowell, 2003; Blackorby et al., 1999, 2005; Burk and Gehrig, 1978; Chakravarty, 1988b, 1990, 2008a; Champernowne and Cowell, 1998; Dutta and Esteban, 1992; Ebert, 1987; Foster and Sen, 1997; Graaff, 1977; Lambert, 2001).

Since I_{AKS} is expressed in terms of a ratio between two functions of the income distribution x, it is reasonable to interpret it as a relative index that depends on income ratios. Since $\lambda(x)$ is linear homogeneous, a necessary condition for I_{AKS} to be a relative index is that E is linear homogeneous as well. Given that E and W are ordinally equivalent, this means that W is a homothetic welfare function. That is,

$$W(x) = \hat{\psi}(E(x)), \tag{1.26}$$

where $\hat{\psi}$ is increasing in its argument.

Conversely, suppose that W is homothetic, that is, $W(x) = \hat{\varphi}(\hat{W}(x))$, where $\hat{W}$ is linear homogeneous and $\hat{\varphi}$ is increasing in its argument. Then we have $x_f = E(x) = \hat{W}(x)/\hat{W}(1^n)$, which is linear homogeneous by linear homogeneity of $\hat{W}$. Hence, I_{AKS} is a relative index. These observations are summarized in the following theorem of Blackorby and Donaldson (1978).

Theorem 1.9. *The Atkinson-Kolm-Sen inequality index I_{AKS} is a relative index if and only if the social welfare function W is homothetic.*

If a relative inequality index has a natural upper bound one, then we can identify its abbreviated welfare function Ξ using the inequality index I_{AKS}. For the Atkinson index $I_{\text{A}}(x)$ in (1.20), this function is the symmetric mean of order $\theta(< 1)$, SM_θ, given by

$$E_{\mathrm{A}}(x)=\Xi_{\mathrm{A}}(\lambda(x),I_{\mathrm{A}}(x))=\mathrm{SM}_{\theta}(x)=\begin{cases}\left(\frac{1}{n}\sum_{i=1}^{n}x_i^{\theta}\right)^{1/\theta}, & \theta<1,\theta\neq 0,\\ \prod_{i=1}^{n}(x_i)^{1/n}, & \theta=0,\end{cases}\tag{1.27}$$

where $x \in D_{+}^{n}$. For $\theta = 0, E_{\mathrm{A}}(x)$ is the geometric mean GM(x). Other examples of relative indices that have natural upper bound 1 are the Gini index I_{G}, the Bonferroni index I_{B} (*see* Bonferroni, 1930) and the Donaldson-Weymark illfare-ranked S-Gini index I_{DWI} (*see* Donaldson and Weymark, 1980, 1983), where

$$I_{\mathrm{G}}(x)=1-\frac{1}{n^2\lambda(x)}\sum_{i=1}^{n}(2(n-i)+1)x_i,\tag{1.28}$$

$$I_{\mathrm{B}}(x)=1-\frac{1}{n\lambda(x)}\sum_{i=1}^{n}\frac{1}{i}\sum_{j=1}^{i}x_j,\tag{1.29}$$

and

$$I_{\mathrm{DWI}}(x)=1-\frac{1}{\lambda(x)}\sum_{i=1}^{n}\left[\left(\frac{i}{n}\right)^{\bar{r}}-\left(\frac{i-1}{n}\right)^{\bar{r}}\right]x_i, 0<\bar{r}<1.\tag{1.30}$$

The Gini index, which is the most popular index of inequality, has a natural geometric interpretation as twice the area enclosed between the Lorenz curve and the diagonal line representing perfect equality. For any unordered income distribution $x \in \Gamma^n$, its equivalent definition is

$$I_{\mathrm{G}}(x)=\frac{1}{2n^2\lambda(x)}\sum_{i=1}^{n}\sum_{j=1}^{n}|x_i-x_j|.\tag{1.31}$$

Pyatt (1976) interpreted this formula in terms of expected value of a game in which each individual is able to compare himself with some other drawn at random from the total population. [*See* Yitzhaki (1998), for alternative formulations of the Gini index.] If we denote the mean of i lowest incomes $(x_1,x_2,\ldots,x_i)$ by λ_i, then I_{B} is the amount by which the mean of the ratios λ_i/λ falls short of unity, where $i=1,2,\ldots,n$ (*see* Nygard and Sandstrom, 1981). For a given x, I_{DWI} decreases as $\bar{r}$ increases over $(0,1)$. As $\bar{r}\to 0$, I_{DWI} converges to the relative maximin index and as $\bar{r}\to 1$, $I_{\mathrm{DWI}}\to 0$. Therefore, as the value of $\bar{r}$ increases the concern for inequality decreases.

With a given rank order of incomes, all these three indices are linear in incomes. That is why none of them satisfies the Diminishing Transfers Principle although they fulfill the Pigou-Dalton Condition. In fact, I_{B} and I_{DWI} satisfy the Positional Transfer Sensitivity Principle as well, but I_{G} des not possess this property. I_{G} is a violator of the Positional Transfer Sensitivity Principle because it assigns equal weight to a given transfer irrespective of wherever it takes place, provided that it occurs between two persons with a fixed rank difference. However, I_{G} and I_{DWI} are population replication invariant but I_{B} is not. Thus, while I_{G} and I_{DWI} are suitable for cross-population comparisons of inequality, I_{B} is not. Assuming a continuous type distribution of income, Aaberge, (2000, 2007) demonstrated that I_G (respectively, I_B) will satisfy the Diminishing Transfers principle if F (respectively, $\log F$) is strictly concave, where F is the distribution function. However, the form of the Bonferroni index used by Aaberge (2000, 2007) only approximates I_B, since I_B is a violator of the Dalton Population Principle "a property of all indices for distributions in the continuum" (Donaldson and Weymark, 1983, p. 358). Aaberge (2000) showed that moments of Lorenz curve generate a family of inequality indices which include I_G. [*See also* Kakwani (1980a), for a discussion on Lorenz curve-based inequality indices].

The reduced form welfare functions, equivalently, the representative incomes associated with these indices are given, respectively, by

$$E_G(x) = \Xi_G(\lambda(x), I_G(x)) = \frac{1}{n^2}\sum_{i=1}^{n}(2(n-i)+1)x_i, \tag{1.32}$$

$$E_B(x) = \Xi_B(\lambda(x), I_B(x)) = \frac{1}{n}\sum_{i=1}^{n}\frac{1}{i}\sum_{j=1}^{i}x_j, \tag{1.33}$$

$$E_{DWI}(x) = \Xi_{DWI}(\lambda(x), I_{DWI}(x)) = \sum_{i=1}^{n}\left[\left(\frac{i}{n}\right)^{\bar{r}} - \left(\frac{i-1}{n}\right)^{\bar{r}}\right]x_i. \tag{1.34}$$

The Gini welfare function E_G and the Bonferroni welfare function E_B are identical if $n = 2$. There have been additional attempts to formalize relationship between the Gini index and social welfare function. Examples along this line are $n^2(1-I_G)\lambda$ (Ben-Porath and Gilboa, 1994; Lambert, 1985; Sheshinski, 1972), $\log\lambda - I_G$ (Kats, 1972), $\lambda(1-I_G)/(1+I_G)$ (Chipman, 1974; Dagum, 1990) and $\lambda/(1+I_G)$ (Kakwani, 1986; Kondor, 1975a; Newbery, 1970). But the central idea in all the cases is the same – the welfare function is increasing in efficiency and decreasing in inequality.

The three welfare functions given by (1.32)–(1.34) are members of the rank dependent general welfare function

$$W_a(x) = \sum_{i=1}^{n} a_i x_i \tag{1.35}$$

where $a = (a_1, a_2, \ldots a_n)$: $a_1 > a_2 > \ldots > a_n > 0$ and $\sum_{i=1}^{n} a_i = 1$ (*see* Ben-Porath and Gilboa, 1994; Donaldson and Weymark, 1980, 1983; Mehran, 1976; Quiggin, 1993; Weymark, 1981; Yaari, 1987, 1988). Thus, W_a is the weighted average of illfare-ranked incomes. It is also referred to as the generalized Gini welfare function. Positivity of a_i guarantees that W_a satisfies the Pareto Principle, that is, increasingness in individual incomes. Decreasingness of the sequence of coefficients $\{a_i\}$ is necessary and sufficient for strict S-concavity of W_a. For $a_i = \sum_{j=i}^{n} 1/jn$, W_a coincides with the Boferroni welfare function Ξ_B. On the other hand, the Gini welfare function Ξ_G drops out as a particular case of W_a if we assume that $a_i = (2(n-i)+1)/n^2$. If we assume that $a_i = ((i/n)^{\bar{r}} - ((i-1)/n)^{\bar{r}})$, the resulting form of W_a becomes the Donaldson-Weymark function Ξ_{DWI}. The social welfare function W_a shows preference for lexicographic equity in the sense that its value increases under a lexicographically equitable transfer if and only if $\sum_{i=1}^{l} a_i/l > a_j$, where $l < j$ and $j > 1$ are arbitrary (Chakravarty, 2007). Clearly, decreasingness of the sequence $\{a_i\}$ implies this condition but the converse is not true. Suppose $a_i = \bar{g}(i/n) - \bar{g}((i-1)/n)$, where $\bar{g} : \{i/n | i = 0, 1, \ldots, n\} \to R^1$ satisfies the conditions that $\bar{g}(i/n) - \bar{g}((i-1)/n)$ is positive, $\bar{g}(0) = 0$ and $\bar{g}(1) = 1$. For the specification $a_i = \bar{g}(i/n) - \bar{g}((i-1)/n)$, W_a becomes lexicographically equity preferring if and only if $g(i/n)/(i/n)$ is increasing (Chakravarty, 2008a). Chateauneuf and Moyes (2006) investigated the welfare implications of lexicographically equitable transfers using the welfare function $W_{CM}(x) = \sum_{i=1}^{n} \hat{g}((n-i+1)/n)(x_i - x_{i-1})$, where $\hat{g} : (0,1) \to (0,1)$ is continuous, nondecreasing, $\hat{g}(0) = 0, \hat{g}(1) = 1$, and $x_0 = 0$. Their demonstration shows that the necessary and sufficient condition for W_{CM} not to decrease under a transfer of this type is that $\hat{g}(t) \leq t$.

Chateauneuf et al. (2002) defined the Strong Diminishing Transfers Principle as a combination of the Positional Transfer Sensitivity and the Diminishing Transfers Principles. That is, a strong diminishing transfer, which is a rank-preserving transfer from an individual with rank $(i+l)$ and income $y_i + \hat{c}$ to someone with rank i and income y_i, should have a greater impact the lower i and y_i are, where $\hat{c} > 0$ and l are given. They considered the rank dependent expected utility type social welfare function $W_{CGW}(x) = \sum_{i=1}^{n} (\hat{g}((n-i+1)/n) - \hat{g}((n-i)/n))U(x_i)$, where the utility function U is increasing. It is then shown that the necessary conditions for W_{CGW} not to decrease under a strong diminishing transfer are nonnegativity of the third-order derivatives of $\hat{g}$ and utility function U.

We now turn to the rank dependent welfare function based on the welfare-ranked permutation of the income distributions. The welfare –ranked permutation x^0 of the distribution $x \in \Gamma^n$ is denoted by $x^0 = (x_1^0, x_2^0, \ldots, x_n^0)$, where $x_1^0 \geq x_2^0 \geq \ldots \geq x_n^0$. This function is parameterized by the sequence of coefficients $\{\hat{a}_i\}$, where $0 < \hat{a}_1 < \hat{a}_2 < \ldots < \hat{a}_n$ and $\sum_{i=1}^{n} \hat{a}_i = 1$. The corresponding welfare function is given by

$$W_{\hat{a}}(x) = \sum_{i=1}^{n} \hat{a}_i x_i^0, \tag{1.36}$$

where $\hat{a} = (\hat{a}_1, \hat{a}_2, \ldots \hat{a}_n)$. Positivity and increasingness of the coefficient sequence $\{a_i\}$ guarantee that $W_{\hat{a}}$ is increasing and strictly S-concave. [See Bossert (1990a), for a characterization of $W_{\hat{a}}$.] Only a subfamily of $W_{\hat{a}}$ remains invariant under replications of the population (Donaldson and Weymark, 1980). In this case, the coefficients in $\hat{a}$ are derived from a single inequality aversion parameter $\delta > 1$. The Donaldson and Weymark welfare –ranked S-Gini welfare function is then given by

$$W_{DWW}(x) = \sum_{i=1}^{n} \left[\left(\frac{i}{n}\right)^{\delta} - \left(\frac{i-1}{n}\right)^{\delta} \right] x_i^0. \tag{1.37}$$

For $\delta = 1$, we get the income average welfare function and as δ approaches plus infinity, the maximin criterion is approximated. For $\delta = 2$, the Gini social welfare function is obtained.

Donaldson and Weymark (1983) extended the welfare-ranked S-Gini index of inequality $I_{\mathrm{DWW}}(x) = 1 - W_{\mathrm{WDW}}(x)/\lambda(x)$ to the distributions in the continuum. The functional form of the Donaldson-Weymark welfare-ranked S-Gini index in this framework is given by

$$I_{\mathrm{DWW}}(F) = 1 - \frac{1}{\lambda(F)} \int_{0}^{\infty} (1 - F(v))^{\delta} \mathrm{d}v, \tag{1.38}$$

where F is the income distribution function and $\lambda(F)$ is the mean income. For $\delta = 2$, (1.38) becomes the Dorfman (1979) formula for the Gini index. $I_{\mathrm{DWW}}(x)$ fulfills the Positional Transfer Sensitivity Principle for all $\delta > 2$. Yitzhaki (1983) investigated a number of properties of $I_{\mathrm{DWW}}(F)$ and demonstrated that when $I_{\mathrm{DWW}}(F)$ is rewritten in terms of the Lorenz curve it becomes equivalent to a formula of Kakwani (1980b). According to Kakwani (1980b), his formula is the continuous analogue of $(1 - \sum_{i=1}^{n} i^{\hat{\varepsilon}} x_i / \sum_{i=1}^{n} i^{\hat{\varepsilon}} \lambda(x))$, where $x \in D^n$ and $\hat{\varepsilon} > 0$ is a parameter. This formula fails to satisfy the Population Principle and for $\hat{\varepsilon} = 1$ it approximates the Gini index. As Donaldson and Weymark (1983) pointed out this formula is not a special case of (when the cumulative distribution function is a step function) of $I_{\mathrm{DWW}}(F)$, but $I_{\mathrm{DWW}}(x)$ is (*see also* Aaberge, 2000, 2001; Lambert, 1985, 2001; Zoli, 1999b).

Thus, the inequality-welfare relationship we have discussed above is exact in the sense that to every homothetic social welfare function, there corresponds a different Atkinson-Kolm-Sen relative index of inequality and conversely, given an inequality index with a natural upper bound one we can determine its associated welfare function.

However, not all inequality indices are bounded above by one, which implies that their welfare functions cannot be expressed in the Atkinson-Kolm-Sen form. In such a situation, we may divide the inequality index by its maximum attainable value, which is achieved when the richest person monopolizes the entire income of the society and all other persons receive zero income, so that the transformed index becomes bounded above by one. [In fact, Blackorby and Donaldson (1978) did this for some indices.] But for an inequality index that reduces under a progressive transfer this normalization is achieved at the cost of population replication invariance. To see this, consider the two-person distribution $x = (0, x_2)$, where $x_2 > 0$. If the inequality index I satisfies the Dalton Population Principle, then $I(x) = I(y)$, where $y = (0, 0, x_2, x_2)$. Now, generate the distribution y^1 from y by transferring $\tilde{\varepsilon}$ amount of income from the third person to the fourth person so that $y^1 = (0, 0, x_2 - \tilde{\varepsilon}, x_2 + \tilde{\varepsilon})$, where $0 < \tilde{\varepsilon} < x_2$. Then by the Pigou-Dalton Transfers Principle, $I(y^1) > I(y) = I(x)$. But this is ruled out in view of the assumption that the value of the inequality index is maximum for x. An additional problem with this normalization is that some indices may not even be defined for zero incomes.

Examples of relative inequality indices that are not bounded above by one are the Theil entropy index I_{TE}, the mean logarithmic deviation I_{TML} (Theil, 1967, 1972) and the coefficient of variation I_{CV}, where

$$I_{\mathrm{TE}}(x) = \frac{1}{n}\sum_{i=1}^{n}\frac{x_i}{\lambda(x)}\log\frac{x_i}{\lambda(x)}, x \in D^n, \tag{1.39}$$

$$I_{\mathrm{TML}}(x) = \frac{1}{n}\sum_{i=1}^{n}\log\frac{\lambda(x)}{x_i}, x \in D^n_+, \tag{1.40}$$

$$I_{\mathrm{CV}}(x) = \frac{\sqrt{n^{-1}\sum_{i=1}^{n}(x_i - \lambda(x))^2}}{\lambda(x)}, x \in D^n. \tag{1.41}$$

Since for I_{TML} to be well-defined, we need positivity of all incomes, the normalization condition considered above does not even apply to I_{TML}. While I_{CV} satisfies transfer neutrality in the sense that it attaches equal weight to transfers at all income positions, the two Theil indices I_{TE} and I_{TML} assign higher weight to transfers at lower income levels.

In view of the above discussion, we assume that the welfare functions associated with these indices are of Shorrocks (1988) type, which do not depend on the upper bound of an inequality index. More generally, we may assume that the abbreviated welfare function associated with any continuous, strictly S-convex, relative inequality index I, including the ones defined in (1.39)–(1.41), is of the form

$$\Xi_{\mathrm{S}}(\lambda(x), I(x)) = \lambda(x)\exp(-I(x)), \tag{1.42}$$

where "exp" is the exponential function. The Shorrocks welfare function Ξ_{S} is continuous, linear homogeneous, and strictly S-concave, but need not be increasing in individual incomes. However, it satisfies the scale improvement condition defined in (1.3). Consequently, it agrees with the dominance condition identified in Theorem 1.6. In fact, it is minimally increasing also, which means that if all individuals enjoy the same income more is preferred to less (Blackorby and Donaldson, 1984a). Minimal increasingness is weaker than any of the Pareto preference conditions and the scale improvement condition.

Evidently, in this case also the relation may be reversed. That is, given the welfare function (1.42), we can generate the associated inequality index uniquely as $I(x) = \log(\lambda(x)/\Xi_{\mathrm{S}}(\lambda(x), I(x)))$ from (1.42). Thus, given any relative inequality index, which may or may not be bounded above by one, we can always associate it with the corresponding reduced form welfare function using the one-to-one relationship (1.42). Clearly, the exact inequality-welfare relationship defined by (1.42) is more general than the one defined by the Atkinson-Kolm-Sen framework. (Axiomatic characterizations of $E(x) = \lambda(x)(1 - I_{\mathrm{AKS}}(x))$ and Ξ_{S} can be found in Chakravarty, 2008a.)

Finally, we discuss a Lorenz curve-based extended Gini index of inequality which was suggested with the objective of being more sensitive to the transfers at the lower end of the distribution (Chakravarty, 1988b). The extended Gini (E-Gini) index, which is based on the difference between the line of equality and the Lorenz curve, is defined as

$$I_{\mathrm{EG}}(F) = 2(\bar{\phi})^{-1}\left(\int_0^1 \bar{\phi}(t - \mathrm{LC}(F,t))\mathrm{d}t\right), \tag{1.43}$$

where the real valued function $\bar{\phi}$ defined on the interval $[0,1]$ is continuous, increasing, strictly convex, $\bar{\phi}(0) = 0$ and $(\bar{\phi})^{-1}$ is the inverse of $\bar{\phi}$. I_{EG} is transfer sensitive in the Shorrocks-Foster (1987) sense, continuous, bounded between zero and two, where the lower bound is achieved in the case of perfect equality. We may define the minimally increasing E-Gini welfare function associated with I_{EG} as $\Xi_{EG} = \lambda(F)\exp(-I_{EG})$. If we choose $\bar{\phi}(v) = v^{\bar{\mu}}$, where $\bar{\mu} > 1$ is a constant, then as $\bar{\mu} \to 1$, I_{EG} approaches the Gini index. An alternative of interest arises from the specification $\bar{\phi}(v) = (\exp(v) - 1)$. In this case, I_{EG} involves a Kolm-Pollak type aggregation. [Dutta (2002) provides further discussion on I_{EG}.]

1.7 Relative Inequality as an Ordinal Concept

In the approaches, we have discussed in Sect. 1.6 the inequality numbers are meaningful. If inequality is regarded as an ordinal concept, then ordinally equivalent inequality indices can lead to different social welfare orderings by the procedures discussed in that section. For instance, the welfare functions $\lambda(x)(1-(I(x))^2)$ and $\lambda(x)\exp(-(I(x))^2)$ cannot be expressed as ordinal transforms of the functions $\lambda(x)(1-I(x))$ and $\lambda(x)\exp(-I(x))$, respectively. The problem of deriving ethical inequality indices with ordinal significance have been discussed by Blackorby and Donaldson (1984b), Ebert (1987), and Dutta and Esteban (1992). Our presentation in this section is based on the Ebert approach (Ebert, 1987) and assumes that $n \in N, n \geq 2$, is arbitrary.

Let $\geq_I$ be a continuous, relative inequality ordering on Γ^n. Continuity implies the existence of a continuous index I on Γ^n and relativity means its scale invariance. Given its ordinal interpretation any increasing transformation of I carries the same information as I itself.

Equity efficiency trade off can be expressed in terms of a continuous ordering $\geq_{EE}$ defined on $\Gamma^1_+ \times Y_I$, where Y_I is the set of indifference classes of $\geq_I$. For any $y \in \Gamma^n$, y_I stands for the indifference class of $\geq_I$ to which y belongs. Consistency of $\geq_{EE}$ with $\geq_I$ requires that for any fixed mean income $\bar{\lambda}$, two arbitrary distributions $x, y \in \Gamma^n$ are ranked by $\geq_I$ in the opposite way as the corresponding indifference classes are ranked by $\geq_{EE}$. Formally, $\geq_{EE}$ is consistent with $\geq_I$ if and only if for all $x, y \in \Gamma^n$, for all $\bar{\lambda} > 0$,

$$y \geq_I x \leftrightarrow [(\bar{\lambda}, x_I) \geq_{EE} (\bar{\lambda}, y_I)]. \tag{1.44}$$

Given $\geq_I$ and $\geq_{EE}$, a social welfare ordering $\geq_W$ can now be defined as follows: For all $x, y \in \Gamma^n$.

$$x \geq_W y \leftrightarrow [(\lambda(x), x_I) \geq_{EE} (\lambda(y), y_I)] \tag{1.45}$$

Continuity of $\geq_I$ and $\geq_{EE}$ ensure continuity of $\geq_W$. Consistency property along with the fact the inequality ordering $\geq_I$ is relative ensures that $\geq_W$ has the following property, which is weaker than homotheticity: For all $x, y \in \Gamma^n$ and for all $c > 0$,

$$\left[\frac{x}{\lambda(x)} \geq_{\mathrm{W}} \frac{y}{\lambda(y)}\right] \leftrightarrow \left[\frac{cx}{\lambda(x)} \geq_{\mathrm{W}} \frac{cy}{\lambda(y)}\right]. \tag{1.46}$$

This procedure can be reversed in the sense that starting from (1.46) we can go back to $\geq_{\mathrm{I}}$. More precisely, for any social welfare ordering $\geq_{\mathrm{W}}$ satisfying (1.46), we can find continuous orderings $\geq_{\mathrm{I}}$ and $\geq_{\mathrm{EE}}$ such that the consistency property is satisfied and $\geq_{\mathrm{I}}$ is relative. The relationship (1.46) specifies the property that a social welfare ordering should possess for deriving an ethical relative inequality index which is ordinally significant. [In a slightly less general framework, Blackorby and Donaldson (1984b), derived equivalent condition for the consistency property (1.44).]

1.8 Absolute Inequality and Welfare

The concept of absolute inequality was introduced by Kolm (1976a,b). Blackorby and Donaldson (1980a) made an investigation for deriving absolute indices from general social welfare functions. Our discussion in this section is divided into two subsections. Unless specified, throughout the section, we will assume that the domain of definition of the inequality index is $\hat{R}^n_+$ ($\hat{R}_+$ in the case of variable population).

1.8.1 The Kolm Approach

Kolm (1976a) suggested an absolute index assuming a separability condition which says that for all income distributions x and for all i, j, l, the ratio between the partial derivatives of $(\lambda(x) - I(x))$ with respect to x_i and x_j is independent of x_l, where $i \neq j \neq l$. If we interpret $(\lambda(x) - I(x))$ as a social welfare function, then this condition means that the marginal social rate of substitution between income accruing to individual i and income accruing to individual j is independent of the income of individual l, where $i \neq j \neq l$ are arbitrary. However, our derivation here does not assume differentiability. We begin by defining the inequality index as

$$I_{\mathrm{KP}}(x) = \lambda(x) - x_{\mathrm{e}}, \tag{1.47}$$

where $x \in \hat{R}^n_+$ and the equally distributed equivalent income x_{e} is defined by (1.18). This nonnegative, continuous, population replication invariant index determines the per capita income that could be saved if society distributed incomes equally without any loss of welfare. By construction, it remains invariant under affine transformations of the utility function U. It achieves its lower bound zero whenever incomes are equally distributed. If we employ x_{e} based on the class of additive welfare functions considered by Pollak (1971) in (1.47), the resulting index becomes the explicit form of the Kolm index (1.48). That is why, we refer to I_{KP} as the Kolm-Pollak index.

The following theorem identifies a unique functional form for I_{KP} if it is desired to be an absolute index.

Theorem 1.10. *The only absolute inequality index of the form (1.47) is given by*

$$I_{\text{KP}}(x) = \lambda(x) + \frac{1}{\beta}\log\frac{1}{n}\sum_{i=1}^{n}(\exp(-\beta x_i)), \tag{1.48}$$

where $\beta > 0$ is a constant.

Proof. Note that $\lambda(x)$ is unit translatable, that is, an equal absolute change in all incomes changes $\lambda(x)$ by the absolute amount itself. Formally, $\lambda(x+c1^n) = \lambda(x) + c$, where c is a scalar such that $x + c1^n \in \hat{R}^n_+$. Therefore, for I_{KP} in (1.47) to be an absolute index, we need unit translatability of x_e. This means that

$$U^{-1}\left(\frac{\sum_{i=1}^{n} U(x_i+c)}{n}\right) = U^{-1}\left(\frac{\sum_{i=1}^{n} U(x_i)}{n}\right) + c, \tag{1.49}$$

where c is a scalar such that $x + c1^n \in \hat{R}^n_+$. The only continuous solution to the functional equation (1.49) is given by

$$U(x_i) = \hat{e}_5 - \hat{e}_6\exp(-\beta x_i). \tag{1.50}$$

where $\hat{e}_5$ and $\hat{e}_6$ are constants (Aczel, 1966, p.153). Increasingness and strict concavity of U demand that $\hat{e}_6 > 0$ and $\beta > 0$. Substituting the form of x_e calculated using U given by (1.50) in (1.47), we get the desired form of I_{KP}. This establishes the necessity form of the theorem. The sufficiency can be verified easily. □

The index I_{KP} satisfies the Transfer Sensitivity Principle for all $\beta \in (0,\infty)$. It reduces under a favorable composite transfer by a larger amount the higher is the value of β. As $\beta \to \infty, I_{\text{KP}}(x) \to \lambda(x) - \min_i\{x_i\}$, the absolute maximin index of inequality.

1.8.2 The Blackorby-Donaldson-Kolm Approach

The Kolm (1976a,b) approach to the measurement of absolute inequality has been substantially generalized and made more formal by Blackorby and Donaldson (1980a) using the Atkinson-Kolm-Sen representative income $x_f = E(x)$ based on the general welfare function $W : \hat{R}^n_+ \to R^1$. In their study Blackorby and Donaldson (1980a) suggested the use of

$$I_{\text{BDK}}(x) = \lambda(x) - E(x), \tag{1.51}$$

as an index of inequality. We refer to I_{BDK} as the Blackorby-Donaldson –Kolm inequality index. Given the basic assumptions about W, I_{BDK} is continuous and strictly

S-convex. It has the same boundedness property and same per capita saving interpretation as I_{KP}. Since $E(\lambda(x)1^n) = \lambda(x)$, we can also interpret it as the size of absolute welfare loss due to inequality. It is population replication invariant if E satisfies the same. In terms of Fig. 1.3, I_{BDK} becomes $OA_6 - OA_8$. Given a functional form for I_{BDK}, we can recover W using (1.51), (1.24), and (1.23).

Since I_{BDK} is defined as the difference between two functions of the income distribution x, it is reasonable to regard it as an absolute index. Since $\lambda(x)$ is unit translatable, a necessary condition for I_{KBD} to be an absolute index is that E is also unit translatable. Given that E and W are ordinally equivalent, this means that W is a translatable welfare function. That is,

$$W(x) = \bar{\psi}(E(x)), \tag{1.52}$$

where $\bar{\psi}$ is increasing in its argument and $E(x+c1^n) = E(x)+c$, where c is a scalar such that $x+c1^n \in \hat{R}^n_+$.

Conversely, suppose that W is translatable, that is, $W(x) = \bar{\varphi}(\bar{W}(x))$, where $\bar{W}$ is unit translatable and $\bar{\varphi}$ is increasing in its argument. Then we have $x_f = E(x) = \bar{W}(x) - \bar{W}(01^n)$, which is unit translatable by unit translatability of $\bar{W}$. Hence, I_{BDK} is an absolute index. The following theorem of Blackorby and Donaldson (1980a) summarizes these observations:

Theorem 1.11. *The Blackorby-Donaldson –Kolm inequality index I_{BDK} is an absolute index if and only if the social welfare function W is translatable.*

The absolute index I_{BDK} tells us how much must be added in absolute terms to the income of each person to reach the same level of welfare that would be achieved if everyone received the mean income of the original distribution. Thus, I_{BDK} gives the per capita cost of inequality. All absolute indices of the form (1.51) imply and are implied by translatable welfare functions. The abbreviated welfare function associated with the Kolm-Pollak index is given by

$$\Xi_{\mathrm{KP}}(\lambda(x), I_{\mathrm{KP}}(x)) = -\frac{1}{\beta}\log\frac{1}{n}\sum_{i=1}^{n}(\exp(-\beta x_i)). \tag{1.53}$$

Some welfare functions are both homothetic and translatable. Such functions are called distributionally homothetic (Blackorby and Donaldson, 1980a). Formally, we say that $W : D^n \to R^1$ is distributionally homothetic if

$$W(x) = \tilde{\psi}(\tilde{W}(x)), \tag{1.54}$$

where $\tilde{\psi}$ is increasing in its argument and $\tilde{W}$ is distributionally homogeneous, that is,

$$\tilde{W}(cx+c'1^n) = c\tilde{W}(x)+c', \tag{1.55}$$

where $c > 0$ and c' are scalars such that $cx+c'1^n \in D^n$. Such welfare functions are compromise welfare functions because they enable us to construct both relative and absolute indices. The Donaldson and Weymark (1980) illfare and welfare-ranked

S-Gini (hence the Gini) and the Bonferroni welfare functions are distributionally homogeneous. The S-Gini (hence the Gini) and the Bonferroni inequality indices are compromise inequality indices-when multiplied by the mean income they become absolute indices. Conversely, these absolute indices when divided by the mean income get converted into their relative counterparts. Thus, the formula for the absolute Bonferroni index is given by $I_{AB}(x) = \lambda(x) - 1/n\sum_{i=1}^{n} 1/i\sum_{j=1}^{i} x_j$. Likewise, the welfare-ranked absolute S-Gini inequality index has the functional form $I_{\text{ADWW}}(x) = \lambda(x) - \sum_{i=1}^{n}[(i/n)^{\delta} - ((i-1)/n)^{\delta}]x_i^0$, which becomes the absolute Gini index for $\delta = 2$, where $x \in \Gamma^n$. Another compromise relative index is the coefficient of variation, which when multiplied by the mean income, becomes the standard deviation $I_{\text{STD}}(x) = \sqrt{n^{-1}\sum_{i=1}^{n}(x_i - \lambda(x))^2}$, the positive square root of the variance I_{V}. However, since the reduced form welfare function $\lambda(x)\exp(-I_{\text{CV}}(x))$ associated with the coefficient of variation is not distributionally homogeneous, we may regard $\lambda(x)\exp(-I_{\text{STD}}(x))$ as the welfare function corresponding to the standard deviation. Chakravarty and Dutta (1987) showed the distributionally homothetic social welfare functions become helpful in measuring the economic distance between two distributions, where economic distance reflects the degree of welfare of one distribution relative to that of another (*see also* Dagum, 1980; Ebert, 1984; Shorrocks, 1982a).

1.9 Decomposable Indices of Inequality

An interesting issue of investigation in inequality measurement is the subgroup decomposition of inequality in the total population. This involves a partitioning of the population into several disjoint subgroups, such as groups by age, sex, race, region, etc., and our objective is to examine how the overall degree of inequality can be subdivided into contributions due to (i) inequality within each of the subgroups and (ii) inequality between groups, that is, due to variations in average levels of income among these subgroups.

Unless specified, we assume throughout the section that the domain of the inequality index is $\Gamma_+ = \bigcup_{n\in N}\Gamma_+^n$, where, as stated earlier, Γ_+^n is the strictly positive part of Γ^n and N is the set of positive integers. An inequality index $I : \Gamma_+ \to R^1$ is called subgroup decomposable if for all $J \geq 2$ and for all $x^1, x^2, \ldots, x^J \in \Gamma_+$,

$$I(x) = \sum_{i=1}^{J} w_i(\underline{\lambda}, \underline{n})I(x^i) + I(\lambda_1 1^{n_1}, \lambda_2 1^{n_2}, \ldots, \lambda_J 1^{n_J}), \tag{1.56}$$

where n_i is the population size associated with the distribution x^i, $n = \sum_{i=1}^{J} n_i$, $\lambda_i = \lambda(x^i) =$ mean of the distribution x^i, $\underline{\lambda} = (\lambda^1, \lambda^2, \ldots, \lambda^J)$, $\underline{n} = (n^1, n^2, \ldots, n^J)$, $w_i(\underline{\lambda}, \underline{n})$ is the positive weight assigned to inequality in the distribution x^i, assumed to depend on the vectors $\underline{n}$ and $\underline{\lambda}$, and $x = (x^1, x^2, \ldots, x^J)$. Thus, the population has been partitioned into J subgroups and overall inequality has been broken down into within-group and between-group components, where $J \geq 2$ is arbitrary. The between-group term $I(\lambda_1 1^{n_1}, \lambda_2 1^{n_2}, \ldots, \lambda_J 1^{n_J})$ is level of inequality that would arise if each income in a subgroup were replaced by the mean income of the subgroup. On the other hand, the within-group term $\sum_{i=1}^{J} w_i(\underline{\lambda},\underline{n})I(x^i)$ is the weighted sum of inequalities in different subgroups. In the literature, subgroup decomposable indices are also referred to as additively decomposable, or simply, additive indices (*see* Foster, 1983, 1985; Shorrocks, 1980, 1984).

Shorrocks (1980, 1984) showed that the only family of relative subgroup decomposable indices is the generalized entropy class:

$$I_S(x) = \begin{cases} \dfrac{1}{n\bar{c}(\bar{c}-1)} \sum_{i=1}^{n} \left[\left(\dfrac{x_i}{\lambda}\right)^{\bar{c}} - 1 \right], \bar{c} \neq 0, 1, \\ \dfrac{1}{n} \sum_{i=1}^{n} \left[\log\left(\dfrac{\lambda}{x_i}\right) \right], \bar{c} = 0, \\ \dfrac{1}{n} \sum_{i=1}^{n} \left[\left(\dfrac{x_i}{\lambda}\right) \log\left(\dfrac{x_i}{\lambda}\right) \right], \bar{c} = 1. \end{cases} \tag{1.57}$$

The parameter $\bar{c}$ reflects different perceptions of inequality. As we have noted in Sect. 1.6.3, the particular cases corresponding to $\bar{c} = 0$ and $\bar{c} = 1$ are the Theil mean logarithmic deviation and the Theil entropy indices of inequality. For $\bar{c} = 2, I_S$ becomes half the squared coefficient of variation. Bourguignon (1979) developed a characterization of the Theil mean logarithmic deviation index using $w_i = n_i/n$. Foster (1983) characterized the entropy index under the assumption that $w_i = (n_i\lambda_i)/(n\lambda)$. The Atkinson (1970) index corresponds to I_S with $\bar{c} = \theta$ via the increasing transformation

$$I_A(x) = \begin{cases} 1 - [\bar{c}(\bar{c}-1)I_S + 1]^{1/\bar{c}}, \bar{c} < 1, \bar{c} \neq 0, \\ 1 - \exp(-I_S(x)), \bar{c} = 0. \end{cases} \tag{1.58}$$

This therefore shows that for any $\bar{c} < 1$, I_S is a transfer sensitive index in the sense of Shorrocks and Foster (1987). This property of I_S also holds if $\bar{c}$ takes values in the interval $[1,2)$. The opposite situation arises if $\bar{c} > 2$. On the other hand, for $\bar{c} = 2$ the index exhibits transfer neutrality, that is, the same weight is attached to a transfer from one person to another at all income positions. The reason behind this is that in this case I_S is monotonically related to the squared coefficient of variation. However, I_S is strictly S-convex for all values of $\bar{c}$ (*see also* Cowell, 1980; Cowell and Kuga, 1981a).

The weight assigned to the inequality of subgroup i in the decomposition of the family I_S is given by

$$w_i(\underline{\lambda},\underline{n}) = \frac{n_i}{n}\left(\frac{\lambda_i}{\lambda}\right)^{\bar{c}}. \tag{1.59}$$

The sum of such weights across subgroups becomes unity only when $\bar{c} = 0, 1$. That is, only in these cases the within-group component is the weighted average of subgroup inequality levels. Thus, in general, the within-group component in the decomposition is not a weighted average of subgroup inequality levels. In fact, apart from the two Theil indices, the weights are not independent of the between-group term.

Foster and Shneyerov (2000) explored the idea of path independent decomposability based on the positive valued general per capita income function PI defined on Γ_+. It is assumed that PI is continuous, increasing, symmetric, population replication invariant, linear homogeneous and $\mathrm{PI}(c1^n) = c$ for any $c > 0$. The smoothed distribution associated with $x^1, x^2, \ldots, x^J \in \Gamma_+$ and the per capita income function PI is defined by

$$\chi(x) = (\mathrm{PI}(x^1)1^{n_1}, \ldots, \mathrm{PI}(x^J)1^{n_J}). \tag{1.60}$$

Thus, in the smoothed distribution each person gets his group's per capita income. It is assumed that the standardized distribution associated with $(x^1, x^2, \ldots, x^J)$ and PI is defined by

$$\mathrm{SD}(x) = \mathrm{PI}(x)\left(\frac{x^1}{\mathrm{PI}(x^1)}, \ldots, \frac{x^J}{\mathrm{PI}(x^J)}\right). \tag{1.61}$$

The standardized distribution involves a rescaling of each group distribution such that the per capita incomes of all groups become the population per capita income $\mathrm{PI}(x)$.

An index of inequality $I : \Gamma_+ \to R^1$ is called path independent decomposable if for all $x^1, x^2, \ldots, x^J \in \Gamma_+$ and $J \geq 2$, $I(x) = I(\chi(x)) + I(\mathrm{SD}(x))$, where $x = (x^1, x^2, \ldots, x^J)$. The term $I(\mathrm{SD}(x))$ corresponds to the level of within-group inequality obtained when all groups under consideration are standardized to the same per capita income. The other term, which remains after smoothing of group distributions, represents between-group inequality. It may be noted that the Theil mean logarithmic deviation index I_{TML} is a path independent decomposable index when the arithmetic mean is used as the per capita income, whereas the variance of logatithms $I_{VL}(x) = \sum_{i=1}^{n} (\log(x_i/GM(x)))^2/n$ fulfills path independent decomposability using the geometric mean GM as the per capita income.

Foster and Shneyerov (2000) showed that the entire class of relative inequality indices satisfying path independence decomposability is a positive multiple of

$$I_{\mathrm{PI}}(x) = \begin{cases} \dfrac{1}{\bar{\upsilon}}\log\dfrac{\mathrm{SM}_{\bar{\upsilon}}(x)}{\mathrm{GM}(x)}, \bar{\upsilon} \neq 0, \\ \dfrac{1}{2}I_{\mathrm{VL}}(x), \bar{\upsilon} = 0, \end{cases} \tag{1.62}$$

where $\mathrm{SM}_{\bar{\upsilon}}$ stands for the symmetric mean of order $\bar{\upsilon}$ [*see* (1.27)]. The I_{PI} index possesses path independent decomposition property relative to the per capita income function $\mathrm{SM}_{\bar{\upsilon}}$. Clearly, I_{PI} measures the extent of inequality in terms of the amount by which the $\mathrm{SM}_{\bar{\upsilon}}$ curve deviates from the geometric mean line in log-income space.

Additive decomposability is quite helpful for analyzing inequality by population subgroups. Extending this property to include arbitrary symmetric mean of order $\bar{\upsilon}$ in its formulation can be regarded a natural generalization of the property. Following Foster and Shneyerov (1999), we say that an inequality index $I : \Gamma_+ \to R^1$ satisfies generalized additive decomposability if there is an $\bar{\upsilon} \in R^1$ and a sequence of positive weights $\{w_i((\mathrm{SM}_{\bar{\upsilon}}(x^1),\ldots,\mathrm{SM}_{\bar{\upsilon}}(x^J)),\underline{n})\}$ such that for any $x^1,x^2,\ldots,x^J \in \Gamma_+$ we have

$$I(x) = \sum_{i=1}^{J} w_i((\mathrm{SM}_{\bar{\upsilon}}(x^1),\ldots\mathrm{SM}_{\bar{\upsilon}}(x^J)),\underline{n})I(x^i) + I(\chi(\mathrm{SM}_{\bar{\upsilon}}(x)),\underline{n}), \tag{1.63}$$

where $\chi(\mathrm{SM}_{\bar{\upsilon}}(x))$ is the smoothed distribution $(\mathrm{SM}_{\bar{\upsilon}}(x^1)1^{n_1},\ldots,\mathrm{SM}_{\bar{\upsilon}}(x^J)1^{n_J})$ and $x = (x^1,x^2,\ldots,x^J)$. Thus, in this generalized decomposition overall inequality is expressed as a weighted sum of subgroup inequality levels plus the inequality in the smoothed distribution, where both the weights and the smoothed distribution are functions of subgroup population sizes and the symmetric mean of order $\bar{\upsilon}$.

Foster and Shneyerov (1999) showed that the only relative inequality index that satisfies the generalized decomposability condition defined above is a positive multiple of the following two-parameter family of inequality indices:

$$I_{\mathrm{FS}}(x) = \begin{cases} \dfrac{1}{\bar{c}(\bar{c}-\bar{\upsilon})}\displaystyle\sum_{i=1}^{n}\left[\left(\frac{\mathrm{SM}_{\bar{c}}(x)}{\mathrm{SM}_{\bar{\upsilon}}(x)}\right)^{\bar{c}} - 1\right], \bar{c}\neq 0, \bar{\upsilon}\neq \bar{c}, \\ \dfrac{1}{\bar{\upsilon}}\displaystyle\sum_{i=1}^{n}\left[\log\left(\frac{\mathrm{SM}_{\bar{\upsilon}}(x)}{\mathrm{GM}(x)}\right)\right], \bar{c}=0, \bar{\upsilon}\neq\bar{c}, \\ \dfrac{1}{n\bar{\upsilon}}\displaystyle\sum_{i=1}^{n}\left[\left(\frac{x_i}{\mathrm{SM}_{\bar{\upsilon}}(x)}\right)^{\bar{\upsilon}}\log\left(\frac{x_i}{\mathrm{SM}_{\bar{\upsilon}}(x)}\right)\right], \bar{c}\neq 0, \bar{\upsilon}=\bar{c}, \\ \frac{1}{2}I_{\mathrm{VL}}(x), \bar{c}=0, \bar{\upsilon}=\bar{c}. \end{cases} \tag{1.64}$$

I_{FS} coincides with the generalized entropy family when $\bar{\upsilon} = 1$, and the limiting indices I_{TML} and I_{TE} are obtained, respectively, when $\bar{c} = 0, \bar{\upsilon} = 1$ and $\bar{c} = 1, \bar{\upsilon} = 1$. The path independent indices arise, respectively, if $\bar{c} = 0, \bar{\upsilon} = 0$ and $\bar{c} = 0, \bar{\upsilon} \neq \bar{c}$. Foster and Ok (1999) presented a picture of the potential conflict between the variance of logarithms and the Lorenz criterion. They demonstrated that this index may regard one distribution whose Lorenz curve is quite close to the line of equality as more unequal than another whose Lorenz curve approaches the line of complete inequality [*see also* Creedy (1977), for a discussion on this index.] Thus, if we impose the Pigou-Dalton Transfers Principle as an axiom here, then the only path independent decomposable member of the family (1.64) is the Theil mean logarithmic deviation index.

Blackorby et al. (1981) argued that between-group inequality can alternatively be defined as the inequality that results if each person receives his subgroup's Atkinson-Kolm-Sen representative income. Let x_f^j be the representative income of this type for subgroup j. Three reference vectors are considered: (i) $x = (x^1,x^2,\ldots,x^J)$, (ii) $(x_f^1 1^{n_1},\ldots,\ldots,x_f^J 1^{n_J})$, (iii) $(x_f 1^n)$. The overall income vector is given by (i), (ii) eliminates within-group inequality by social indifference and (iii) eliminates between-group inequality with social indifference. It may be worthwhile to mention here the Population Substitution Principle which requires replacement of income of each member of a subgroup j by x_f^j with a matter of independence(Blackorby and Donaldson, 1984a). Given the basic assumptions about the social welfare function, we have $x_f^j = (\hat{\xi})^{-1}(\sum_{i \in SG_j} \hat{\xi}(x_i)/n_j)$, where SG_j is the set of persons in subgroup j and the real valued function $\hat{\xi}$ defined on the set of positive real numbers is continuous, increasing and strictly concave.

The within-group inequality index $I_{\mathrm{AKS}}^{\mathrm{WI}}$ is defined as the fraction of income saved in moving from (i) to (ii) and the between-group index $I_{\mathrm{AKS}}^{\mathrm{BI}}$ is the fraction saved in moving from (ii) to (iii). Formally,

$$I_{\mathrm{AKS}}^{\mathrm{WI}} = \frac{n\lambda(x) - \sum_{i=1}^{J} n_i x_f^i}{n\lambda(x)} = \sum_{j=1}^{J} \frac{n_j \lambda_j}{n\lambda}\left(1 - \frac{x_f^j}{\lambda_j}\right) = \sum_{j-1}^{J} \frac{n_j\lambda_j}{n\lambda} I_{\mathrm{AKS}}(x^j) \qquad (1.65)$$

and

$$I_{\mathrm{AKS}}^{\mathrm{BI}} = \frac{\sum_{i=1}^{J} n_i x_f^i - n x_f}{n\lambda(x)}. \qquad (1.66)$$

The overall Atkinson-Kolm –Sen index $I_{\mathrm{AKS}}(x) = 1 - x_f/\lambda(x)$ is the sum of these two subindices (*see also* Ebert, 1999a). This decomposition is meaningful only if the representative income is additively separable.

An absolute inequality index is subgroup decomposable if and only if it is a positive multiple of one of the two following indices:

$$I_{\mathrm{EXP}}(x) = \frac{1}{n}\sum_{i=1}^{n}[e^{\tilde{\upsilon}(x_i - \lambda(x))} - 1], \tilde{\upsilon} \neq 0,$$
$$I_{\mathrm{V}}(x) = \frac{1}{n}\sum_{i=1}^{n} x_i^2 - \lambda^2, \qquad (1.67)$$

where $x \in R_+^n$ (*see* Chakravarty and Tyagarupananda, 2008). The index I_{V} in (1.67) is the variance, which attaches equal weight to a progressive transfer at all income positions. In contrast, for any $\tilde{\upsilon} < 0$, the absolute exponential index I_{EXP} favors transfers at the lower end of the distribution. The opposite situation is observed for $\tilde{\upsilon} > 0$. Assuming that $\beta = -\tilde{\upsilon} > 0$, the Kolm-Pollak index of absolute inequality is related to I_{EXP} through the ordinal transformation

$$\log(1 + I_{\mathrm{EXP}}(x)) = \beta I_{\mathrm{KP}}(x). \qquad (1.68)$$

Thus, these two indices essentially convey the same information. The weight attached to the inequality of subgroup i in the decomposition of I_{EXP} is $w_i(\underline{\lambda}, \underline{n}) = (n_i \exp(\tilde{\upsilon}\lambda_i))/n\exp(\tilde{\upsilon}\lambda)$ and they do not add up to one across subgroups.

Blackorby et al. (1981) considered the per capita counterpart to their decomposition for the Atkinson-Kolm-Sen index. The within-group inequality index has been defined as the per capita income saved in moving from (i) to (ii). Formally, for $x^1, \ldots, x^J \in R_+$, $I_{\mathrm{BDK}}^{\mathrm{WI}} = \lambda(x) - \sum_{i=1}^{J}(n_i x_f^i/n) = \sum_{i=1}^{J}(n_i/n)(\lambda_i - x_f^i)$, which is simply the weighted average of Blackorby-Donaldson-Kolm subgroup inequality indices, where $x = (x^1, \ldots, x^J) \in R_+^n$ and $\sum_{i=1}^{J} n_i = n$. As before n_i is the population size of the distribution x^i, and x_f^i and λ_i are, respectively, its representative income and mean income. The per capita income saved in moving from (ii) to (iii) is the intergroup inequality index, that is, $I^{\text{BI}}_{\text{BDK}} = \sum_{i=1}^{J}(n_i x^i_f/n) - x_f$. It is immediate that the overall per capita index I_{BDK} is the sum of the subindices $I^{\text{WI}}_{\text{BDK}}$ and $I^{\text{BI}}_{\text{BDK}}$. Again, the representative income should be additively separable.

Zheng (2007a) demonstrated that the decomposable class of inequality indices satisfying the unit consistency axiom is a two-parameter extension of the one-parameter generalized entropy class. According to the unit consistency axiom, ordinal inequality rankings remain unaffected when incomes are expressed in different units (Zheng, 2007a,d). This means that a unit consistent index is appropriate for comparison of inequality across countries that have different currency units. Thus, if the income distribution in country I is more unequal than that in country II when incomes are expressed in currency of country I, then a reversal of inequality ranking when incomes are expressed in currency of country II is regarded as a violation of unit consistency. An inequality index $I : \Gamma_+ \to R^1$ is called unit consistent if for all $x, y \in \Gamma_+$, $I(x) < I(y)$ implies $I(cx) < I(cy)$, where $c > 0$ is any scalar. Evidently, a relative inequality index is unit consistent. But there are other indices as well with this property.

Zheng (2007a) showed that the only unit consistent relative inequality index that satisfies subgroup decomposability is a positive multiple of

$$I_{\text{ZU}}(x) = \begin{cases} \dfrac{1}{n\bar{c}(\bar{c}-1)(\lambda(x))^{\bar{\eta}}} \sum_{i=1}^{n} [x_i^{\bar{c}} - (\lambda(x))^{\bar{c}}], \bar{c} \neq 0, 1, \\ \dfrac{1}{n(\lambda(x))^{\bar{\eta}}} \sum_{i=1}^{n} \left[\log\left(\dfrac{\lambda(x)}{x_i}\right)\right], \bar{c} = 0, \\ \dfrac{1}{n(\lambda(x))^{\bar{\eta}-1}} \sum_{i=1}^{n} \left[\left(\dfrac{x_i}{\lambda(x)}\right)\log\left(\dfrac{x_i}{\lambda(x)}\right)\right], \bar{c} = 1, \end{cases} \tag{1.69}$$

where the real numbers $\bar{c}$ and $\bar{\eta}$ are constants. Clearly, for $\bar{c} = \bar{\eta} \neq 0, 1$, I_{ZU} coincides with I_{S}. If $\bar{c} = 2$ and $\bar{\eta} = 0$, I_{ZU} becomes the half the variance. Thus, the variance is an absolute unit consistent inequality index. The weights attached to within-group inequalities in the decomposition of the variance take the form $\{n_i/n\}$. Therefore, for absolute indices if we insist on unit consistency and the requirement that the intragroup term should be weighted average of subgroup inequality levels, then we must accept transfer neutrality as a postulate.

It may be noted that in general the Gini index is not subgroup decomposable. In case subgroup income ranges overlap, it is necessary to add an extra term to make the decomposition usable (Bhattacharya and Mahalanobis, 1967). Mehran (1975) interpreted this extra term in terms of dominance of income one group over that of another. Lambert and Aronson (1993) provided interesting graphical analysis that enables us to understand the term in greater details and we refer to it as the Lambert-Aronson measure of overlap. If subgroup income ranges are nonoverlapping, then the Gini index can be neatly decomposed into between and within-group components. [*See* Ebert (1988b), for a characterization.]

Another issue that needs to be mentioned is component aggregation of inequality indices. The major issue addressed along this line is the investigation of contributions of different sources to total inequality. To discuss this briefly, suppose that there are J disjoint and exhaustive components of income and x_j^i denotes the income of individual j from source $i, 1 \leq i \leq J$. The distribution of incomes from source i is $x^i = (x_1^i, \ldots, x_n^i) \in \Gamma_+^n$ and that of total incomes is $x = \left(\sum_{i=1}^J x_1^i, \ldots, \sum_{i=1}^J x_n^i\right)$. Shorrocks (1982b) assumed that the inequality index I satisfies a consistent decomposition rule in the sense that it can be written as $I(x) = \sum_{i=1}^J \overline{E}(x^i, x)$, where $\overline{E}(x^i, x)$ is the contribution of source i to total inequality. The unique decomposition coefficient characterized by Shorrocks (1982b) is given by $\overline{E}(x^i, x)/I(x) = (\text{Cov}(x^i, x))/I_V(x))$, where $\text{Cov}(x^i, x)$ is the covariance between x^i and $x \neq \lambda 1^n$, and I_V stands for the variance. This unique decomposition rule enables us to calculate the contributions of different sources to total inequality (*see also* Fei et al., 1978, 1979; Fields, 1979; Lerman and Yitzhaki, 1985; Pyatt et al., 1980; Silber, 1989).

1.10 Measurement of Inequality When Needs Differ

In our presentation so far, we have assumed that the population under consideration is homogeneous with respect to any characteristic other than income. But individuals are likely to differ when they belong to households of different types or they have different preference relations. Thus, it is clear that for a heterogeneous population there will be asymmetric treatments of individuals for characteristics other than income. For inequality and welfare comparisons in the presence of heterogeneity additional value judgments are necessary to take into account factors like family size, physical handicap, and rural/urban location.

Atkinson and Bourguignon (1987) developed sequential dominance condition for making comparisons of welfare in the presence of social heterogeneity. Our presentation here is based on Lambert and Ramos (2002). Suppose that there are J household types in the society ranked in nonincreasing order of needs. Each type is homogeneous with respect to its needs. Thus, type $i = 1$ is the neediest type. For instance, the society may be partitioned into three types of households, families with children, families without children and single-person families. Houshold overall money income distributions F and G will be compared. The type-specific distribution functions corresponding to F and G are denoted, respectively, by F_i and G_i and the respective density functions are f_i and g_i, $1 \leq i \leq J$. The social welfare functions are assumed to be separable across types so that

$$W(F) = \sum_{i=1}^{J} \hat{\pi}_i \int_0^\infty U_i(v) f_i(v), \tag{1.70}$$

where $\hat{\pi}_i$ is the proportion of type i households and the utility functions U_i's are different across types. Similarly, for the distribution function $G, W(G) = \sum_{i=1}^{I} \hat{\pi}_i \int_0^\infty U_i(v) g_i(v)$. (For a nonadditive formulation, see Ok and Lambert, 1999.)

The needs structure is expressed by conditions relating to the utility functions U_i and U_{i+1} of adjacent types, $1 \le i \le (J-1)$. The marginal utility difference $U_i'(v) - U_{i+1}'(v)$ is the increase in utility of a household of type i for one unit increase in income over that of a household of next-less-needy type $(i+1)$ when they are at the same income level v. (For any U_i, U_i', and U_i'' will stand, respectively, for its first and second derivatives, where $1 \le i \le J$) Let W_{IA} be the set of social welfare functions of the form (1.70) with the restriction that for all v, $U_i'(v) - U_{i+1}'(v) > 0$ and $U_J'(v) > 0$, $1 \le i \le (J-1)$. We write W_{IIA} for the set of all welfare functions in W_{IA} when the additional restriction $U_i''(v) - U_{i+1}''(v) < 0, \quad 1 \le i \le (J-1), \quad U_J''(v) < 0$ for all v, is satisfied. That is, for the utility functions in W_{IIA} the rate of decrease in utility from granting an extra unit of resource to a needy household i is less than that of a household of next-less-needy type $(i+1)$ when they are at the same income level.

The following theorem of Atkinson and Bourguignon (1987) can now be stated:

Theorem 1.12. *(i)* $W(F) \ge W(G)$ *for all* $W \in W_{\text{IA}}$ *if and only if* $\sum_{1 \le i \le j} \hat{\pi}_i (F_i(v) - G_i(v)) \le 0$ *for all* $1 \le j \le J$, *and for all* $v \in [0, \infty)$. *(ii)* $W(F) \ge W(G)$ *for all* $W \in W_{\text{IIA}}$ *if and only if* $\sum_{1 \le i \le j} \hat{\pi}_i \left(\int_0^s (F_i(v) - G_i(v))\,\mathrm{d}v\right) \le 0$ *for all* $1 \le j \le J$, *and for all* $s \in [0, \infty)$.

If there is only one type of households, then conditions (i) and (ii) of the Atkinson-Bourguignon theorem reduce simply to weak first and second-order dominances, respectively. To understand these conditions more explicitly, let ${}^jF$ be the income distribution function for the jth merged subpopulation, so that $\left[\sum_{1 \le i \le j} \hat{\pi}_i\right]^j F(v) = \left[\sum_{1 \le i \le j} \hat{\pi}_i F_i(v)\right]$. Similarly, we define ${}^jG$. Then condition (i) states that the level of welfare under F is not lower than that under $G(W(F) \ge W(G))$ for all welfare functions $W \in W_{\text{IA}}$ if and only if for each set of the j most needy types, $1 \le j \le J$, ${}^jF$ weakly first-order (rank) dominates ${}^jG$. Likewise, according to condition (ii), $W(F) \ge W(G)$ for all welfare functions $W \in W_{\text{IIA}}$ if and only if for each set of the j most needy types, $1 \le j \le J$, ${}^jF$ weakly second-order (generalized Lorenz) dominates ${}^jG$. We can therefore refer to these conditions as sequential rank dominance and sequential generalized Lorenz dominance, respectively. The procedure is to consider the neediest group first and then add the second neediest group and so on until all the groups are included. It is necessary to check at each stage for rank or generalized dominance. Lambert and Ramos (2002) developed conditions for sequential dominance in terms of intersecting generalized Lorenz curves (*see also* Ebert, 1997, 1999b, 2000; Lambert, 2001). Jenkins and Lambert (1993) respecified the dominance conditions to allow for demographic differences.

To propose a summary measure of inequality in a heterogeneous framework, assume again that there are J types and number of households of type i is n_i. Let x_j^i be the income of household j of type i. The households are now arranged in non-decreasing order of needs. The total number of households is $\sum_{i=1}^J n_i = n$. We write x^i for the vector $(x_1^i, \ldots x_{n_i}^i)$ and x for $(x^1, \ldots, x^J)$. The mean income $\lambda(x)$ associated with x is now defined as $\sum_{i=1}^J \sum_{j=1}^{n_i} x_j^i / n$. The continuous, increasing, strictly concave utility function of households of type i is U_i. Following Ebert (2007), the equally distributed equivalent income x_e^i of this type of households is defined as

$$x_{\mathrm{e}}^{i} = U_i^{-1}\left(\frac{\sum_{j=1}^{n_i} U_i(x_j^i)}{n_i}\right). \tag{1.71}$$

In the second step it is assumed the social welfare function W is defined on the vector $(x_{\mathrm{e}}^1, \ldots, x_{\mathrm{e}}^J)$. Formally,

$$W(x) = \hat{\mathrm{K}}^{-1}\left(\sum_{i=1}^{J} \hat{w}_i n_i \hat{\mathrm{K}}(x_{\mathrm{e}}^i)\right), \tag{1.72}$$

where $\hat{K}$ is again continuous, increasing and strictly concave, and $\hat{w}_1, \ldots \hat{w}_{J-1}, \hat{w}_J$ are positive welfare weights. Since there are n_i households of type i, its total contribution to welfare is $n_i\hat{K}(x_{\mathrm{e}}^i)$. This is weighted by $\hat{w}_i$ to reflect the need of type i households. The formulation shows that the welfare function has been assumed to be separable.

We can check from the definition of x_{e} in (1.18) that nx_{e} is the minimum amount of aggregate income required to arrive at an income distribution which is socially indifferent to the existing distribution. (This is more generally true for the representative income defined in (1.24).) Below we consider the heterogeneous counterpart to x_{e} using this idea. This function is defined as the minimal amount of total income necessary to yield a distribution which is ethically indifferent to the existing distribution x. Formally,

$$\Phi(x) = \min_{\gamma_1^1, \ldots, \gamma_{n_J}^J} \sum_{i=1}^{J} \sum_{j=1}^{n_i} \gamma_j^i \quad \text{such that } W(\gamma_1^1, \ldots, \gamma_{n_J}^J) = W(x). \tag{1.73}$$

The function Φ parallels the individual expenditure function in consumer theory. It is continuous and increasing. If there is only one type of household then $\Phi(x) = nx_{\mathrm{e}}$. Ebert (2007) suggested the use of

$$I_{\mathrm{EHR}}(x) = \frac{\lambda(x) - (\Phi(x)/n)}{\lambda(x)}, \tag{1.74}$$

as an index of proportionate welfare loss. Likewise,

$$I_{\mathrm{EHA}}(x) = \lambda(x) - (\Phi(x)/n) \tag{1.75}$$

represents the absolute welfare loss per household. These indices can be regarded as heterogeneous population counterparts to the Atkinson-Kolm-Sen and Blackorby-Donaldson-Kolm indices of inequality.

As Ebert (2007) demonstrated I_{EHR} becomes a relative inequality index if and only if it has the form

$$I_{\mathrm{EHR}}(x) = \frac{1 - \left(\sum_{i=1}^{J} n_i \bar{w}_i / \left(\sum_{j=1}^{J} n_j \bar{w}_j\right) \left(1/n_i \sum_{j=1}^{n_i} (x_j^i/\bar{w}_i)^{\bar{\varepsilon}_i}\right)^{\bar{\varepsilon}/\bar{\varepsilon}_i}\right)^{1/\bar{\varepsilon}}}{\left(\sum_{i=1}^{J} \sum_{j=1}^{n_i} \left(\bar{w}_i / \sum_{i=1}^{J} \bar{w}_i n_i\right) x_j^i/\bar{w}_i\right)}, \tag{1.76}$$

where $x_j^i > 0$, $\bar{w}_i = (\hat{w}_i)^{1/(1-\bar{\varepsilon})}$ and $\bar{\varepsilon}, \bar{\varepsilon}_i \in (-\infty, 1)$ for all $1 \le j \le n_i$ and $1 \le i \le J$. If an exponent is equal to zero, then we need to use the corresponding geometric mean. Similarly, I_{EHA} satisfies translation invariance if and only if

$$I_{\text{EHA}}(x) = \frac{1}{n}\sum_{i=1}^{J}\sum_{j=1}^{n_i}\left(x_j^i - \frac{\log \hat{w}_i}{\hat{\upsilon}}\right) + \frac{1}{\hat{\upsilon}}\log\left(\sum_{i=1}^{J}\frac{n_i}{n}\left(\frac{1}{n_i}\sum_{j=1}^{n_i}\exp\left(-\hat{\upsilon}_i\left(\frac{\hat{\upsilon}x_j^i - (\log \hat{w}_i)}{\hat{\upsilon}}\right)\right)\right)\right), \quad (1.77)$$

where $x_j^i \in R^1$ and $\hat{\upsilon}, \hat{\upsilon}_i \in (0, \infty)$ for all $1 \le j \le n_i$ and $1 \le i \le J$. I_{EHR} and I_{EHA} are, respectively, the heterogeneous forms of the Atkinson and the Kolm-Pollak indices of inequality. If we assume that there is only one type, then I_{EHR} in (1.76) coincides with the Atkinson index I_{A} in (1.20) under the situation $\theta = \bar{\varepsilon} = \bar{\varepsilon}_i$ for all $1 \le i \le J$. Analogously, I_{EHA} in (1.77) becomes the Kolm-Pollak index I_{KP} in (1.48) under the assumption $\beta = \hat{\upsilon} = \hat{\upsilon}_i$ for all $1 \le i \le J$. The parameters in (1.76) and (1.77) represent respective inequality aversion. The constants $\bar{w}_i$ and $(\log \hat{w}_i)/\hat{\upsilon}$, which can be determined by welfare weights and inequality aversion parameters, may be interpreted as implicit relative and absolute equivalence scales. Given that the welfare function is ordinal, relative scales are unique up to a scale transformation and the absolute scales can be changed by a constant. Consequently, without loss of generality, we can assume that household1, the least needy household, is the reference type by setting $\hat{w}_1 = 1$, $\bar{w}_1 = 1$ and $(\log \hat{w}_1)/\hat{\upsilon} = 0$. Then the implicit equivalent income of an equivalent adult in household j of type i will be given, respectively, by $x_j^i/\bar{w}_i$ and $x_j^i - (\log \hat{w}_i)/\hat{\upsilon}$ (Ebert, 2007).

Alternative forms of redistributive principles have been suggested in the heterogeneous set up (*see* Bourguignon, 1989; Ebert, 2000, 2004b, 2007; Hammond, 1976a; Shorrocks, 2004). Here, following Ebert (2007), we consider a simple form of transfer principle between types. According to this principle, a transfer of income from a less needy and richer household to a needier and poorer household such that the post transfer income of the donor is higher than that of recipient, should reduce inequality. Formally,

Weak Between-Type Transfers Principle: A transfer of income $\hat{c} > 0$, changing x_j^i to $x_j^i - \hat{c}$ and x_l^{i+1} to $x_l^{i+1} + \hat{c}$ such that $x_j^i - \hat{c} > x_l^{i+1} + \hat{c}$, will decrease inequality.

Ebert (2007) made a detailed investigation of the implications of transfers in terms of parameter restrictions. Assuming that there are only two types i and $i+1$, the parameters $(\bar{\varepsilon}, \bar{\varepsilon}_i, \bar{\varepsilon}_{i+1})$ have to be related. He showed that I_{EHR} satisfies the Weak Between-Type Transfers Principle if and only if (i) $[\bar{\varepsilon}_{i+1} \le \bar{\varepsilon} \le \bar{\varepsilon}_i]$ for $\bar{\varepsilon}_{i+1} > 0$, (ii) $[\bar{\varepsilon}_{i+1} = \bar{\varepsilon} \le 0 < \bar{\varepsilon}_i]$ for $\bar{\varepsilon}_{i+1} \le 0$ and $\bar{\varepsilon}_i > 0$, or (iii) $[\bar{\varepsilon}_{i+1} = \bar{\varepsilon} = \bar{\varepsilon}_i]$ for $\bar{\varepsilon}_{i+1} \le 0$ and $\bar{\varepsilon}_i \le 0$; and $\bar{w}_i \le (1/n_i)^{(1-\bar{\varepsilon}/\bar{\varepsilon}_i)/(1-\bar{\varepsilon})}(1/n_{i+1})^{(\bar{\varepsilon}/\bar{\varepsilon}_{1+1}-1)/(1-\bar{\varepsilon})}(\bar{w}_{i+1})$. The corresponding restrictions in the case of I_{EHA} are $\hat{\upsilon}_i = \hat{\upsilon} = \hat{\upsilon}_{i+1}$ and $(\log \hat{w}_i)/\hat{\upsilon} \le (\log \hat{w}_{i+1})/\hat{\upsilon}$. To illustrate this for I_{EHR}, suppose that $n_1 = n_2 = 100$. We can choose $\bar{\varepsilon}_1 = 11/12$, $\bar{\varepsilon}_2 = 10/21$, $\bar{\varepsilon} = 1/2$, and set $\bar{w}_1 = 1$ and $\bar{w}_2 = 2.5$. Then these restrictions are fulfilled (Ebert, 2007). In the general case of J types and other notions of transfer principles, the restrictions turn out to be more complicated.

One important aspect which we did not discuss in this chapter is the problem of estimation of inequality indices and related issues. Excellent contributions along this line came from Kakwani (1980a, 1993), Beach and Davidson (1983), Slottje (1989), Bishop et al. (1989), Bishop et al. (1997), Davidson and Duclos (2000), Zheng (2002), and others. Since our objective has been to analyze the axiomatic approaches to the measurement of inequality, we did not discuss this issue here. However, this definitely does not mean that this aspect of inequality measurement is less important. Several articles in the volume, edited by Silber (1999), deal with the issue in details.

Chapter 2
Inequality and Income Poverty

2.1 Introduction

Poverty elimination is still one of the major economic policies in many countries of the world. In order to evaluate the efficacy of an antipoverty policy, it is necessary to know how much of poverty is there and observe the changes in the level of poverty over time. Poverty elimination programs also require identification of the causal factors of poverty, for example, the subgroups of population that are most afflicted by poverty. Quantification of the extent of poverty becomes necessary to address these problems. More precisely, we need an indicator of poverty that will enable us to analyze these issues.

According to Sen (1976a), poverty measurement problem involves two distinct but not unrelated exercises: (i) identification of the poor, that is, to isolate the set of poor persons from the set of nonpoor persons and (ii) to aggregate the information available on the poor into an overall indicator of poverty. That is, we need to know who are poor and how poor are the poor? While identification can be referred to as perception of poverty, the aggregation of characteristics of the poor is known as "measurement of poverty." When income is regarded as the only attribute of well-being, identification problem is solved by specifying a "poverty line," an exogenously given level of income required to maintain a subsistence standard of living. A person is identified as poor if his income does not exceed the poverty line. Thus, the poverty line is a line of demarcation that separates the set of poor persons from the set of nonpoor persons. The aggregation exercise, loosely speaking, consists of aggregating the income shortfalls of the poor from the poverty line into an overall indicator of poverty.

The index of poverty that has been used by most countries is the headcount ratio, the proportion of population with incomes not above the poverty line. This index has been criticized by Watts (1968) and Sen (1976a) on the ground that it does not consider the income distribution of the poor. For instance, consider two income distributions with the same population size and the same number of poor. Suppose that in the former, the poor have almost no income, whereas in the latter, the incomes

S.R. Chakravarty, *Inequality, Polarization and Poverty: Advances in Distributional Analysis,* Economic Studies in Inequality, Social Exclusion and Well-Being 6,
DOI: 10.1007/978-0-387-79253-8_2,

of the poor are marginally below the poverty line. Evidently, poverty in the former distribution is more acute than that in the latter. But the headcount ratio will treat the two distributions as identically poor.

Another often-used index is the income gap ratio, the relative gap between the poverty line and the average income of the poor. This index may not represent the poverty status correctly. To see this, consider again two income distributions with the same population size. Assume that the first distribution has only one poor person with zero income, while in the second, there is more than one poor person with zero income, so that the two distributions have the same average income of the poor. We can definitely argue that in this case the first distribution is less poverty stricken than the second. But the income gap ratio will regard them as equally poor.

Using an axiomatic approach, Sen (1976a) suggested a more sophisticated index of poverty that avoids the above shortcomings. His path breaking contribution has motivated many researchers to focus on the issue of poverty measurement.[1] As a consequence, the literature now contains several poverty indices. In designing new poverty indices, most of the researchers have adopted Sen's axiomatic approach and proposed new poverty axioms in addition to those of Sen.

Often from policy perspective, it may be necessary to identify the subgroups of the population that are most susceptible to poverty. Subgroup decomposable poverty indices become helpful in identifying such subgroups. According to subgroup decomposability, for any partitioning of the population with respect to a homogeneous characteristic, say, age, sex, region, and race, overall poverty is given by the population share weighted average of subgroup poverty levels (Anand, 1977; Chakravarty, 1983c; Foster et al., 1984).

Now, for a set of reasonable axioms, there may be several poverty indices. Quite often there is arbitrariness in the choice of a particular index of poverty, which in turn implies arbitrariness of the conclusions based on that index. Therefore, it will be worthwhile to reduce the degree of arbitrariness by choosing all poverty indices that satisfy a set of reasonable desiderata. Thus, instead of choosing individual poverty indices, we look for a set of postulates for poverty indices that implicitly determines a family of indices. It then becomes possible to rank two income distributions unambiguously by all members of this class. Clearly, this kind of research has grown out of existence of too many poverty indices. However, in some situations, a class of indices may not be able to compare all income distributions, that is, there may not be unanimous agreement among these indices about the ranking of some income distributions. Thus, while a single poverty index completely orders all the income distributions, the ordering generated by a class of indices is partial. For some distributions, it is not possible to conclude unambiguously whether one has more or less poverty than another by all members of the class. This notion of poverty

[1] Alternatives to and variations of the Sen index have been suggested, among others, by Takayama (1979), Thon (1979), Blackorby and Donaldson (1980b), Kakwani (1980a,b), Clark et al. (1981), Chakravarty (1983a,b,c,1997a), Foster et al. (1984), and Shorrocks (1995). This literature has been surveyed by Foster (1984), Seidl (1988), Chakravarty (1990), Ravallaion (1994a), Foster and Sen (1997), Zheng (1997), Dutta (2002), and Chakravarty and Muliere (2004). Our presentation in some sections of the chapter relies, to some extent, on Chakravarty and Muliere (2004).

ordering is known as poverty-measure ordering (*see* Atkinson, 1987, 1992; Jenkins and Lambert, 1993, 1997, 1998a,b; Shorrocks, 1998; Spencer and Fisher, 1992; Zheng, 2000b).

The definition of a poverty line is crucial both for poverty indices and poverty orderings. The determination of such an income or consumption threshold on which the definition of poverty relies has been an issue of debate for quite sometime. Often the construction of a poverty line may involve a significant degree of arbitrariness. The ranking of two income distributions by a poverty index may be different for two distinct poverty lines. It will, therefore, be useful to investigate whether it is possible to rank two income distributions unanimously by a given index for all poverty lines in some reasonable interval. This area of research on partial poverty orderings arises from uncertainty about fixation of the poverty line. This second notion of ordering of distributions by a given poverty index for a range of poverty lines is referred to as poverty-line ordering (*see* Foster and Shorrocks, 1988a,b; Foster and Jin, 1998; Zheng, 2000b).

Investigation has also been made in the literature whether poverty rankings remain unaffected when all the incomes and the poverty lines are expressed in different units of measurement. Indices satisfying this condition are called unit consistent (Zheng, 2007c).

Standards of living as well as size and composition of populations are likely to change over time. Therefore, it may become necessary to reformulate public policies like expenditure on public health, public funding of education, budget allocation for removal of poverty, resource conservation, designing the social security system etc., that are affected by change in population composition and size directly and indirectly.[2] This in turn necessitates the examination of impacts of population change on poverty (Chakravarty et al., 2006).

Duration of poverty in a society is an important aspect for understanding the experience of poverty. Increased duration of poverty can have detrimental effects on society's well-being. Therefore, it becomes necessary to understand and respond to the persistence of poverty over time.

The objective of this chapter is to present an extensive and analytical discussion on income distribution-based poverty measurement problems. The poverty axioms suggested in the literature and their desirability, alternative indices of poverty and their properties, different notions of poverty ordering, the issue of poverty measurement in the presence of population growth, and the measurement of poverty over time are examined in detail.

2.2 Axioms for an Index of Income Poverty

This section presents a discussion on alternative poverty axioms and their implications. For a population of size $n \geq 1$, a typical income distribution is given by

[2] The issue of population size in evaluating welfare has been considered, among others, by Parfit (1984), Broome (1996), and Blackorby et al. (2005).

$x = (x_1, \ldots, x_n)$, where x_i is the income of person i. Assuming that all income distributions are illfare-ranked, the set of income distributions in this n-person economy is D^n and the set of all possible income distributions $D = \bigcup_{n \in N} D^n$, where N is the set of positive integers. Unless specified we will define all the axioms and the indices on the domain D^n (or D). Recall that for all illfare-ranked income distributions, all increments/reductions in incomes, and transfers between two persons will be rank preserving.

The problem of identification of the poor requires the specification of an exogenously given poverty line z, an income level necessary to maintain a subsistence standard of living. This absolutist notion of poverty contrasts with the relativist view in which the poverty line is made responsive to the income distribution. For instance, a household with less than 40% of the median income may be regarded as relativist poor [see Ravallion (1994a) and Foster and Sen (1997) for further discussion][3].

We assume that the exogenously given poverty line z is positive and takes values in some subset $[z_-, z_+]$ of the real line, where $z_- > 0$ and $z_+ < \infty$ are the minimum and maximum poverty lines. For any income distribution x, person i is said to be strongly poor if $x_i \leq z$. Person i is weakly poor if the inequality $\leq$ in $x_i \leq z$ is replaced by $<$. In the literature, the former definition is more commonly used (*see* Donaldson and Weymark, 1986; Bourguignon and Fields, 1997). Person i is called nonpoor or rich if he is not poor. Assume that using the either definition of the poor, there are q poor persons in the society. For any, $x \in D^n$, let x^p be the income distribution of the poor. Since x is illfare-ranked, $x^p = (x_1, x_2, \ldots, x_q)$. For any $x \in D^n$, we denote the set of poor persons in x by $z(x)$. Thus, $z(x) = \{1, 2, .., q\}$.

For a given population size n, a poverty index P is a real valued function defined on $D^n \times [z_-, z_+]$. Thus, given any income distribution, $x \in D^n$ and a poverty line $z \in [z_-, z_+]$, $P(x,z)$ determines the extent of poverty associated with x. A poverty index will be called a relative or an absolute index according as it satisfies the scale invariance or translation invariance condition stated below.

Scale Invariance: For all $x \in D^n, z \in [z_-, z_+]$, $P(x,z) = P(cx, cz)$, where $c > 0$ is any scalar such that $cz \in [z_-, z_+]$.

Translation Invariance: For all $x \in D^n, z \in [z_-, z_+]$, $P(x,z) = P(x + c1^n, z + c)$, where c is any scalar such that $x + c1^n \in D^n$ and $(z + c) \in [z_-, z_+]$.

Thus, a relative poverty index is invariant under equal percentage changes in all the incomes and the poverty line, whereas an absolute poverty index remains unaltered under equal absolute changes in all the incomes and the poverty line.

The following axioms have been suggested in the literature for an arbitrary poverty index P, which may be of relative or absolute variety. Unless specified, we assume that the poverty line z is given arbitrarily.

Focus Axiom: For all $x, y \in D^n$, if $z(x) = z(y)$ and $x_i = y_i$ for all $i \in z(x)$, then $P(x,z) = P(y,z)$.

---

[3] Discussions on problems regarding the determination of an appropriate poverty line can be found in Atkinson (1983a), Sen (1981, 1983), Paul (1989), Ravallion (1994a), Pradhan and Ravallion (2000), and Sharma (2004). For references to the earlier literature, see Atkinson (1983a) and Chakravarty (1990).

This axiom was formally proposed by Sen (1981), but it was implicitly used in Sen (1976a). It says that the poverty index should not depend on the incomes of the nonpoor persons. However, it does not demand that the poverty index is independent of the number of the nonpoor persons. Assuming that in poverty measurement, we are concerned with the insufficiency of the incomes of the poor, this axiom seems to be sensible. Chakravarty (1983a) referred to this axiom as "Independence of the Incomes of the Rich" (*see also* Clark et al., 1981). A poverty index satisfying this axiom will be called focused.

Normalization Axiom: For any $x \in D^n$ if the set $z(x)$ is empty, then $P(x,z) = 0$.

According to this axiom, if there is no poor person in the society, the value of the poverty index is zero. This is a cardinal property of the poverty index.

The next axiom will ensure that minor inaccuracy in income data and negligible imprecision of an appropriate poverty line will not give rise to a huge jump in the poverty level.

Continuity Axiom (CON): $P(x,z)$ is jointly continuous in (x,z).

Symmetry Axiom: For all $x,y \in D^n$, if y is obtained from x by a permutation of the incomes, then $P(x,z) = P(y,z)$.

The interpretation of this axiom is similar to its inequality counterpart. It enables us to define the poverty index on the ordered distributions, as we have done.

Population Replication Invariance Axiom: For all $x \in D^n, P(x,z) = P(y,z)$, where y is the l-fold replication of x, $l \geq 2$ being any integer.

This axiom parallels the Population Principle employed in the context of inequality measurement. It was introduced into the poverty measurement literature by Chakravarty (1983a) and Thon (1983a).

Assuming that the income distribution is given, consider an increase in the poverty line. In such a case, the income gaps of the poor persons from the poverty-line increase. This in turn leads to a higher level of poverty. The following axiom of Clark et al. (1981) and Chakravarty (1983a) specifies this formally.

Increasing Poverty-Line Axiom: For a given $x \in D^n$, $P(x,z)$ is increasing in z.

Weak Monotonicity Axiom: For all $x,y \in D^n$, if $x_j = y_j$ for all $j \neq i, i \in z(x)$, and $x_i > y_i$, then $P(x,z) < P(y,z)$.

This axiom of Sen (1976a) is concerned with the effect of reducing a poor person's income. Note that here the distribution y is obtained from the distribution x by reducing the income of poor person i, under the ceteris paribus assumption. The axiom demands that this income reduction has increased poverty. A stronger version of this axiom was suggested by Donaldson and Weymark (1986). It demands decreasingness of the poverty index if the income of a poor person goes up. Thus, it includes the possibility that the beneficiary of the income increase may cross the poverty line and become rich.

Strong Monotonicity Axiom: For all $x,y \in D^n$, if $x_j = y_j$ for all $j \neq i, i \in z(x)$ and $x_i < y_i$, then $P(y,z) < P(x,z)$.

Clearly, for either definition of the poor, the strong axiom implies its weak version. It follows that for the strong definition of the poor, a focused poverty index satisfying the Strong Monotonicity Axiom will achieve its lower bound if all the incomes of the poor are at the poverty line. If a focused, continuous poverty index fulfills the Strong Monotonicity Axiom, then under the strong definition of the poor, we cannot simultaneously decrease the value of the index, as demanded by monotonicity, and keep it constant, as required by continuity, when the income of a person at the poverty-line increases. This shows that under the strong definition of the poor, there is no focused poverty index that meets the Strong Monotonicity and Continuity Axioms (Donaldson and Weymark, 1986). However, under the weak definition of the poor, continuity ensures that the two versions of the monotonicity axiom are equivalent. If we adopt the strong definition of the poor, for a focused poverty index, continuity is not consistent with the weak form of the monotonicity axioms.

The third axiom proposed by Sen (1976a) is a transfer axiom, which requires poverty to increase under a transfer of income from a poor person to anyone who has a higher income. Following Donaldson and Weymark (1986), we distinguish among four transfer axioms.

Minimal Transfer Axiom: For all $x, y \in D^n$, if y is obtained from x by a regressive transfer between two poor persons such that the recipient is not becoming rich as a result of the transfer, then $P(x,z) < P(y,z)$.

This self-explanatory axiom considers a regressive transfer between two poor persons keeping the number of poor persons unchanged. Likewise, a progressive transfer between two poor persons should reduce poverty. The next axiom also keeps the set of poor persons unchanged but in this case the regressive transfer may take place from a poor person to a rich person.

Weak Transfer Axiom: For all $x, y \in D^n$, if y is obtained from x by a regressive transfer from a poor person with no one becoming rich as a result of the transfer, then $P(x,z) < P(y,z)$.

The next axiom, which has been suggested by Sen (1976a), is also stated using a regressive transfer. But it allows the possibility that the recipient, if he is poor, may cross the poverty line.

Strong Upward Transfer Axiom: For all $x, y \in D^n$, if y is obtained from x by a regressive transfer from a poor person to someone who is richer, then $P(x,z) < P(y,z)$.

In the most general case, we may consider a poor person receiving a progressive transfer crosses the poverty line.

Strong Downward Transfer Axiom: For all $x, y \in D^n$, if x is obtained from y by a progressive transfer with at least the recipient being the poor, then $P(x,z) < P(y,z)$.

The essential idea underlying the transfer axioms is that poverty increases or decreases according as the transfer is regressive or progressive. By definition, the Minimal Transfer Axiom is the weakest among the four transfer axioms. For either definition of the poor, the Strong Downward Transfer Axiom is sufficient for the Strong Upward Transfer Axiom, which in turn implies the Weak Transfer Axiom from which the Minimal Transfer Axiom follows. If the recipient of a transfer considered under the Weak Transfer Axiom is a rich person, then for a focused poverty index, the transfer has the same effect as income reduction under the Weak Monotonicity Axiom. Therefore, for a focused poverty index, the Weak Transfer Axiom is equivalent to the Minimal Transfer and Weak Monotonicity Axioms

(Zheng, 1997). Note that the Strong Upward Transfer Axiom records an increase in poverty even if a poor recipient of the transfer crosses the poverty line. This "makes poverty measurement, in an important way, independent of the number below the poverty line" (Sen, 1981, p.186, n.1). Therefore, in later works, Sen (1981, 1982) opted for the Weak Transfer Axiom. However, if we maintain Continuity and the Weak Transfer Axioms, the focused poverty index will satisfy the Strong Upward Transfer Axiom for either definition of the poor. For the weak definition of the poor, Continuity and the Strong Upward Transfer Axiom, under Focus, imply the Strong Downward Transfer Axiom (Donaldson and Weymark, 1986). Since the Weak Transfer Axiom and Continuity are quite reasonable, the use of the Strong Upward and Downward Transfers Axioms are justifiable as well (Zheng, 1997). For the strong definition of the poor, no focused poverty index can satisfy the Strong Downward Transfer Axiom.

Kakwani (1980b) noted that the Sen (1976a) index is not more sensitive to transfers at the lower end of the income profile. He suggested three sensitivity axioms, one on monotonicity and two on transfers. They are presented below formally.

Monotonicity Sensitivity Axiom: If $x', x'' \in D^n$ is obtained from $x \in D^n$ by reducing, respectively, the incomes of the poor persons i and j by the same amount, where $x_i < x_j$, then $P(x',z) - P(x,z) > P(x'',z) - P(x,z)$.

Positional Transfer Sensitivity Axiom: For all $x \in D^n$ and for any pair of poor individuals i and j, suppose that the distribution x' (respectively x'') is obtained from x by a regressive transfer of income from the ith (respectively jth) person to the $(i+l)$th (respectively $(j+l)$th) poor person where $i < j$ and $z(x) = z(x') = z(x'')$. Then $P(x',z) - P(x,z) > P(x'',z) - P(x,z)$.

Diminishing Transfer Sensitivity Axiom: For all $x \in D^n$, if y is obtained from x by a regressive transfer of income from the poor person with income x_i to the poor person with income $x_i + \hat{c}$, then for a given $\hat{c} > 0$, the magnitude of increase in poverty $P(y,z) - P(x,z)$ is higher the lower is x_i, where $z(x) = z(y)$.

Kakwani's first axiom demands that a poverty index should be more sensitive to a reduction in the income of a poor person, the poorer the person happens to be. The second axiom is the poverty counterpart to the Positional Transfers Principle considered in Chap. 1. It says that the poorer the donor of the regressive transfer, the higher is the increase in poverty, given that the number of persons between the recipient and the donor of the transfer is fixed. The third axiom is the poverty analogue to Kolm's (1976a,b) Diminishing Transfers Principle and argues that more weight should be assigned to transfers lower down the income profile. Note that the regressive transfers considered in the later two axioms do not change the set of poor persons. We can also consider a poverty version of the Shorrocks and Foster (1987) Transfer Sensitivity Axiom proposed for inequality indices. However, since the Diminishing Transfer Sensitivity Axiom is quite intuitive and easy to understand, we will regard it as sufficient for evaluation of a poverty index.

The next two axioms are concerned with partitioning of the population into subgroups and relationship of overall poverty with subgroup poverty levels.

Subgroup Consistency Axiom: For all $n, l \in N$, $x^1, x^2 \in \Gamma^l; y^1, y^2 \in \Gamma^n$, if $P(x^1,z) = P(x^2,z)$ and $P(y^1,z) < P(y^2,z)$, then $P(x^1,y^1,z) < P(x^2,y^2,z)$.

Subgroup Decomposability Axiom: For $x^i \in \Gamma^{n_i}$, $i = 1,2,..,J$, we have

$$P(x,z) = \sum_{i=1}^{J} \frac{n_i}{n} P(x^i,z), \tag{2.1}$$

where $x = (x^1, x^2, \ldots, x^J) \in \Gamma^n$ and $\sum_{i=1}^{J} n_i = n$.

The first of these two axioms was introduced by Foster and Shorrocks (1991). It has the same intuitive appeal as the monotonicity axioms. While the latter deals with changes in individual poverty, the former is concerned with subgroup poverty. Thus, if the poverty level in a subgroup of the population reduces, given that the poverty levels in the other subgroups remain constant, it is natural to expect that global poverty will reduce.

The second axiom is quite useful for practical purposes (*see* Anand, 1977, 1983; Chakravarty, 1983c, 1990; Foster and Shorrocks, 1991; Foster et al., 1984; Kakwani, 1980a). It says that for any division of the population into nonoverlapping subgroups with respect to characteristics like region, religion etc., national poverty becomes the weighted average of subgroup poverty levels, where the weights are the population shares of different subgroups. Note that here n_i is the population size of subgroup i and $P(x^i,z)$ is its poverty level. The contribution of subgroup i to total poverty is then given by the quantity $(n_i/n)P(x^i,z)$. This is precisely the amount by which overall poverty will reduce if poverty in the ith subgroup is eliminated. This in turn shows that the percentage contribution of subgroup i to total poverty is $[\{100n_i/(nP(x,z))\}P(x^i,z)]$. This axiom, therefore, becomes helpful in identifying the subgroups that are more affected by poverty and hence in designing antipoverty policies. Clearly, according to this notion of policy, an assessment of poverty becomes dependent on the implicit valuation of the index. However, following Sen (1985a), the nonwelfarist approach to policy applications has become quite popular. Therefore, it seems worthwhile to investigate what kind of policy would be implied by the use of a particular poverty index.

Essential to the Subgroup Decomposability Axiom is independence between poverty levels of different subgroups. Sen (1992, p. 106, n.12) questioned the appropriateness of this assumption because he thought one group's poverty level may be affected by poverty characteristics of other groups. However, because of its immense popularity and usefulness, we will regard this axiom as one of the basic requirements of poverty indices. It may be mentioned that all subgroup decomposable poverty indices are subgroup consistent and under certain assumptions, all subgroup consistent indices are increasing transformations of some subgroup decomposable indices (Foster and Shorrocks, 1991).

By repeated application of the decomposability axiom, we can write the poverty index as

$$P(x,z) = \frac{1}{n} \sum_{i=1}^{n} \zeta(x_i,z), \tag{2.2}$$

where $\zeta(x_i,z) = P(x_i,z)$ is the poverty level of person i. Therefore, $\zeta(x_i,z)$ can be referred to as the individual poverty function. Note that the functional form of the individual poverty index $\zeta(x_i, z)$ does not depend on i. It may also be worthwhile to observe that the index in (2.2) is symmetric and population replication invariant.

Kundu and Smith (1983) introduced two population monotonicity axioms, one for poverty growth and the other for nonpoverty growth.

Poverty Growth Axiom: For all $n \in N, x \in D^n$, if y is obtained from x by adding a poor person to the population, then $P(x,z) < P(y,z)$.

Nonpoverty Growth Axiom: For all $n \in N, y \in D^n$, if x is obtained from y by adding a rich person to the population, then $P(x,z) < P(y,z)$.

The first (second) of these two axioms says that poverty should increase (decrease) under migration of a poor (nonpoor) person to the society. By the formulation, the latter axiom requires a focused poverty index to be a decreasing function of the nonpoor population size. That is, a focused poverty index satisfying this postulate is independent of incomes of the rich but dependent on their population size. Kundu and Smith (1983) demonstrated that for the weak definition of the poor, there is no poverty index that satisfies these two axioms and the Strong Upward Transfer Axiom simultaneously. They argued that the source of the problem here is the transfer postulate and advocated for use of some weaker form of the postulate. But we have seen how the transfer postulate can be justified by some reasonable criteria. It may be noted that these two axioms treat a poor and a nonpoor asymmetrically. More precisely, for a focused index while we do not consider the income of the nonpoor entrant, we take into account the income of the poor migrant. Zheng (1997) demonstrated that the Poverty Growth Axiom will be satisfied if the entrant's income is not higher than that of the poorest person, whereas a focused, population replication invariant poverty index satisfying the Strong Monotonicity Axiom will be affirmatively responsive to the Nonpoverty Growth Axiom. This shows that the latter of the two axioms may be regarded as a reasonable axiom for a poverty index in some specific situation. He also showed that the only subgroup decomposable poverty index that satisfies the two axioms is a linear transformation of the headcount ratio. According to Sen (1981), the problem arises because the formulation of the axioms relies on the position of the poverty line, which is not true for the transfer axiom.

In the following theorem, we show that many seemingly unrelated conditions for poverty ranking are equivalent. A variant of the theorem was stated in Chakravarty and Muliere (2004).

Theorem 2.1. *Let $x, y \in D^n$, where $z(x) = z(y) = \{1, 2, .., q\}$, be arbitrary. Then under the weak definition of the poor, the following statements are equivalent:*

(i) x^p can be obtained from y^p by a finite sequence of rank-preserving income increments of the poor and a finite sequence of rank-preserving progressive transfers among the poor or simply by rank-preserving income increments of the poor.

(ii) y^p can be obtained from x^p by a finite sequence of rank-preserving income reductions of the poor and a finite sequence of rank-preserving regressive transfers among the poor or simply by a finite sequence of rank-preserving income reductions of the poor.

(iii) $P(x,z) < P(y,z)$ *for all symmetric, focused poverty indices* $P : D^n \times [z_-, z_+] \to R^1$ *that satisfy the Weak Monotonicity and Weak Transfer Axioms.*

(iv) $P(x,z) < P(y,z)$ *for all focused poverty indices* $P : D^n \times [z_-, z_+] \to R^1$ *that are decreasing and strictly S-convex in the incomes of the poor.*

(v) $W(x^p) > W(y^p)$*, where W is any increasing, strictly S-concave social welfare function defined on the set of income distributions of the poor.*

(vi) $\sum_{i=1}^{q} U(x_i) > \sum_{i=1}^{q} U(y_i)$ *for any increasing, strictly concave individual income utility function U of the poor.*

(vii) $\sum_{i=1}^{q} \zeta(x_i,z) < \sum_{i=1}^{q} \zeta(y_i,z)$ *for all individual poverty functions* ζ *that are decreasing and strictly convex in the incomes of the poor.*

(viii) x^p *is generalized Lorenz better than* y^p*, that is,* $x^p \geq_{\mathrm{GL}} y^p$*.*

(ix) x^p *second-order stochastic dominates* y^p*.*

(x) $\sum_{i=1}^{j} (z - x_i) \leq \sum_{i=1}^{j} (z - y_i)$ *for all* $1 \leq j \leq q$*, with* $<$ *for some* $j \leq q$*.*

(xi) There exists a bistochastic matrix A of order q such that $x^p \geq y^p A$*.*

(xii) There exists a finite number $T^1, T^2, \ldots, T^J$ *of T-transformations such that* $x^p \geq y^p T^1 \ldots T^J$*, where the order of each* T^i *matrix is* $q \times q$*.*

Proof. Equivalence between the conditions (v) and (viii) follows from the Shorrocks (1983a) theorem. Equivalence between the conditions (vi) and (viii) follows from a theorem of Marshall and Olkin (1979, p. 12). We also know that condition (ix) is equivalent to condition (viii) (*see* Chap. 1). Hence, conditions (v), (vi), (viii), and (ix) are equivalent. Condition (iv) is an alternative way of writing condition (v), whereas condition (vii) is the (equivalent) poverty analogue to condition (vi). Since for a focused, symmetric poverty index, we allow only rank-preserving transfers among the poor, the poverty index is strictly S-convex if it satisfies the Weak Transfer Axiom. If the index satisfies the Weak Monotonicity Axiom, we need its decreasingness also. Hence, condition (iii) implies condition (iv). Arguing in an analogous way, we can show that the converse is also true (see also Foster, 1984). Equivalence between conditions (i) and (viii) was established by Foster and Shorrocks (1988b, Lemma 2). Condition (ii) is an alternative way of expressing condition (i). Likewise, condition (x) expresses condition (viii) in a different but technically equivalent way. Proof of equivalence between the conditions (vi) and (xi) can be found in Marshall and Olkin (1979, p. 12). Demonstration of equivalence between conditions (xii) and (viii) can also be found in Marshall and Olkin (1979, p. 28). Hence, all the twelve conditions stated in the theorem are equivalent. □

Condition (xii) says that we postmultiply y^p by the product of a finite number (J) of T-transformation matrices and then x^p can be obtained from the resulting distribution by increasing some incomes. That is, x^p can be derived from y^p by reducing income inequality among the poor and then increasing some incomes below the poverty line. Condition (x) of the theorem says that the sum of poverty gaps $\sum_{i=1}^{j} (z - y_i)$ of the bottom j/q proportion of the poor under y is as high as the corresponding sum $\sum_{i=1}^{j} (z - x_i)$ under x and for at least one proportion, it is higher. This intuitively appealing condition is equivalent to 11 other conditions for poverty ranking. In view of equivalence of welfare dominance [condition (v)] with poverty dominance [condition (iii)], Theorem 2.1 says that we can regard Focus, Symmetry, the Weak Monotonicity, and Transfer Axioms as basic axioms for a poverty index. The other basic axioms can be Continuity, the Population Replication Invariance, Increasing Poverty Line, and Subgroup Decomposability Axioms because of their intuitive appeal. [An experimental questionnaire investigation on acceptability of different poverty axioms was made by Amiel and Cowell (1997).]

2.3 Poverty Indices

In this section, we present a discussion on alternative indices of poverty suggested in the literature. The presentation is divided into several subsections. Unless specified, the discussion of different indices relies on the assumptions that all income distributions are illfare-ranked and that there are q poor persons in the society.

2.3.1 The Classical Indices

Probably the most extensively used index of poverty is the headcount ratio, the proportion of persons that falls in poverty in the population, that is, the ratio of the total population with incomes not above the poverty line. Given that q denotes the number of poor in the society, the headcount ratio is defined as

$$P_{\mathrm{H}}(x,z) = \frac{q}{n}. \tag{2.3}$$

P_{H} possesses a joint invariance characteristic – it is a relative index as well as an absolute index. In fact, a general result along this was established by Foster and Shorrocks (1991). Their demonstration shows that under certain conditions, the only subgroup consistent poverty index that satisfies this joint invariance property and continuity in individual incomes (restricted continuity) is a continuous, increasing transformation of P_{H}. A stronger version of this result proved by Zheng (1994) also shows that the poverty indices that are both relative and absolute are related to P_{H}. P_{H} ignores actual incomes of the poor in its formulation. For instance, it regards the distributions $x = (0,0,20)$ and $y = (9,9,20)$, where the poverty line is 10, as identically poor. It, therefore, violates all versions of the monotonicity and transfer axioms. This in turn demonstrates that there is no distribution-sensitive poverty index that can be both relative and absolute. Since this index makes no distinction between a poor person and a poorer poor person, its application as a tool for the purpose of poverty alleviation purpose is not appropriate. This is because the policymakers are likely to recommend that the most pauper persons (with the highest income shortfalls from the poverty line) deserve the maximum share of a given anti-poverty budget on a priority basis. However, P_{H} is unable to identify such groups.

Another commonly used index of poverty is the income gap ratio, the average of the relative income shortfall of the poor from the poverty line. This index is formally defined as

$$P_{\mathrm{IGR}}(x,z) = \frac{\sum_{i=1}^{q}(z-x_i)}{qz}. \tag{2.4}$$

This index is also referred to as the normalized poverty gap. It is a summary indicator of poverty depths $(z-x_i)$ of different poor individuals in the society. Since qzP_{IGR} determines the aggregate income shortfall of the poor from the poverty line, from policy point of view, qzP_{IGR} gives us the total amount of money required to put all the poor persons at the poverty line. By concentrating on the average gap $(\sum_{i=1}^{q}(z-x_i)/q)$, this index ignores the distribution of income among the poor. To see this, let $x = (0,14,15,20)$ and $y = (0,0,0,20)$ be two income distributions and suppose that the poverty line is 10. Then P_{IGR} treats the two distributions as equally poor. Clearly, a sensible focused poverty index should regard y as more poverty stricken than x. The main problem is that the income gaps of the poor are aggregated linearly in P_{IGR}. This in turn implies that the index is insensitive to the redistribution of income among the poor. More precisely, it is a violator of the transfer axioms that do not modify the set of poor persons, although it meets the weak form of the monotonicity axioms. Further, it is not subgroup decomposable. The headcount ratio is, however, subgroup decomposable but may not increase if the poverty-line increases. The product $P_{\mathrm{H}}P_{\mathrm{IGR}}$ of these two indices, which is popularly known as the poverty gap ratio, can as well be an index of poverty. But it is also a violator of the transfer principles, although it is increasing in poverty line.

2.3.2 The Sen Index

We have noted that independently P_{H} and P_{IGR} are subject to many shortcomings. Sen (1976a) showed how these two indices along with $I_{\mathrm{G}}^{\mathrm{p}}$, the Gini index of the income distribution of the poor, can give an adequate picture of poverty. For a large number of poor, the Sen index is given by

$$P_{\mathrm{S}}(x,z) = P_{\mathrm{H}}[P_{\mathrm{IGR}} + (1-P_{\mathrm{IGR}})I_{\mathrm{G}}^{\mathrm{p}}]. \tag{2.5}$$

The original form of the Sen index contains an additional factor $(q/(q+1))$ in the second term of the third bracketed term. Since this additional factor can be approximated by one for a fairly large q, we will refer to the more commonly used form P_{S} as the Sen index. The presence of the Gini index in (2.5) ensures that P_{S} is sensitive to the income distribution of the poor. Under ceteris paribus assumption, an increase in the value of $I_{\mathrm{G}}^{\mathrm{p}}$ increases P_{S}. $I_{\mathrm{G}}^{\mathrm{p}}$ has not been directly incorporated in P_{S}. Sen began by assuming that the poverty index is the normalized weighted sum of the income gaps of the poor from the poverty line. Then $I_{\mathrm{G}}^{\mathrm{p}}$ dropped out as an implication of the assignment of the ith poor person's rank in the income distribution of the poor as the weight on his poverty gap $(z-x_i)$ and the normalization condition that when all the poor persons enjoy the same income, the extent of poverty is determined by the poverty gap ratio, $P_H P_{IGR}$. Assignment of ranks as weights to individual poverty gaps captures the idea that the higher is the gap, the more is the weight. The relative index P_S is focused, symmetric, population replication invariant, increasing in poverty line, and satisfies the weak forms of the transfer and monotonicity principles. However, it is not subgroup decomposable.

2.3.3 Some Alternatives and Variants of the Sen Index

Alternatives and variations of the Sen index have been suggested from several perspectives. For instance, use of an alternative index of inequality in P_S is one possibility. We can also explore the possibility of weighting the gaps in a different way.

Blackorby and Donaldson (1980b) observed that we can rewrite P_S as the product of the headcount ratio and proportionate shortfall of the Gini representative income of the poor $E_G(x^p)$ from the poverty line. (See Sect. 1.6.3 for definition of the representative income and its specific forms.) We can rewrite P_S as

$$P_S(x,z) = P_H\left[1 - \frac{E_G(x^p)}{z}\right]. \tag{2.6}$$

Recall from our discussion in Sect. 1.6.3 that indifference surfaces of E_G are numbered so that $E_G(z1^q) = z$. Hence P_S is the product of the proportion of persons in poverty and the proportionate gap between the welfare level of the income distribution of the poor where each of them enjoys the poverty-line income and that of the actual income distribution of the poor, when welfare evaluation is done with the Gini welfare function. This shows a direct welfare interpretation of P_S. An ordinal transformation of the welfare function does not change the value of the poverty index (*see also* Xu and Osberg, 2002).

A natural generalization of P_S will be to replace $E_G(x^p)$ with an arbitrary representative income $E(x^p)$, determined using a continuous, increasing, strictly S-concave, and homothetic social welfare function defined on the income distributions of the poor. The resulting index is the Blackorby-Donaldson relative poverty index P_{BD} (Blackorby and Donaldson, 1980b). Formally,

$$P_{BD}(x,z) = P_H\left[1 - \frac{E(x^p)}{z}\right]. \tag{2.7}$$

Note that we can rewrite $E(x^p)$ as $E(x^p) = \lambda(x^p)(1 - I_{AKS}(x^p))$, the product of the Atkinson (1970)-Kom (1969)-Sen (1973) index of equity $(1 - I_{AKS}(x^p))$ of the poor and their mean income $\lambda(x^p)$ under the assumption that $\lambda(x^p) > 0$ (*see* Sect. 1.6.3). This shows that the general relative index P_{BD} (hence the Sen index) is increasing in the level of inequality $I_{AKS}(x^p)$ among the poor under ceteris paribus assumptions. It is also sensitive to the headcount ratio and how poor the poor are (because of its explicit dependence on the relative gap). It possesses the same welfare interpretation that we provided for P_S. Blackorby and Donaldson (1980b) discussed the relationship between the social welfare functions of the poor with those for the whole society. They concluded that the social welfare function must be completely strictly recursive in the sense that the ordering over incomes of any subset of the poor people must be separable from the income of anyone who is richer. But P_{BD} is not continuous, population replication invariant, and subgroup decomposable. However, it is symmetric, focused, and satisfies the weak versions of the monotonicity and transfer axioms, although not their strong counterparts (Chakravarty, 1983a, 1990, 1997a; Foster and Shorrocks, 1991; Zheng, 1997). To understand the reason for violation of the Strong Upward Transfer Axiom, consider an upward transfer that makes the recipient rich. This brings a decline in P_H but the change in the other component may not be so significant to indicate an unambiguous change in the product of the two terms in (2.7).

For every homothetic social welfare function of the poor, we have a corresponding poverty index of the type P_{BD}. For instance, assume that the representative income $E(x^p)$ of the poor is of the form $\sum_{i=1}^{q} x_i(q+1-i)^r/i^r$, where $r > 0$. Then the corresponding index turns out to be the one suggested by Kakwani (1980b), which is given by

$$P_K(x,z) = \frac{q}{nz\sum_{i=1}^{q} i^r} \sum_{i-1}^{q} (z-x_i)(q+1-i)^r. \tag{2.8}$$

The original form of the Sen index corresponds to the particular case $r = 1$. On the other hand, if $r = 0$, the Kakwani index P_K reduces to the form $P_H P_{IGR}$, the poverty gap ratio. The relative index P_K index was introduced with the objective that it will fulfill the Diminishing Transfer Sensitivity Axiom. Kakwani (1980b) demonstrated that for a given income distribution, a positive value of r exists for which this objective is fulfilled. But for any given r, there exists an income distribution for which P_K is not sensitive to the transfers, the way the axiom demands. However, it meets the positional version of the transfer sensitivity axiom for all $r > 1$.

Giorgi and Crescenzi (2001) suggested a variant of P_S by replacing the Gini index in (2.5) by the Bonferroni inequality index. We can rewrite it in terms of the Bonferroni representative income of the poor. The resulting index is given by

$$P_{GC}(x,z) = P_H \left(1 - \frac{1}{qz} \sum_{i=1}^{q} \frac{1}{i} \sum_{j=1}^{i} x_j \right). \tag{2.9}$$

This index has the advantage of satisfying the Positional Transfer Sensitivity Axiom. However, P_S does not fulfill this property since it involves the Gini index as its inequality component. P_K and P_{GC} behave in the same way as P_{BD} with respect to the Continuity, Monotonicity, Replication Invariance, and (Upward and Downward) Transfer Axioms.

An alternative way of employing inequality indices for construction of poverty indices was suggested by Hamada and Takayama (1977) and Takayama (1979) using censored income distributions. A censored income distribution replaces income of each nonpoor person by the poverty line z and maintains the income of a poor person at its existing level. Formally, the censored income corresponding to the income level x_i is defined as

$$x_i^* = \min\{x_i, z\}. \tag{2.10}$$

We denote the censored income distribution corresponding to x by x^*. Thus, $x^* = (x_1, x_2, \ldots .x_q, z, z, .., z)$. Takayama (1979) defined the Gini index of x^* as an index of poverty. More precisely, the Takayama index is defined as

$$P_{\mathrm{T}}(x,z) = 1 - \frac{1}{n^2 \lambda(x^*)} \sum_{i=1}^{n} (2(n-i)+1)x_i^*. \tag{2.11}$$

Hamada and Takayama (1977) also suggested the use of various censored income distribution-based inequality indices as poverty indices. All such indices have a clear merit – they do not ignore the existence of persons above the poverty line but ignore information on their income and count them in with the poverty line. But for either definition of the poor, these indices violate the weak form of the monotonicity axiom. To see this, suppose that all persons in the society are poor. Then multiplication of all the incomes by a positive scalar less than one keeps these indices unchanged. But the Weak Monotonicity Axiom demands increasingness of the poverty index in this situation. Under the weak definition of the poor, they also violate the strong form of the axiom (Chakravarty, 1983a, 1990).

Chakravarty (1983a, 1997a) suggested a general index by combining the Blackorby and Donaldson (1980b) and the Takayama (1979) approaches. This index is defined as the relative gap between the poverty line z and the representative income $E(x^*)$ based on the censored income distribution x^*, where E is calculated using a continuous, increasing, strictly S-concave, and homothetic social welfare function. Formally, this index is given by

$$P_{\mathrm{C}}(x,z) = 1 - \frac{E(x^*)}{z}. \tag{2.12}$$

By construction, the Chakravarty index P_{C} is focused, normalized, continuous, and symmetric. Since homotheticity of the welfare function implies that E is linear homogeneous, P_{C} is a relative index. Linear homogeneity of E along with its increasingness ensures that P_{C} is increasing in poverty line. It satisfies both forms of the monotonicity axiom and all versions of the transfer principle. If we assume that E is population replication invariant, then P_{C} is so. However, in general, it is not subgroup decomposable. Since $E(z1^n) = z, P_{\mathrm{C}}$ can be interpreted as the proportionate size of welfare loss due to existence of poverty. This loss becomes zero if there is no poor person in the society.

We can rewrite P_{C} as

$$P_{\mathrm{C}}(x,z) = 1 - \frac{\lambda(x^*)(1 - I_{\mathrm{AKS}}(x^*))}{z}. \tag{2.13}$$

This shows that we can transform the Atkinson-Kom-Sen relative inequality index of a censored income distribution $I_{\mathrm{AKS}}(x^*)$ into a poverty index in a fairly natural way. Given a poverty line, for two censored income distributions x^* and y^* with the same mean, the ranking of the distributions generated by P_C coincides with that generated by I_{AKS}. Formally, $I_{AKS}(x^*) \geq I_{AKS}(y^*) \leftrightarrow P_C(x,z) \geq P_C(y,z)$ P_C has a relationship with P_{BD} as well: if the social welfare function is completely strictly recursive, then $P_{BD}(x,z) < P_C(x,z) < (z - E(x^p)/z$. If we do welfare evaluation with the Rawlsian maximin rule $\min_i\{x_i\}$ (Rawls, 1971) and the income sum criterion $\sum_{i=1}^n x_i$, then the bounds are actually attained. However, these welfare functions are S-concave, but not strictly so. Pyatt (1987) investigated properties of P_C using affluence and basic income, and examined the implications when the society equivalent income is given by the sum of equivalent basic income and equivalent income of affluence.

Evidently, to every homothetic social welfare function, there corresponds a different poverty index in (2.12). These indices will differ in the way we aggregate the censored incomes into an indicator of welfare. For instance, suppose that welfare evaluation is done with the Gini welfare function. Then P_C turns out to be the continuous extension of the Sen index characterized by Shorrocks (1995):

$$P_{Sh}(x,z) = \frac{1}{n^2 z}\sum_{i=1}^{n}(z - x_i^*)(2(n-i)+1). \tag{2.14}$$

In addition to being population replication invariant, P_{Sh} fulfills all the postulates that are fulfilled by P_C in its general form. We can rewrite the formula for P_{Sh} using the Gini index of the censored income distribution $I_G(x^*)$ as $P_{Sh}(x,z) = P_H P_{IGR} + (1 - P_H I_{IGR}) I_G(x^*)$. This shows explicit dependence of the index on the per capita poverty gap index $P_H P_{IGR}$ and the inequality index $I_G(x^*)$. Since $I_G(x^*)$ is bounded above by one, under ceteris assumption, an increase in P_H or P_{IGR} will lead to an increase in poverty.

Earlier Thon (1979) suggested an index that has similar properties as P_{Sh}. In fact, the failure of P_S to verify the strong upward version of the transfer postulate motivated Thon to propose his index. If we employ the representative income $\sum_{i=1}^n 2(x_i^*(n+1-i))/(n(n+1))$ in (2.12), the resulting formula becomes the Thon index (Thon, 1979):

$$P_{Th}(x,z) = \frac{2}{(n+1)nz}\sum_{i=1}^{n}(z - x_i^*)(n+1-i). \tag{2.15}$$

The difference between P_{Sh} and P_{Th} arises from the assignment of different weights on the income gap of a poor. While Thon employed the rank of a person in the total population, Shorrocks used Gini type weight in the entire population. Thus, the simple alternations in the weighting scheme in P_S makes P_{Sh} and P_{Th} to satisfy several axioms which P_S violates (*see also* Xu and Osberg, 2001).

None of the members of P_C we have discussed so far are sensitive to income transfers lower down the scale. The second Clark et al. index, which drops out as a member of P_C, when welfare evaluation is done with the symmetric mean of order $\theta < 1$, fulfills this objective (*see* Clark et al., 1981). The functional form for this index is given by

$$P_{\mathrm{CHU}}(x,z) = \begin{cases} 1 - \frac{[1/n\sum_{i=1}^{n}(x_i^*)^{\theta}]^{1/\theta}}{z}, & \theta < 1, \theta \neq 0, \\ 1 - \frac{\prod_{i=1}^{n}(x_i^*)^{1/n}}{z}, & \theta = 0, \end{cases} \tag{2.16}$$

where $x \in D_+^n$. This index can be regarded as the poverty counterpart to the Atkinson (1970) inequality index, when applied to the censored income distribution. It is population replication invariant and retains all the properties of P_{C}. For any given income distribution, an upward income transfer will increase the value of the index by a larger amount the lower is the value of θ. For any finite value of $\theta < 1$, the social indifference curve will be strictly convex to the origin and it becomes more and more convex as the value of θ decreases. For $\theta = 0$, we get the symmetric Cobb-Douglas poverty index. As $\theta \to -\infty$, the poverty index becomes $1 - \min_i\{x_i^*/z\}$, the relative maximin poverty index. On the other hand, when $\theta \to 1$, P_{CHU} coincides with $P_{\mathrm{H}}P_{\mathrm{IGR}}$, which ignores many important features of a satisfactory poverty index, including redistribution of income.

From Theorem 2.1, it follows that if we adopt the weak definition of the poor, a decreasing and strictly S-convex function of the incomes of the poor can be a suitable index of poverty under appropriate formulation. Suppose we consider an illfare function H defined on the income gaps of the poor. Assume that $H((z-x_1),\ldots\ldots,(z-x_q))$ is continuous, increasing, strictly S-convex, and homothetic in its arguments. (Recall that z is given.) We now define the representative income gap g_{e} as that level of poverty gap which if suffered by each poor person will make the existing profile of gaps socially indifferent. More precisely, $H(g_{\mathrm{e}}1^q) = H((z-x_1),\ldots\ldots,(z-x_q))$. Given assumptions about H, we can determine g_{e} uniquely. As a general relative poverty index, Chakravarty (1983b) suggested the use the following representative gap-based index:

$$P_{\mathrm{CRG}} = P_{\mathrm{H}}\frac{g_{\mathrm{e}}}{z}. \tag{2.17}$$

P_{CRG} is a generalization of the first Clark et al. (1981) index, which is based on the assumption that H is given by sum of rth power ($r > 1$) of the gaps, that is, $H((z-x_1),\ldots(z-x_q)) = \sum_{i=1}^{q}(z-x_i)^r$. Then g_{e} becomes the symmetric mean of order $r > 1$ of the poverty gaps, which when substituted into (2.17) gives the first Clark et al. index. Assuming that the set of poor persons is fixed, it satisfies the diminishing sensitivity version of the transfer principle. However, like P_{S}, it is a violator of the upward strong form of the transfer axiom (*see* Thon, 1983b).

Now, consider the illfare function that uses the Sen-type weights. More precisely, H is of the form $H((z-x_1),\ldots(z-x_q)) = \sum_{i=1}^{q}(z-x_i)(q+1-i)$. Then $g_{\mathrm{e}} = \left(2\sum_{i=1}^{q}(z-x_i)(q+1-i)/(q(q+1))\right)$, which on substitution into (2.17) yields the original form of the Sen (1976a) index. If all the poor persons have zero income, then the representative income gap g_{e} is given by z. (Assume that the income vector 01^q of the poor persons is in the domain.) Note that g_{e} is a specific representation of the illfare function H. If we assume that all the incomes are nonnegative, then the original version of the Sen index becomes the product of two ratios: the headcount ratio and the ratio between the actual illfare and the (maximal) illfare that would arise if all the poor persons are at the zero income level. This gives us an illfare interpretation of the original Sen index. We have also noted in Theorem 2.1 that, under certain assumptions, all indices of the form (2.17) can be used for poverty ranking of income distributions.

According to Vaughan (1987), poverty indices can be viewed as measuring the size of welfare loss that results from the existence of poverty. This is quite similar to the interpretation we have provided for P_C and P_{BD} (and hence for P_S). His formulation incorporates social welfare function directly into the construction of poverty indices. The Vaughan relative poverty index is defined as:

$$P_{VR}(x,z) = 1 - \frac{W(x)}{W(\tilde{x})}, \tag{2.18}$$

where $\tilde{x}$ is derived from x by replacing all the incomes of the poor by the poverty line. This is a quite general index and many indices may be embedded into it. Increasingness of W will ensure nonnegativity of P_{VR}. A sufficient condition for P_{VR} to be a relative index is homogeneity of W of some arbitrary degree. Likewise, additional restrictions on W will be necessary for fulfillment of different axioms.

2.3.4 Subgroup Decomposable Poverty Indices

As we have argued in Sect. 2.2, the subgroup decomposable indices enable us to identify the more poverty stricken population subgroups on a priority basis for implementing poverty alleviation program. Equation (2.2) shows that the general form of an index satisfying the decomposability axiom is given by the symmetric average of the individual poverty functions. If we assume that the index is of relative type, then the individual poverty function must be of the form $\zeta(x_i,z) = \zeta(x_i/z,1) = h(x_i/z)$ say, where $h : R^1_+ \to R^1$. If we impose further axioms, it is possible to narrow down the functional form of the index. For instance, if we assume that the index is focused, continuous, normalized, and satisfies the weak form of the monotonicity axiom and the strong upward version of the transfer principle, then it will be of the form

$$P_D(x,z) = \frac{1}{n}\sum_{i=1}^{n} h\left(\frac{x_i}{z}\right), \tag{2.19}$$

where $h : R^1_+ \to R^1$ is continuous, decreasing, strictly convex. and $h(v) = 0$ for all $v \geq 1$ (*see* Foster and Shorrocks, 1991). Assume that first $q \leq n$ persons are poor.

As an illustrative example, suppose that $h(v) = -\log v$, where $v > 0$. Then the resulting subgroup decomposable index becomes the Watts index of poverty (Watts, 1968):

$$P_W(x,z) = \frac{1}{n}\sum_{i=1}^{q} \log\left(\frac{z}{x_i}\right). \tag{2.20}$$

Blackburn (1989) showed that we can rewrite P_W in terms of the Theil (1967) mean logarithmic deviation index of inequality of the poor $I_{TML}(x^p) = \frac{1}{q}\sum_{i=1}^{q} \log[(\mu(x^p))/x_i]$ as

$$P_W(x,z) = P_H[I_{TML}(x^p) - \log(1 - P_{IGR})]. \tag{2.21}$$

Thus, for a given values of P_H and P_{IGR}, a reduction in the Theil inequality index on the right-hand side of (2.21) is equivalent to a reduction in the Watts index and vice versa. Zheng (1993) interpreted this index as the size of absolute welfare loss due to poverty and characterized it in such a framework using a set of axioms. Tsui (1996) noted that the change in P_W can be neatly disaggregated into growth and redistributive components. Another interesting observation is that for a given poverty line, P_W is related to the member of the Clark et al. (1981) index P_{CHU} in (2.16) for $\theta = 0$ as follows: $P_{CHU} = 1 - \exp(-P_W)$. Therefore, the two indices produce the same poverty ranking of income distributions when the poverty line is fixed.

Next, for the functional form $h(v) = 1 - v^e, 0 < e < 1$, P_D coincides with the additively decomposable index characterized by Chakravarty (1983c):

$$P_{CD}(x,z) = \frac{1}{n}\sum_{i=1}^{q}\left[1 - \left(\frac{x_i}{z}\right)^e\right]. \tag{2.22}$$

The subgroup decomposable Chakravarty index P_{CD} satisfies the diminishing form of the transfer principle and all higher order sensitivity axioms. As the value of the parameter e decreases, the index becomes more sensitive to transfers at the lower part of the profile. For $e = 1$, P_{CD} becomes the poverty gap ratio, whereas for $e = 0$, $P_{CD} = 0$. If we replace z by the mean income λ, normalize the index over [0,1] and sum over uncensored income distributions then a clear link of P_{CD} is established with the normalized Theil (1967) entropy index (Chakravarty, 1990; Zheng, 1997). In order to establish relationship between P_{CHU} and P_{CD}, note that $n[z(1-P_{CHU})]^\theta = \sum_{i=1}^{n}(x_i^*)^\theta$ and $z^e[q - nP_{CD}] = \sum_{i=1}^{q} x_i^e$. Hence, assuming that the poverty line is given, the ranking of two distributions by P_{CD} coincides with that generated by P_{CHU} for $0 < \theta < 1$. Thus, in this particular case, the two indices convey the same information in terms of ranking. However, P_{CHU} is a nondecomposable index because of the specific type of aggregation employed in it.

Finally, suppose that $h(v) = (1 - v)^\alpha$, where $\alpha > 1$, then P_D becomes the Foster et al. index (Foster et al., 1984):

$$P_{FGT}(x,z) = \frac{1}{n}\sum_{i=1}^{q}\left(\frac{z - x_i}{z}\right)^\alpha. \tag{2.23}$$

Except P_{CD}, all poverty indices proposed after Sen (1976a) and prior to P_{FGT} are not subgroup decomposable. The difference between P_S and P_{FGT} is that while the former uses the relative rank of the ith poor as the weight on his poverty gap, the latter employs the $(\alpha - 1)$th power of his normalized gap $(z - x_i)/z$ as the weight on this gap itself. The index can be rewritten as the product of the headcount ratio q/n and average of the transformed normalized gaps of the poor: $\sum_{i=1}^{q}(z - x_i/z)^\alpha/q$. Thus, it is sensitive to the proportion of population in poverty and how poor this proportion is. As $\alpha \to 0$, the index approaches P_H, whereas for $\alpha = 1$, it coincides with the poverty gap ratio $P_H P_{IGR}$ A larger value of α gives greater emphasis to the poorer of the poor in the aggregation. For $\alpha > 2$, P_α satisfies all the axioms satisfied by P_{CD}. For $\alpha = 2, P_\alpha$ can be written as

$$P_{\text{FGT}}(x,z) = P_{\text{H}} \left\lfloor (I_{\text{IGR}})^2 + (1 - P_{\text{IGR}})^2 (I_{\text{CV}}(x^p))^2 \right\rfloor, \tag{2.24}$$

where $I_{\text{CV}}(x^p)$ is the coefficient of variation of the income distribution of the poor. This explicitly shows that for $\alpha = 2, P_{\text{FGT}}$ does not exhibit transfer sensitivity. However, the formula in (2.24) recognizes its explicit relationship with an index of inequality in a positive monotonic way. As $\alpha \to \infty, P_{\text{FGT}}$ approaches q_0/n, where q_0 is the number of persons with zero income, while the transformed index $(P_{\text{FGT}})^{1/\alpha}$ tends to the relative maximin index of poverty. Note that we can convert P_{FGT} into the inequality index $(\sum_{i=1}^{n} |(\lambda(x) - x_i)/\lambda(x)|^\alpha)/n$ by a straightforward transformation. For $\alpha = 1$, it becomes the relative mean deviation or the Kuznets ratio and when $\alpha = 2$ the squared coefficient of variation is obtained. It becomes a transfer sensitive index of inequality in the sense of Shorrocks and Foster (1987) if α takes on values in the open interval $(2, \infty)$.[4]

Zheng (2000a) defined the measure of distribution-sensitivity for an individual poverty index $\zeta(v,z)$, for all $v < z$, as follows:

$$\text{DS}_\zeta(v,z) = -\frac{\zeta_{vv}(v,z)}{\zeta_v(v,z)}, \tag{2.25}$$

where ζ_v and ζ_{vv} denote, respectively, the first and second partial derivatives of the function ζ with respect to its first argument.

The distribution-sensitivity measure $\text{DS}_\zeta(v,z)$ is quite similar to the Arrow (1971)-Pratt (1964) absolute risk aversion measure $\text{AP}(v) = -U''(v)/U'(v)$ for a utility function U, where v represents wealth and, U' and U'' are, respectively, the first and second derivatives of U. Taking cue from Pratt (1964), Zheng (2000b) argued that the following result concerning DS_ζ for the weak definition of the poor can be demonstrated.

Theorem 2.2. *For a given poverty line z and two individual poverty functions ζ and $\hat{\zeta}$, the following statements are equivalent:*

(a) $\text{DS}_\zeta(v,z) > \text{DS}_{\hat{\zeta}}(v,z)$ *for all* $v \in [0,z)$.

(b) $\zeta(v,z)$ *is a strictly convex function of* $\hat{\zeta}(v,z)$ *for* $v \in [0,z)$.

Theorem 2.2 says that ζ will indicate a higher increase in poverty than $\hat{\zeta}$ for a regressive transfer between two poor persons.

We can also interpret the distribution-sensitivity measure in terms of poverty aversion. A poverty averse policymaker will regard the reduction in social welfare of the poor less if one unit of income is taken from a poor person than from a poorer poor person. Thus, poverty aversion has essentially the same flavor as distribution-sensitivity (*see also* Seidl, 1988).

[4] Ebert (1988c) characterized indices of this type using alternative sets of axioms. See also Ebert and Moyes (2002) for discussion on P_{FGT}.

From the functional form of the second Clark et al. (1981) index, it appears that we can regard $\zeta(v,z) = \lfloor 1-(v/z)^{\theta} \rfloor /\theta$ with $\theta < 1$, as its individual poverty function. Its measure of distribution-sensitivity is $\mathrm{DS}_{\theta}(v,z) = (1-\theta)/v$. As the value of θ reduces, the index becomes more distribution-sensitive. We can interpret $(1-\theta)$ as a measure of poverty aversion: for a given income, the lower is the value of θ, the more poverty averse the index becomes. Since the Watts index corresponds to the case $\theta = 0$, the Clark et al. index with negative θ is more distribution-sensitive than the Watts index, which in turn has higher distribution-sensitivity than the Chakravarty index because of its increasing relationship with the Clark et al. index for positive θ. This provides an interesting comparison among the three indices.

Since for the Foster et al. index $\zeta(v,z) = (1-v/z)^{\alpha}$, its distribution-sensitivity measure is $DS_{\alpha}(v,z) = (\alpha-1)/(z-v)$. Thus, as the value of α increases, distribution-sensitivity increases and $(\alpha-1)$ can be regarded as an indicator of poverty aversion. It may be checked that for given (z,α,θ), neither of the Clark et al. and the Foster et al. indices is always more distribution-sensitive than the other.

2.3.5 Absolute Indices of Poverty

Absolute indices often become very useful because of their policy implications. The absolute poverty index suggested by Blackorby and Donaldson (1980b) enables us to determine the total monetary cost of poverty. It is formally defined as

$$P_{\mathrm{BDA}}(x,z) = q(z-E(x^p)), \tag{2.26}$$

where the representative income of the poor $E(x^p)$ is evaluated according to a continuous, increasing, strictly S-concave, and translatable social welfare function of the poor. Since E is unit translatable, if each poor in the society were given $(z-E(x^p))$ amount of money then the Blackorby-Donaldson absolute poverty index P_{BDA} will be zero at an aggregate cost of $q(z-E(x^p))$. Therefore, this index gives us the monetary cost of poverty. However, it shares all the shortcomings of its relative sister P_{BD} (*see also* Bossert, 1990b).

While P_{BDA} determines the aggregate cost of poverty, Chakravarty (1983a) suggested a per capita absolute poverty index. It is given by the difference between the poverty line and the society representative income which is calculated using a continuous, increasing, strictly S-concave, and translatable social welfare function defined on the censored income distributions. Formally,

$$P_{\mathrm{CA}}(x,z) = z - E(x^*). \tag{2.27}$$

Unit translatability of E shows that if each person in the censored income distribution x^* were given $(z-E(x^*))$ amount of money, then absolute poverty, as measured by P_{CA}, will be zero at an aggregate cost of $n(z-E(x^*))$. Thus, P_{CA} determines the per capita absolute poverty cost. This index shares all the properties of its relative counterpart P_C. We can illustrate the index using the Gini and the Kolm (1976a)-Pollak (1971) welfare functions defined on the censored income distributions. It may be worthwhile to mention here that the use of any absolute inequality index defined on the censored income distributions will not be suitable for measuring poverty because of its failure to fulfill the monotonicity axioms.

We can also define absolute indices using the illfare function of the poor. Since these functions are defined directly on income gaps, they are translation invariant. This in turn shows that any well-defined aggregation of the gaps will give us an absolute index. For instance, the index $(\sum_{i=1}^{q} \exp(r(z-x_i))/q$, where $r > 0$ is a parameter, is an absolute index that satisfies all the poverty axioms specified in condition (iii) of Theorem 2.1. We can also use the representative gap g_e calculated using a continuous, increasing, and strictly S-convex function to construct a wide class of absolute indices, namely, $(q/n)g_e$ (Chakravarty, 1983b). One member of this class is the absolute version of the Sen (1976a) index, which, as we show in Sect. 2.6, becomes quite helpful in poverty comparisons in a very general setup.

The Vaughan absolute index $P_{VA}(x,z) = W(\tilde{x}) - W(x)$, where $\tilde{x}$ is the same as in (2.18), has been proposed to determine the size of absolute welfare loss due to existence of poverty (Vaughan, 1987). Clearly, as in the relative case, we need more information on the welfare function W to examine the properties of P_{VA}.

The Zheng absolute individual poverty function $\xi(v,z) = \exp(\tilde{\omega}(z-v)) - 1$ has a constant distribution-sensitivity $(\mathrm{DS}_{\zeta}(v,z) = \tilde{\omega} > 0)$ (Zheng, 2000b). It can be verified that at a lower income level, this index is more poverty averse than the Foster et al. (1984) index but is less poverty averse than the Clark et al. (1981) index.[5]

2.4 Population Growth and Poverty

Population replication invariant poverty indices view changes in the number of poor persons in terms of changes in the fraction of population in poverty. However, a common person may not like to look at the change in such a simple way. The distinction between the two views can be explained by an illustration provided by Kanbur (2001). It was observed that in Ghana between 1987 and 1991, the head-count ratio came down by about 1% per year, while the number of the poor increased because the total population was growing by approximately 2% per year. The policy recommenders regarded the former as a measure of the success of their "structural adjustment" policies. However, the common people criticized these policies, at least partly, because they could see more poor people around.

---

[5] Many of the indices discussed in this section have been applied to study the incidence of poverty in India. For a review of this literature, see Maiti (1998). See also Deaton (2008). Dominguez and Velazquez (2007) employed several indices to analyze poverty intensity in 15 countries of the European Union using European Commission Household Panel data. Bresson and Labar (2007) studied decomposition of poverty in China for the period 1990–2003. See Slesnick (1993) for a study of poverty in the USA.

Chakravarty et al. (2006) characterized the following family of poverty indices that accommodates alternative views on poverty change resulting from population growth in a common framework:

$$P_{\mathrm{CKM}}(x,z) = \delta_1 \left[\sum_{i=1}^{n} h\left(\frac{x_i^*}{z}\right) - \delta_2 n \right], \tag{2.28}$$

where h is the same as in (2.19), and $\delta_1 > 0$ and δ_2 are constants. Consequently, P_{CKM} is symmetric, continuous, and satisfies both forms of the monotonicity axiom and the Strong Upward Transfer and the Diminishing Transfer Sensitivity Axioms. However, it is not invariant under replications of the population because of the aggregation rule and the presence of the population-size dependent term $\delta_2 n$. In fact, the latter is the major source of difference between the population replication invariant index P_{D} in (2.19) and P_{CKM}. This is because if $\delta_2 = 0$, we can convert P_{CKM} into a population replication invariant index simply by dividing by the population size n. The presence of the term $\delta_2 n$ in the latter enables us to consider alternative views on poverty change as a consequence of change in the population size n. If q is fixed, δ_2 can be interpreted as the amount by which poverty goes down when the number of rich persons increases by one. Hence, in this situation, nonnegativity of δ_2 is a reasonable assumption. However, if we allow both the numbers of poor and rich to increase simultaneously, then there is a trade off between the reduction in poverty resulting from higher number of rich and increase in poverty because of higher number of poor. As we note below, the value of δ_2 may be helpful in resolving this issue. The constant $\delta_1 > 0$ can be regarded as a scale parameter: under ceteris paribus assumption, an increase in the value of δ_1 increases poverty. Therefore, without loss of generality, we can set $\delta_1 = 1$.

For a given income distribution over a given population size, an increase in the value of δ_2 decreases P_{CKM}. If we assume that $\delta_2 = 0$, P_{CKM} is independent of the size of the nonpoor population and their income distribution. In this case, P_{CKM} can be taken as an aggregate version of P_{D}. Consequently, for $h(v) = -\log v$, $h(v) = 1 - v^e$, and $h(v) = (1-v)^{\alpha}$, P_{CKM} becomes, respectively, the aggregate form of the Watts (1968), the Chakravarty (1983c), and the Foster et al. (1984) index. Note that if $\delta_2 = 0$, an l-fold replication of the population will augment the poverty index $(l-1)$ times, which is demanded by the Replication Scaling Principle of Subramanian (2002). Subramanian also introduced a Population Growth Principle which requires that if all the poor persons in the society have the same income and a person having this identical income migrates to the society and if there is at least one nonpoor person in the society, then poverty must go up. It is easy to verify that this principle of population growth is verified by the index P_{CKM} under the assumption that $\delta_2 = 0$.

If $\delta_2 = 0$, an increase in the number of poor increases the index P_{CKM} unambiguously. Next, for $\delta_2 > 0$, the index records a reduction in poverty if the population size increases keeping the number of poor and their income distribution fixed. This therefore shows that the formulation puts the two Kundu and Smith (1983) axioms into a common framework. The major difference between the Kundu and Smith formulation and the present one, which generates P_{CKM}, is that in the former, the two population growth criteria are assumed at the outset, whereas in the latter, the two views follow separately as implications of the functional form P_{CKM}.

Now, consider the following form of the poverty index involving the number of poor and the population size:

$$P_{HA}(x,z) = q - \delta_2 n. \tag{2.29}$$

Consider two distributions x^1 and x^2 over population sizes n_1 and n_2, respectively. Let q_1 and q_2 satisfying the restrictions $q_1 > q_2$ and $(q_1/n_1) = (q_2/n_2)$ be the numbers of poor persons in x^1 and x^2, respectively. These restrictions imply that $n_1 > n_2$. Then $P_{HA}(x^1,z) > P_{HA}(x^2,z)$ demands that $\delta_2 < ((q_1 - q_2)/(n_1 - n_2))$ which is positive. Hence, δ_2 is bounded above by a positive real number.

Next, suppose that the number of poor is the same in both the distributions but the headcount ratio in the former is higher. That is, $q_1 = q_2$ but $(q_1/n_1) > (q_2/n_2)$. This in turn gives $n_1 < n_2$. Then $P_{HA}(x^1,z) > P_{HA}(x^2,z)$ requires that $\delta_2(n_1 - n_2) < 0$, implying positivity of δ_2.

The following proposition of Chakravarty et al. (2006) summarizes the above observation:

Proposition 2.1. *There exists a positive value of δ_2 such that the poverty index of the form (2.29) will satisfy the following conditions simultaneously:*

(i) For a given headcount ratio, if the absolute number of poor goes down, then poverty should decline.
(ii) For a given absolute number of poor and the income distribution of the poor population, if the headcount ratio goes down, then poverty should decline.

Note that the satisfaction of condition (i) does not require positivity of δ_2. It can hold as well for negative values of δ_2. Thus, a negative value of δ_2 may be sufficient to make sure that the trade off between poverty reduction resulting from a reduction in the number of poor and poverty increase due to a reduction in the number of rich works out in favor of diminishing poverty. In other words, the effect of poverty reduction as a consequence of lower number of poor outweighs that of poverty increase following from a smaller rich population size. In such a situation, Proposition 2.1 will become an impossibility result stating that conditions (i) and (ii) of Proposition 2.1 cannot be fulfilled simultaneously [since we always need positivity of δ_2 for condition (ii) to hold]. Note also that since for simultaneous satisfaction of (i) and (ii), δ_2 should be very small, the number of poor becomes the major determinant of poverty ranking here.[6]

An alternative poverty index that fulfills these two views simultaneously is the Arriaga index $P_{AR}(x,z) = q^2/n$. It was introduced by Arriaga (1970) as an urbanization index. In the Arriaga framework, the numerator of P_{AR} is the square of total

---

[6] The numerical illustration provided by Chakravarty et al. (2006) using data sets from South Asia and Africa confirms this.

resident population in the urban community. (If there is more than one urban community, then it will be the sum of squares of such population sizes across communities.) Since the fulfillment of the two conditions by P_{AR} does not depend on any parameter, no impossibility result emerges in the underlying framework.

Since both P_{HA} and P_{AR} are based on the number of poor persons, they fail to meet the monotonicity and transfer axioms. The following alternative to P_{HA} which meets the strong versions of the monotonicity and transfer axioms meets also the two conditions of Proposition 2.1:

$$P_{HAA}(x,z) = \frac{1}{n^{\delta_3}} \sum_{i=1}^{n} h\left(\frac{x_i^*}{z}\right), \tag{2.30}$$

where h is same as in (2.19) and $0 < \delta_3 < 1$. For a given (x,z), an increase in δ_3 will lead to a reduction in the value of P_{HAA}, which we can rewrite as $n^{(1-\delta_3)}\left[\sum_{i=1}^{n}(h(x_i^*/z)/n)\right]$. For a given headcount ratio for condition (i) to hold, under a reduction in the absolute number of poor, a corresponding proportionate contraction of the nonpoor population size is necessary. Under this contraction, a population replication invariant poverty index remains unaltered. If we replicate the population l times, the third bracketed term remains unchanged, but the multiplicative factor becomes $(nl)^{(1-\delta_3)}$, which is greater than $(n)^{(1-\delta_3)}$. Hence $P_{HAA}(x,z) < P_{HAA}(y,z)$, where y is the l-fold replication of x. Thus, condition (i) is verified. Next, when the number of poor persons and their income distribution are given, a reduction in the headcount ratio results from an increase in the number of rich persons. It is quite easy to check that the P_{HAA} decreases in such a case. The following proposition of Chakravarty et al. (2006) summarizes these observations:

Proposition 2.2. *A poverty index of the form (2.30) will satisfy the conditions (i) and (ii) stated in Proposition 2.1 simultaneously.*

However, one limitation of P_{HAA} is that it may not indicate an unambiguous direction of change in poverty if there is an increase in the number of poor.

2.5 Poverty Orderings

Our discussion in Sect. 2.3 shows the existence of a large number of poverty indices satisfying different sets of axioms. Poverty assessment of two distributions can certainly be conflicting by two different indices. As the determination of a poverty line is subjective, variation in poverty line can be identified as a major source of disagreement in ranking of distributions. While for a given poverty line, a poverty index will rank two distributions unambiguously, for two distinct poverty lines, ranking of the distributions may be different. Therefore, it will be worthwhile to investigate whether a given poverty index can order two income distributions in an unambiguous way for a range of poverty lines. This concept of poverty ordering of distributions by a given index for all poverty lines in some reasonable interval is referred to as poverty-line ordering (Zheng, 2000b).

Foster and Shorrocks (1988a,b) developed conditions under which unanimous poverty comparisons can be made by members of P_{FGT} when poverty lines are allowed to vary. To discuss the Foster-Shorrocks results, suppose that the income distributions are defined on the continuum. Let $F : [0,\infty) \to [0,1]$ be the cumulative distribution function. Then $F(v)$ is the proportion of persons with income less than or equal to v. We retain our assumptions about F made in Chap. 1. Suppose that the poverty lines are allowed to vary over the interval $(0,\infty)$. For a given $z \in (0,\infty)$ and a poverty index P, the poverty level associated with the distribution function F is denoted by $P(F,z)$. Then of two distribution functions F and G defined on the same domain $[0,\infty)$, G poverty line dominates F with respect to the index P if and only if $P(F,z) \le P(G,z)$ for all $z \in (0,\infty)$ with $<$ for some z.

Suppose that poverty assessment is made with the counting measure, that is, the headcount ratio. Thus, $P(F,z) = F(z)$. Then G poverty line dominates F with respect to the headcount ratio if and only if $F(z) \le G(z)$ for all $z \in (0,\infty)$ with $<$ for some z. But this is same as the condition that F first-order stochastic dominates G.

Next, assume that poverty evaluation is done with the poverty gap ratio $P(F,z) = \int_0^z ((z-v)/z)\mathrm{d}F(v) = \int_0^{F(z)} (z - F^{-1}(t))\mathrm{d}t$, where F^{-1} is the inverse distribution function defined in Chap. 1. This shows that G poverty line dominates F by the poverty gap ratio if and only if F second-order stochastic dominates G, which is equivalent to the condition that $F \ge_{\mathrm{GL}} G$.

While these two results involve two members of P_{FGT}, the following general result in terms of P_{FGT} has been demonstrated by Foster and Shorrocks (1988a) along this line.

Theorem 2.3. *For two income distribution functions F and G defined on the same domain and a nonnegative integer α, the following statements are equivalent:*

(a) $P_{\mathrm{FGT}}(F,z) \le P_{\mathrm{FGT}}(G,z)$ for all $z \in (0,\infty)$, with $<$ for some z.
(b) F dominates G by the $(\alpha+1)$th degree stochastic dominance criterion.

Thus, the poverty ranking of two distributions by the member of P_{FGT} defined in (2.24) is same as third-order stochastic dominance. An implication of the P_{FGT} orderings is that if the index generates an unambiguous ranking of two distributions for $\alpha = \alpha_1$, then it is capable of ranking the two distributions in the same direction for $\alpha = \alpha_2$ if $\alpha_1 \le \alpha_2$. If the dominance relation holds for some member of the Foster et al. (1984) class, say for $\alpha = \alpha_1$, then it is not necessary to check dominance for higher values of α. The direction of dominance will not change. This means that the P_{FGT} orderings are nested. Thus, if one distribution is regarded as less poor than another by the headcount ratio, then the same will be true for the poverty gap ratio as well. While the nested characteristic of the Foster-Shorrocks result requires that α should be an integer, Tungodden (2005) extended this to the case where α can be an arbitrary nonnegative real number. In view of equivalence between stochastic dominance and welfare dominance, the P_{FGT} orderings enable us to provide welfare interpretation of the P_{FGT} family. Assuming that the poverty line is bounded above, Foster and Shorrocks (1988b) derived results analogous to Theorem 2.3.

Foster and Jin (1998) developed poverty-line ordering of distributions using indices that are based on utility gaps. Formally, a utility gap-based poverty index is defined as

$$P_{\mathrm{U}}(x,z) = \frac{\tilde{a}(z)}{n} \sum_{i=1}^{n} (U(z) - U(x_i^*)), \tag{2.31}$$

where U is the identical individual utility function and $\tilde{a}(z) > 0$ is a normalization coefficient. Thus, P_{U} aggregates the utility gaps of the poor from the poverty line. This general Dalton type index contains many well-known indices as special cases. For instance, if $U(v) = \log v, \tilde{a}(z) = 1$, then P_{U} becomes the Watts (1968) index. On the other hand, for $U(v) = \log v, \tilde{a}(z) = 1/\log z$, P_{U} coincides with the Hagenaars (1987) index. Finally, the Chakravarty (1983c) index drops out as a member of P_{U} if we assume that $U(v) = v^e$ and $\tilde{a}(z) = z^e$. For any $x \in D_+^n$, we denote the utility distribution of x by $U^x = (U(x_1), U(x_2), \ldots, U(x_n))$.

The following theorem of Foster and Jin (1998) provides a characterization of the utility gap -based indices in terms of the poverty-line ordering.

Theorem 2.4. *Let U be continuous and increasing, and $x, y \in D_+^n$ be arbitrary. Then the following conditions are equivalent:*

(a) $P_{\mathrm{U}}(x,z) \leq P_{\mathrm{U}}(y,z)$ for all $z \in (0,\infty)$ with $<$ for some z.
(b) $U^x \geq_{\mathrm{GL}} U^y$, that is, U^x generalized Lorenz dominates U^y.

Theorem 2.4 says that if the distribution y poverty line dominates the distribution x, then the utility distribution of x will be generalized Lorenz superior to the utility distribution of y. The converse is true as well. Since the utility gap-based Dalton type poverty index and the generalized Lorenz curve remain invariant under replications of the population, we can use Theorem 2.4 for cross-population poverty comparisons of income distributions.

An alternative direction of research on poverty ranking involves identification of a family of poverty indices that will rank different distributions unambiguously when the poverty line is given. This is referred to as poverty-measure ordering. Given the poverty line, we need to specify a set of axioms such that all the poverty indices fulfilling these axioms will rank the distributions in the same direction. That is, we need to check whether, for a given poverty line, it is possible to compare two distributions unanimously by all members belonging to the class of indices satisfying these axioms.

Atkinson (1987) developed conditions on poverty-measure ordering for subgroup decomposable indices with a common arbitrary poverty line. He considered the range $[z_-, z_+]$ for the poverty lines, where, as before, $z_- > 0$ and $z_+ < \infty$ are the minimum and maximum poverty lines. The poverty line arbitrarily varies within this range. Instead of considering a single poverty index, he focused attention on a given class of poverty indices. The two theorems presented below summarize the poverty-measure orderings developed by Atkinson (1987).

For presenting the theorems, we follow Zheng (2001) and consider poverty indices that are additively separable, so that

$$P(F,z) = \int_0^{\infty} \zeta(v,z)\mathrm{d}F(v), \tag{2.32}$$

where the individual poverty function $\zeta(v,z)$ is zero if $v \geq z$, it is positive otherwise.

Theorem 2.5. *Consider two income distribution functions F and G defined on the same domain and assume the weak definition of the poor. Then (i) the necessary and sufficient condition for $P(F,z) < P(G,z)$ to hold for all individual poverty functions that are continuous on $[0,\infty)$ and decreasing in the incomes of the poor, and a given poverty line $z \in [z_-, z_+]$ is that F first-order stochastic dominates G over $[0,z]$, and (ii) the necessary and sufficient condition for $P(F,z) < P(G,z)$ to hold for all individual poverty functions that are continuous on $[0,\infty)$ and decreasing in the incomes of the poor, and all poverty lines $z \in [z_-, z_+]$ is that F first-order stochastic dominates G over $[0,z_-]$ and F weakly first-order stochastic dominates G over $[z_-, z_+]$.*

Theorem 2.6. *Consider two income distribution functions F and G defined on the same domain and assume the weak definition of the poor. Then the necessary and sufficient condition for $P(F,z) < P(G,z)$ to hold for all individual poverty functions that are continuous on $[0,\infty)$, decreasing and strictly convex in the incomes of the poor, and a given poverty line $z \in [z_-, z_+]$ is that F second-order stochastic dominates G over $[0,z]$, (ii) the necessary and sufficient condition for $P(F,z) < P(G,z)$ to hold for all individual poverty functions that are continuous on $[0,\infty)$, decreasing and strictly convex in the incomes of the poor, and all poverty lines $z \in [z_-, z_+]$ is that F second-order stochastic dominates G over $[0,z_-]$ and F weakly second-order stochastic dominates G over $[z_-, z_+]$.*

These two theorems have very strong implications. If a dominance relation holds, then no individual poverty index with the relevant properties needs to be consulted in ordering the distributions under considerations. The dominance conditions are quite easy to implement and our discussion in Chap. 1 shows that they have very nice welfare theoretic interpretations (*see also* Howes, 1993). Zheng (1999) extended Theorem 2.6 to the case of third-order dominance. Clearly, the poverty index in this case is required to be diminishing transfer sensitive.

Spencer and Fisher (1992), Jenkins and Lambert (1997, 1998a,b), and Shorrocks (1998) derived conditions for ranking one distribution as having more poverty than another in terms of dominance condition that relies on the poverty gap profile. The aggregate normalized poverty gap of the cumulative population proportion i/n for the distribution x is $\sum_{j=1}^{i}(z-x_j^*)/nz$, where $1 \leq i \leq n$. Given the poverty line z, this is the ordinate $\mathrm{PG}(x,z,i/n)$ of the poverty gap profile at the cumulative population proportion i/n. The poverty gap profile $\mathrm{PG}(x,z,t)$ of x, where $0 \leq t \leq 1$, is completed by setting $\mathrm{PG}(x,z,0) = 0$ and by defining

$$\mathrm{PG}\left(x,z,\frac{i+\tau}{n}\right) = (1-\tau)\mathrm{PG}\left(\mathrm{x},\mathrm{z},\frac{\mathrm{i}}{\mathrm{n}}\right) + \tau\mathrm{PG}\left(\mathrm{x},\mathrm{z},\frac{\mathrm{i}+1}{\mathrm{n}}\right), \tag{2.33}$$

for all $0 \leq \tau \leq 1$ and $1 \leq i \leq (n-1)$. This curve is nondecreasing and concave (*see* Fig. 2.1). The 45° line represents the situation where all the persons have zero

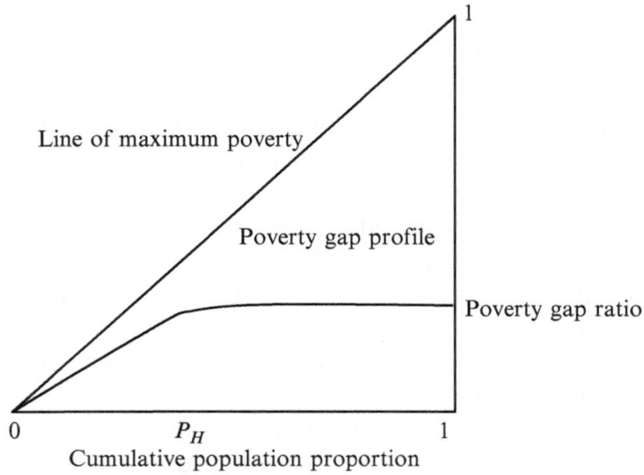

Fig. 2.1 Poverty gap profile

income. This is the line of maximum poverty. The vertical distance between the 45° line and the poverty gap profile is the generalized Lorenz curve of the normalized distribution x^*/z. Shorrocks (1998) has shown that P_{Sh}, the continuous version of the Sen index P_S, can be expressed as the area under the poverty gap profile expressed as a fraction of the area under the 45° line. The headcount ratio, which represents the poverty intensity, is the population proportion at which the curve becomes flat (given that there is no person with exactly the poverty-line income). The poverty gap ratio, the relative gap between the poverty line and the mean of the censored income distribution, is the maximum height of the curve. The curvature of the curve between the origin and the headcount ratio is an indicator of inequality among the poor because in this position the curve is not flat. Since the curve depicts these three important components of poverty, Jenkins and Lambert (1997, 1998a,b) renamed the curve as the TIP (three Is of poverty) curve and analyzed it in greater details. We may also refer to the curve as the illfare curve of the society. Spencer and Fisher (1992) called the absolute poverty gap profile $z\mathrm{PG}(x,z,t)$ absolute rotated Lorenz curve of the censored income distribution x^*.

Given two income distributions $x, y \in D^n$, we say that y poverty gap profile dominates x, which we denote by $y \geq_{\mathrm{PG}} x$, if for a given poverty line z, $\mathrm{PG}(x,z,t) \leq \mathrm{PG}(\mathrm{y},\mathrm{z},\mathrm{t})$ for all $0 \leq t \leq 1$ with $<$ for some t. The following theorem of Spencer and Fisher (1992), Jenkins and Lambert (1997, 1998a,b), and Shorrocks (1998) gives an implication of poverty gap profile dominance in terms of illfare indices.

Theorem 2.7. *Let $x, y \in D^n$ be arbitrary. The poverty line $z \in [z_-, z_+]$ is assumed to be given. Then the following conditions are equivalent:*

(i) $y \geq_{\mathrm{PG}} x$.
(ii) $H((1 - x_1^*/z), (1 - x_2^*/z), \ldots, (1 - x_n^*/z)) < H((1 - y_1^*/z), (1 - y_2^*/z), \ldots, (1 - y_n^*/z))$ *for all illfare indices* $H : [0,1]^n \to R^1$ *that are increasing and strictly S-convex in the relative poverty gaps* $(1 - x_i^*/z)$.

The theorem shows an interesting application of the illfare functions we have considered in Sect. 2.3. Clearly, it can be regarded as an extension of the equivalence between conditions (iv) and (x) of Theorem 2.1 to the censored income distributions (*see also* Foster and Sen, 1997, pp. 192–193).[7] This equivalent condition can be used to check poverty ranking of distributions for a large class of poverty indices. Spencer and Fisher (1992) referred to the illfare functions as the aggregate hardship functions. Jenkins and Lambert (1998b) also demonstrated equivalence between censored generalized Lorenz dominance and TIP curve dominance. Finally, it may be worthwhile to mention that Atkinson (1992) and Jenkins and Lambert (1993) studied poverty-measure orderings when the poverty line is adjusted for differences in family composition. Contributions along this line have also been made by Chambaz and Maurin (1998) and Zoli and Lambert (2005).

As Zheng (2000b) noted all the poverty indices that are covered by Theorem 2.6 can be expressed in terms of their distribution-sensitivity measures. He considered the poverty-measure ordering based on the class of minimum distribution-sensitive indices. The reason for concentrating on such a class is that minimum distribution-sensitive indices may be able to increase the completeness or power of poverty ordering beyond second-degree dominance (*see also* Zheng, 1999). He restricted attention on the set of all subgroup decomposable focused poverty indices $\mathrm{SP}(\hat{\zeta}(v,z)) = \{P(x,z) = (1/n)\sum_{i=1}^{n}\zeta(x_i,z)|\mathrm{DS}_{\zeta}(v,z) \geq \mathrm{DS}_{\hat{\zeta}}(v,z) \text{ for all } v \in [0,z)\}$, where, as before, the individual poverty function $\zeta(v,z) > 0$ on $[0,z)$, $\zeta(v,z) = 0$ for $v \geq z$. Further, ζ is decreasing, strictly convex in the incomes of poor and continuous on $[0,\infty)$. If $\hat{\zeta}(v,z) = (z-v)$, then $\mathrm{SP}(\hat{\zeta}(v,z))$ and the family of distribution-sensitive poverty indices considered by Atkinson (1987) coincide. Zheng (2000b) then showed that for two income distributions x and y over a given population and a given poverty line z, y has at least as high poverty level as x for all poverty indices belonging to this particular set if and only if $\sum_{i=1}^{j}\hat{\zeta}(y_i,z) \geq \sum_{i=1}^{j}\hat{\zeta}(x_i,z)$ for all $1 \leq j \leq n$. Clearly, this result can be regarded as a generalization of the Spencer and Fisher (1992), Jenkins and Lambert (1997, 1998a,b), and Shorrocks (1998) theorem because in the latter, we set $\hat{\zeta}(x_i,z) = (1 - x_i^*/z)$. He also showed how to compare poverty orderings with different $\hat{\zeta}$ functions. It is shown that the necessary and sufficient condition for the set of distributions ordered by $\mathrm{SP}(\hat{\zeta}_1(\mathrm{v},\mathrm{z}))$ be included in the set ordered by $\mathrm{SP}(\hat{\zeta}_2(\mathrm{v},\mathrm{z}))$ is that $\hat{\zeta}_2$ is a convex function of $\hat{\zeta}_1$. An implication of this result is that if $\hat{\zeta}_2$ is an increasing and convex function of $\hat{\zeta}_1$, then the poverty ordering by $\mathrm{SP}(\hat{\zeta}_2(v,z))$ will have at least as much power as that by $\mathrm{SP}(\hat{\zeta}_1(v,z))$. Recall that for the second Clark et al. (1981), the Watts (1968), the Chakravarty (1983c), the Foster et al. (1984), and the constant distribution-sensitivity indices, the individual poverty functions are given, respectively, by $(1-(v/z)^{\theta}/\theta$, where $\theta < 1$; $\log(z/v)$; $(1-(v/z)^{\theta})$, where $0 < \theta < 1$; $(1-(v/z))^{\alpha}$, where $\alpha > 1$; and $\exp(\tilde{\omega}(z-v)) - 1$ with $\tilde{\omega} > 0$. It then turns

[7] In fact, Shorrocks (1998) referred to the poverty gap profile as deprivation profile. He looked at the issue from a quite general perspective and used the curve for ranking societies in terms of bads such as unemployment duration and wage discrimination, in addition to poverty. See also Xu and Osberg (1998).

out that the poverty ordering by SP($\hat{\zeta}(v,z)$) with $\hat{\zeta}$ being anyone of these indices has more power than the Atkinson second-degree stochastic dominance criterion. (This is because for a given $z > 0$, the individual poverty functions $(1-(v/z)^{\theta})/\theta$, where $\theta < 1$, and $(\exp(\tilde{\omega}(z-v))-1)$ are increasing and strictly convex functions of $(z-v)$.) The poverty ordering associated with the Clark et al. index for $\theta < 0$ has more power than that with the Watts index, which in turn has more power than that with the Chakravarty index. The power of the poverty ordering induced by the Foster et al. index increases with the value of α. The power of poverty ordering with the constant distribution-sensitivity index is not comparable with that of any other index.

2.6 Unit Consistent Poverty Indices

The unit consistency axiom, introduced by Zheng (2007c), demands that the poverty rankings of income distributions remain unaltered if all the incomes and the poverty line are expressed in different units of measurement. To illustrate this, suppose that when incomes and poverty lines are expressed in euros, region I is regarded as poorer than region II. It is reasonable to expect that the regional poverty ranking does not change if incomes and poverty lines are expressed in terms of one thousand euros. A unit consistent poverty index will achieve this objective. Thus, unit consistency ensures that measurement of incomes and poverty lines in different units will not lead to contradictory conclusions.

A poverty index $P : D_+ \times [z_-, z_+]$ is said to be unit consistent if for $x, y \in D_+$ and two given poverty lines $z_1, z_2 \in [z_-, z_+]$, $P(x,z_1) < P(y,z_2)$ implies $P(cx, cz_1) < P(cy, cz_2)$, where $c > 0$ is any scalar such that $cz_1, cz_2 \in [z_-, z_+]$.

Since for a relative poverty index P, $P(cx,cz) = P(x,z)$, all relative poverty indices are unit consistent. But the converse is not true. However, people may not always like to view income shortfalls from the poverty line in relative terms. Sometimes they may like to look at poverty in terms of absolute shortfalls and, as argued earlier, in this case, we concentrate on absolute indices. Therefore, it might be worthwhile to look for absolute indices that satisfy unit consistency.

In order to identify unit consistent absolute poverty indices, we consider some specific type of indices. Following Zheng (2007c), we say that a poverty index P is semi-individualistic if for any $(x,z) \in D_+ \times [z_-, z_+]$, $P(x,z) = (1/n)\sum_{i=1}^{q} \zeta(x_i, n, q, i, z)$, where the nonnegative semi-individualistic poverty function $\zeta(x_i, n, q, i, z)$ is invertible, twice differentiable, decreasing in $x_i < z$, also $\lim_{v \to z-} \zeta(v, n, i, z) = 0$ and $\zeta(v, n, q, i, z) = 0$ if $v \geq z$. Because of dependence of ζ on n, q, and i in addition to v and z, it is referred to as semi-individualistic, instead of individualistic in which case dependence is assumed only on (v,z). Thus, a semi-individualistic poverty function for person i does not change in response to a change in another person's income as long as i's rank in the distribution and the number of poor persons remain unaltered.

Zheng (2007c) showed that an absolute semi-individualistic poverty index is unit consistent if and only if it is of the form

$$P_{ZA}(x,z) = \frac{1}{n}\sum_{i=1}^{q} \tilde{f}(n,q,i)(z-x_i)^{\bar{f}(n,q)}, \tag{2.34}$$

for some positive functions $\tilde{f}(n,q,i)$ and $\bar{f}(n,q)$.

If $\bar{f}(n,q) = 1$ and $\tilde{f}(n,q,i) = 2(q+1-i)/(q+1)$, then P_{ZA} becomes the absolute form of the Sen (1976a) index, which we have discussed in Sect. 2.3.5. On the other hand, if $\tilde{f}(n,q,i) = 1$ and $c(n,q) = \alpha$, then P_{ZA} coincides with the absolute version of the Foster et al. (1984) index. Finally, for $\bar{f}(n,q) = 1$ and $\tilde{f}(n,q,i) = (2(n-i)+1)/n$, P_{ZA} will be the absolute variant of P_{Sh}, the continuous form of the Sen index characterized by Shorrocks (1995), which is a member of the general Chakravarty (1983a) index.

Next, we consider poverty indices within a more specified framework to study implications of unit consistency. Recall that the Dalton (1920) index of inequality is based on utility ratio. Chakravarty (1983c) and Hagenaars (1987) applied the Dalton index to the measurement of poverty. For all $x \in D_+$ and $z \in [z_-, z_+]$, a generalized Dalton-Chakravarty-Hagenaars poverty index $P_{DCH}(x,z)$ is defined as

$$P_{DCH}(x,z) = \frac{1}{n}\sum_{i=1}^{q} \frac{(\tilde{\phi}(z) - \tilde{\phi}(x_i))}{\tilde{\varphi}(z)}, \tag{2.35}$$

where the real valued functions $\tilde{\phi}$ and $\tilde{\varphi}$ are assumed to be twice differentiable. If we assume that $\tilde{\phi}$ and $\tilde{\varphi}$ are identical then P_{DCH} reduces to the general form of the Hagenaars index.

By construction, P_{DCH} is subgroup decomposable and semi-individualistic. The set of all poverty indices defined by (2.35) is a proper subset of the set of all subgroup decomposable indices and the latter set is a proper subset of the set of semi-individualistic indices. Therefore, the framework that defines P_{DCH} is narrower than the framework for semi-individualistic indices.

It may be noted that for all subgroup decomposable unit consistent poverty indices, the individual poverty function will be homogeneous of some arbitrary degree in its arguments (Zheng, 2007c). However, this does not identify any specific form of the index. If we restrict our attention to P_{DCH} in (2.35), then it is possible to isolate some functional forms uniquely. Zheng (2007c) showed that a generalized Dalton-Chakravarty-Hagenaars poverty index $P_{DCH}(x,z)$ satisfies unit consistency if and only if it is of the form

$$P_{DCH}(x,z) = \begin{cases} \frac{1}{r_1}\frac{1}{nz^{r_2}}\sum_{i=1}^{q}[z^{r_1} - x_i^{r_1}], r_1 \neq 0, \\ \frac{1}{nz^{r_2}}\sum_{i=1}^{q}\log\left(\frac{z}{x_i}\right), r_1 = 0, \end{cases} \tag{2.36}$$

where r_1 and r_2 are constants.

The logarithmic member of this family is a parametric extension of the Watts (1968) index, while the other member is a two parameter generalization of the second Clark et al. (1981) and the Chakravarty (1983c) indices. The entire family may be regarded as the poverty counterpart to the generalized entropy family of inequality indices. Note that the family contains the absolute poverty gap ratio $(\sum_{i=1}^{q}(z-x_i))/n$ as a member. In fact, the only member of the P_{DCH} in (2.36) that satisfies absolute scale invariance and unit consistency simultaneously is a positive multiple of this index.

2.7 Measuring Chronic Poverty

Our analysis so far has ignored one important aspect of poverty, its duration. Looking at poverty trends using a particular index of poverty does not tell us whether individuals are persistently poor or they have been able to move out of poverty. The duration aspect of poverty deserves attention for several reasons. For instance, longer duration in poverty may lead to worse health status for individuals, particularly, for children and aged persons. Long exposure to poverty has quite important implications for future strategies of individuals or households.

A distinction has been made between transitory and chronic poverty in the context of intertemporal poverty measurement. The former is a consequence of a short-term fall in the level of living of an individual, while the latter arises from low long-term well-being of the person. For instance, a person in the short-term transition period between two jobs may be in poverty over the unemployment duration period. This can be referred to as transitory poverty. In contrast, chronic poverty deals with the prolonged concept of poverty.[8]

Identification of chronically poor persons and aggregation of their characteristics require panel data on income. Broadly, two different approaches for identifying chronically poor persons have been suggested in the literature (*see* Yaqub, 2000a,b; McKay and Lawson, 2003). The first is the components approach that separates the permanent component of income from its transitory component and identifies a person as chronically poor if his permanent income falls below the poverty line (*see* Jalan and Ravallion, 1998; Calvo and Dercon, 2007). This approach is not sensitive to the time for which a person remains in poverty (Foster, 2008).

The second approach, which is referred to as the spells approach, identifies a person as chronically poor in terms of the number of spells of poverty he experiences. That is, this approach depends on a duration threshold as well as an income threshold. More precisely, a person is identified as chronically poor by the spells approach if he is in income poverty for a fraction of the total duration not less than the duration threshold. For instance, if we have data for 8 years and the duration threshold

[8] For further discussions along this line, see Rodgers and Rodgers (2006), Ravallion (1988), Jalan and Ravallion (1998, 2000), Hulme and Shepherd (2003a,b), McKay and Lawson (2003), Clark and Hulme (2005), Hulme and McKay (2005), Duclos et al. (2006), and Kurosaki (2006).

is .5, then we say that a person is chronically poor if his incomes are not above the poverty line for at least 4 years.[9]

Axiomatic approaches to the measurement of chronic poverty have been suggested, among others, by Hoy and Zheng (2006), Calvo and Dercon (2007), Bossert et al. (2008), and Foster (2008). In this section, we follow the axioms proposed by Foster (2008) and consider the subgroup decomposable chronic poverty index.

Suppose there are observations on incomes of a set $\{1,2,..,n\}$ of individuals over the periods $\{1,2,..,K\}$. Let $x_{ij} \geq 0$ be the income of person $i \in \{1,2,..,n\}$ in period $j \in \{1,2,..,K\}$. The row vector $x_{i.}$ represents the incomes of person i in different periods. The $n \times K$ matrix X shows the incomes of different persons in K periods. Thus, the jth column of X shows the income distribution among n persons in period j. We denote the duration threshold by $z_K > 0$ and, as before, the income threshold, the poverty line, is denoted by $z > 0$. It is assumed that the incomes have been properly deflated to take into account the intertemporal variations so that the same poverty line can be used to identify the poor in each period. Person i becomes chronically poor if he remains in poverty for $K_i \geq K z_K$ periods. That is, for person i, the inequality $x_{ij} \leq z$ is satisfied for K_i values of j, where $(K_i/K) \geq z_K$. Let $CP(z, z_K)$ be the set of chronically poor persons.

To illustrate the issue numerically, suppose that $K = 4, n = 4, z_K = .6$, and $z = 9$. The income distributions of the four persons in different periods are given, respectively, by $x_{1.} = (7,4,8,15), x_{2.} = (3,8,3,4), x_{3.} = (9,10,3,20)$, and $x_{4.} = (4,25,5,6)$. Note that person 1 has incomes below the threshold z in three periods and hence $K_1 = 3$. Likewise $K_2 = 4$ and $K_4 = 3$. However, person 3 is not chronically poor because $K_3 = 2$. The headcount ratio, $P_{\mathrm{H}}(X, z, z_K)$, for this example is then given by $3/4$ since there are three persons who are chronically poor.[10]

Now, suppose we reduce person 1's income in period 4 to 8. This increases K_1 to 4. Clearly, the headcount ratio remains unchanged although we have increased the time duration of poverty for person 1. In order to make some adjusted form of the headcount ratio sensitive to time monotonicity, let us consider another counting index, the average of the fractional durations K_i/K of the chronically poor. We denote this index by $P_{\mathrm{AD}}(X, z, z_K)$. It is the fraction of the total time period for which the average chronically poor person remains in poverty. For the original example we have considered, this index becomes $2.5/3$. If we multiply the two indices, we get the duration adjusted headcount ratio $P_{\mathrm{HAD}}(X, z, z_K) = P_{\mathrm{H}}(X, z, z_K) P_{\mathrm{AD}}(X, z, z_K)$ that becomes sensitive to the changes in the duration of a person in poverty (Foster, 2008). For our example, the value of this adjusted index is $10/16$. This value is the total number of periods, 10, for which all the chronically poor persons experience poverty as a fraction of the total number of periods $16 (= Kn)$ for the entire population.

---

[9] See Bane and Ellwood (1986), Gaiha (1989, 1992), Gaiha and Deolikar (1993), Morduch (1994), Baluch and Masset (2003), and Carter and Barrett (2004) for discussion on duration issues.

[10] For applications of the headcount/headcount ratio, see The Chronic Poverty Report (2004–2005), Gaiha and Deolikar (1993), and Mehta and Shah (2003).

Since the h function in (2.19) captures the depth of poverty in an analytical way, taking cue from the above discussion, we can say that the subgroup decomposable chronic poverty index is given by

$$P_{\mathrm{CP}}(X,z,z_K) = \frac{1}{Kn} \sum_{i \in \mathrm{CP}(z,z_K)} \sum_{j=1}^{K} h\left(\frac{x_{ij}^*}{z}\right), \tag{2.37}$$

where the real valued function h is the same as in (2.19). This index is the sum of transformed censored income shortfalls $h(x_{ij}^*/z)$ of the chronically poor persons divided by the maximum value this sum can take. If we assume that $z_K = 0$, then P_{CP} takes into account all the poverty spells of all persons. In contrast, for a positive given value of z_K, it considers the spells of only chronically poor persons, as determined by z and z_K. Consequently, the difference $P_{\mathrm{CP}}(X,z,z_K) - P_{\mathrm{CP}}(X,z,0)$ is based on spells of those who are not chronically poor. Therefore, this difference is an indicator of transitory poverty. Thus, the subgroup decomposable transitory poverty index is given by

$$P_{\mathrm{TP}}(X,z,z_K) = P_{\mathrm{CP}}(X,z,z_K) - P_{\mathrm{CP}}(X,z,0). \tag{2.38}$$

Clearly, we can have chronic poverty variants of the Watts (1968), Chakravarty (1983c), and Foster et al. (1984) indices for appropriate specifications of the functions h. Thus, the functional form for the Watts chronic poverty index will be $1/Kn \sum_{i \in \mathrm{CP}(z,z_K)} \sum_{j=1}^{K} \log(z/x_{ij}^*)$. The corresponding functional forms for the Chakravarty and the Foster et al. indices are given, respectively, by $1/Kn \sum_{i \in \mathrm{CP}(z,z_K)} \sum_{j=1}^{K} (1 - (x_{ij}^*/z)^e)$ and $1/Kn \sum_{i \in \mathrm{CP}(z,z_K)} \sum_{j=1}^{K} (1 - x_{ij}^*/z)^{\alpha}$. This Foster et al. form was suggested and analyzed by Foster (2008). Each of these indices can be used to generate the corresponding transitory poverty index.

The general index P_{CP}, in addition to satisfying the standard income-based axioms for a specific time period, satisfies Time Anonymity, Time Focus, Time Monotonicity, and Chronic Poverty Transfer Axioms introduced by Foster (2008). The first axiom says that if there is a permutation of incomes across time, poverty does not change. That is, if $Y = X\Pi$ for a $K \times K$ permutation matrix Π, then $P(X,z,z_K) = P(Y,z,z_K)$. According to the second axiom, an increase in the nonpoor income of a chronically poor person does not alter the level of poverty. That is, if there is some period j' and person i' who is chronically poor in Y and if $x_{ij} > y_{ij} > z$ for $(i,j) = (i',j')$ and $x_{ij} = y_{ij}$ for all $(i,j) \neq (i',j')$, then $P(X,z,z_K) = P(Y,z,z_K)$. The third axiom demands that if a chronically poor person is out of poverty in a spell and if because of reduction in income, the person becomes poor in that spell, then poverty should go up. Technically, if there is some period j' and a person i' who is chronically poor in X and $y_{ij} \leq z < x_{ij}$ for $(i,j) = (i',j')$ and $x_{ij} = y_{ij}$ for all $(i,j) \neq (i',j')$, then $P(X,z,z_K) < P(Y,z,z_K)$. Finally, let Y_{CP}^* be the censored submatrix of Y representing the y_{ij} values of the chronically poor persons, that is, the (i,j)th entry of Y_{CP}^* is $\min\{z, y_{ij}\}$, where person i is chronically poor and let $X_{\mathrm{CP}}^* = AY_{\mathrm{CP}}^*$ for some nonpermutation bistochastic matrix A of order q, the number of chronically poor persons. Then the fourth axiom says that $P(X_{\mathrm{CP}}^*, z, z_K) \leq P(Y_{\mathrm{CP}}^*, z, z_K)$. In words, if there is a redistribution of income among the chronically poor persons, then chronic poverty does not increase. [This formulation, which is based on Kolm (1977), Tsui (2002), and Bourguignon and Chakravarty (2003), is slightly different from that of Foster (2008).] The general index also fulfills the Normalization and Nondecreasingness in Duration Threshold Axioms. According to the first of these two axioms, $P(X,z,z_K)=0$ if the set $\mathrm{CP}(z,z_K)$ is empty. That, is, the value of the chronic poverty index is zero, if nobody is chronically poor in the society. The second axiom says that chronic poverty does not decrease if there is an increase in the duration threshold.

Let us now illustrate the index $1/Kn\sum_{i\in \mathrm{CP}(z,z_K)}\sum_{j=1}^{K}(1-(x_{ij}^*/z)^e)$ using the numerical example considered above when $e=0.5$. Since the calculation is based on censored incomes, we first determine the censored distributions corresponding to x_i's. These distributions are: $x_{1.}^*=(7,4,8,9), x_{2.}^*=(3,8,3,4), x_{3.}^*=(9,9,3,9)$, and $x_{4.}^*=(4,9,5,6)$. Let ρ_i be the intertemporal poverty profile of person i. That is, the jth entry of ρ_i is $\rho_{ij}=(1-(x_{ij}^*/z)^{0.5})$, the level of person i's poverty in period j. For instance, $\rho_{11}=(1-(x_{11}^*/z)^{0.5})=(1-(7/9)^{0.5})=0.118$. The ρ-vectors for the chronically poor persons 1, 2, and 4 become $\rho_1=(0.118,0.333,0.057,0), \rho_2=(0.423,0.057,0.423,0.333)$, and $\rho_4=(0.333,0,0.255,0.183)$, respectively. Now, the level of chronic poverty for this example is calculated by taking the sum of these 12 ρ_{ij} values, which is 2.515, and then dividing the sum by 16. Thus, the required poverty level is $(2.515/16)=0.157$. To calculate the transitory poverty, we also have to consider $\rho_3=(0,0,0.423,0)$, the poverty profile of person 3 who is not chronically poor. The total poverty level for the example will be $((2.515+0.423)/16)=0.184$. Hence, the level of transitory poverty is $(0.184-0.157)=0.027$.

Bossert et al. (2008) argued that the length of poverty spells is an important component of intertemporal poverty analysis. For instance, consider the following two per period individual poverty profiles: $\rho_1=(1/8,0,1/3,2/5)$ and $\rho_2=(1/8,1/3,2/5,0)$. The third entry in the vector ρ_1 gives the level of poverty experienced by person 1 in period 3, where the poverty level is calculated using a given poverty index. Similarly, other entries can be explained. They argued that since in the first profile the person experiences a break from poverty rather than being in poverty for three consecutive periods, the first profile should depict less poverty than the second one. Further, their formulation does not rely on the assumption that the poverty line is fixed over time. They also developed an axiomatic characterization of an intertemporal poverty index that takes this into account. Note that the general poverty index in (2.37) regards the two profiles as identically poor. The functional form of the Bossert et al. (2008) index is given by

$$P_{\mathrm{BCD}}(\rho_1,\rho_2,..,\rho_n)=\frac{1}{nK}\sum_{i=1}^{n}\sum_{j=1}^{K} r^{d^j(\rho_i)-1}\rho_{ij}, \tag{2.39}$$

where $d^j(\rho_i)$ is the maximum number of consecutive periods including j with positive (zero) per period poverty values in ρ_i and $r\geq 1$ is a parameter. The value of the poverty index P_{BCD} increases as r increases.

To illustrate the formula, let $r=2$. For example, we have considered here, $d^1(\rho_1)=d^2(\rho_1)=1, d^3(\rho_1)=d^4(\rho_1)=2$ and $d^1(\rho_2)=d^2(\rho_2)=d^3(\rho_2)=3$,

$d^4(\rho_2) = 1$. For person 1, the length of the first poverty spell is one and hence $d^1(\rho_1) = 1$. This is followed by a nonpoverty spell of length one, which gives $d^2(\rho_1) = 1$. For the next two periods, he is in poverty and hence $d^3(\rho_1) = d^4(\rho_1) = 2$. A similar explanation holds for $d^j(\rho_2)$ values. It is easy to see that the individual poverty function $\sum_{j=1}^{K} r^{d^j(\rho_i)-1}\rho_{ij}/K$ is higher for person 2. The value of the aggregate poverty index in (2.39) turns out to be 0.628.

Chapter 3
Measuring Income Deprivation

3.1 Introduction

A person's feeling of deprivation with respect to an attribute of well-being arises from the comparison of his situation in the society with those of the persons that are better-off in the attribute. Evidently, high deprivation may generate tensions in the society which ultimately may lead to conflicts. A natural objective of the society should, therefore, be to make deprivation as low as possible. In this chapter, for simplicity, we will study only income deprivation.

The concept of deprivation was introduced into the income distribution literature by Sen (1973, 1976a). According to Sen (1973), in any pairwise comparison, the person with lower income may have a feeling of depression on finding that his income is lower. Assuming that the extent of depression suffered by an individual is proportional to the difference between the two incomes concerned, the average of all such depressions in all pairwise comparisons becomes the Gini index. A more formal treatment of this result was provided by Hey and Lambert (1980). Kakwani (1980a) interpreted the coefficient of variation from a similar perspective under the assumption that an individual's extent of depression is proportional to the square of the income difference. Tsui and Wang (2000) characterized a transformation of the Donaldson and Weymark (1980, 1983) S-Gini indices as a deprivation index using the concept of "net marginal deprivation." Net marginal deprivation demands that a rank-preserving increase in a person's income will generate two effects: (1) the feeling of deprivation among those poorer than him will increase and (2) his deprivation with respect to those richer than him will decrease. This approach bears some similarity with the Berrebi and Silber (1981) formulation.

A person in subgroup i of persons with i lowest incomes in the society may regard the subgroup highest income as his source of envy and the sum of gaps between the subgroup highest income and all lower incomes can be taken as an aggregate depression index of the subgroup. Aggregation of depressions across subgroups generates the absolute Bonferroni inequality index as the summary index of depression for the population as a whole (Chakravarty, 2007).

S.R. Chakravarty, *Inequality, Polarization and Poverty: Advances in Distributional Analysis*, 85
Economic Studies in Inequality, Social Exclusion and Well-Being 6,
DOI: 10.1007/978-0-387-79253-8_3,

Sen (1976a) argued that for any person, an increasing function of the number or share of the persons who have higher incomes can be taken as the level of deprivation. Alternatively, one might use the individual's income shortfall from a reference income level as an indicator of his deprivation. Yitzhaki (1979) considered the former notion and showed that one plausible index of average deprivation in a society is the absolute Gini index (*see also* Hey and Lambert, 1980). In either case, the position of the individual on income hierarchy plays an important role in the determination of his deprivation. Runciman (1966) discussed these two notions of deprivation earlier in a more general context (*see also* Weiss and Fershatman, 1998). In this general framework, an individual's assessment of a social state depends on the positions of those who are more favorably treated than him.

Bossert and D'Ambrosio (2007) considered time as a dimension in the determination of individual deprivation. In their framework, individual deprivation depends on two components, the average income shortfall of a person from all persons who are richer than him in the current period and the number of persons who were not richer than him in the previous period but are now better-off than him. Thus, this approach incorporates the idea that a person feels deprived not only because he is poor now but also because he was not poorer in the earlier period. They also developed axiomatic characterizations of deprivation indices that capture these ideas.

Chakravarty et al. (1995), Chakravarty (1997b, 2008b), and Chakravarty and Mukherjee (1999) looked at alternative implications of deprivation dominance induced by Kakwani's (1984a) relative deprivation curve (RDC), which is obtained by plotting the normalized cumulative sum of income shortfalls of different individuals from richer individuals against the corresponding cumulative population proportions. Chakravarty (1997b, 2008b) also studied satisfaction dominance in details, where the notion "satisfaction" may be regarded as the dual of the notion of deprivation. These issues have been examined further, among others, by Zoli (2000), Chakravarty and Moyes (2003), Chateauneuf and Moyes (2004, 2006), Moyes (2007), and Zheng (2007b).

Marshall et al. (1967) and Marshall and Olkin (1979) developed conditions on pairwise absolute and relative (ratio) income differences that are sufficient for Lorenz dominance. Preston (1990) provided some characterizations of these conditions along with an empirical illustration. The absolute difference and ratio criteria are, in fact, special cases of Zheng's (2007b) general utility gap dominance. He investigated a weak dominance concept which imposes conditions only on the gap between each person's utility and some reference utility.

According to Temkin (1986, 1993), a person has a complaint if he has lower income than others and inequality can be viewed in terms of such complaints. The greater is the difference between the income of a person and income of those richer than him, the greater will be his complaint. Similarly, the higher is the number of persons richer than him, the higher is his complaint. Social inequality then aggregates the complaints of different individuals concerning the income gaps and the numbers of persons. More precisely, inequality is defined as an increasing function of the total numbers and sizes of complaints of different individuals in the society. An important case here is that the highest income of the society is the reference point for all and everybody except the richest has a legitimate complaint. Cowell and Ebert (2004) used this structure to derive a complaint-based dominance criterion and a new class of inequality indices (*see also* Cowell, 2008, and Cowell and Ebert, 2008). Some implications of the complaint dominance relation have also been examined.

This chapter provides a comprehensive and analytical treatment of alternative notions of deprivation. Particularly, we examine the alternative notions of redistributive principles that take us from a more deprived distribution to a less deprived one under general assumptions about the mean income and the population size.

3.2 Deprivation and Satisfaction

For a population of size $n > 2$, a typical income distribution is given by $x = (x_1, \ldots, x_n)$, where $x_i > 0$ is the income of person i. Assuming that all income distributions are illfare-ranked, the set of income distributions in this n-person economy is D_+^n and the set of all possible income distributions is $D_+ = \underset{n \in N}{\cup} D_+^n$, where N is the set of natural numbers.

Let us now combine the two notions of deprivation explored in the introduction to arrive at a single indicator. Essential to the construction of this indicator is the existence of higher incomes than the income of the person under consideration and they constitute a source of frustration for the person. Given that $x \in D_+^n$ is illfare-ranked, according to the first notion, a measure of deprivation felt by person i is $(n-i)/n$. An alternative measure of deprivation for person i can be $(\lambda_{n-i}(x) - x_i)/\lambda(x)$, where $\lambda_{n-i}(x)$ is the mean income of the $(n-i)$ persons richer than i in the distribution x. We can arrive at a combined indicator from these two measures by a multiplicative aggregation. The resulting indicator then becomes

$$\mathrm{RD}_i(x) = \left(\frac{n-i}{n}\right)\left(\frac{\lambda_{n-i}(x) - x_i}{\lambda(x)}\right) = \left(\frac{n-i}{n}\right)\sum_{j=i+1}^{n}\frac{(x_j - x_i)}{\lambda(x)(n-i)} = \sum_{j=i+1}^{n}\frac{(x_j - x_i)}{n\lambda(x)}. \tag{3.1}$$

This is the Kakwani (1984a) measure of deprivation of person i. It determines the sum of income share shortfalls of person i from all persons who are not poorer than him.

Note that RD_i is homogeneous of degree zero in incomes, that is, it is a relative indicator of individual deprivation. Alternatively, we may assume that the individual deprivation indicator is an absolute measure. Multiplying RD_i by the mean we arrive at the following simple specification, which looks at deprivation in terms of absolute income differentials:

$$\mathrm{AD}_i(x) = \sum_{j=i+1}^{n}\frac{(x_j - x_i)}{n}. \tag{3.2}$$

This absolute counterpart to RD_i is the Yitzhaki measure of deprivation of person i (Yitzhaki, 1979). It indicates the total income shortfall of person i from all those who are not worse-off, as a fraction of the population size n.

The following are some of the properties of the functions RD_i and AD_i (*see* Chakravarty, 1997b, 2008b; Ebert and Moyes, 2000).

1. They are continuous, symmetric, population replication invariant, and nonnegative, where the lower bound zero is achieved whenever there is no feeling of deprivation.
2. When deprivation is measured by these two indicators, the richest individual with income x_n does not feel deprived at all.
3. They are decreasing under a rank-preserving increase in x_i.
4. An increase in any income higher than x_i that does not change the income ranks increases them.
5. An increase in any income lower than x_i, keeping the income hierarchy positions unaltered, does not change AD_i but decreases RD_i.
6. They decrease under a rank-preserving income transfer of income from a person with income higher than x_i to someone with income lower than x_i.
7. They remain unaltered if a rank-preserving income transfer takes place among persons richer/poorer than person i.

Note that we can rewrite $\mathrm{RD}_i(x)$ in (3.1) as

$$\mathrm{RD}_i(x) = \frac{n\lambda(x) - \left(\sum_{j=1}^{i} x_j + (n-i)x_i\right)}{n\lambda(x)} = 1 - \mathrm{LC}\left(x, \frac{i}{n}\right) - \frac{(n-i)x_i}{n\lambda(x)}, \quad (3.3)$$

where $\mathrm{LC}(x,(i/n))$ is the ordinate of the Lorenz curve of x at the cumulative population proportion i/n. We define the complement

$$\mathrm{RS}_i(x) = \frac{\sum_{j=1}^{i} x_j + (n-i)x_i}{n\lambda(x)} \quad (3.4)$$

of $\mathrm{RD}_i(x)$ in (3.3) from unity as the relative satisfaction function of person i. The function RS_i can be interpreted as follows. Person i does not have any feeling of frustration if he compares his income x_i with the lower incomes $x_1,\ldots,x_{i-1}$. This justifies the inclusion of first term $\sum_{j=1}^{i} x_j$, which depends on $x_1,\ldots,x_{i-1},x_i$, in the numerator of the right-hand side of (3.4). Next, we can eliminate person i's frustration about the higher incomes $x_{i+1},\ldots,x_n$ by replacing each of them by x_i. This then generates the distribution $(x_1,x_2,\ldots,x_i,x_i,\ldots,x_i)$ censored at x_i. In the censored income distribution $(x_1,x_2,\ldots,x_i,x_i,\ldots,x_i)$ corresponding to $(x_1,x_2,\ldots,x_{i-1},x_i,\ldots,\ldots,x_n)$, person i does not feel frustrated because of absence of incomes that are higher than x_i. Given the position of an individual in the income distribution ladder, he can be regarded as being either satisfied or frustrated. Since in the censored distribution in addition to person i there are $(n-i)$ persons with income x_i and they are all treated in a symmetric manner, we simply add $(n-i)x_i$ to $\sum_{j=1}^{i} x_j$ to arrive at the numerator of RS_i. Thus, the definition of RS_i relies on the assumption that an individual derives satisfaction from the observation that nobody in the society is richer than him and there are people who are as well-off as he is. By multiplying RS_i

with the mean income, we get the generalized satisfaction function GS_i. That is, $\mathrm{GS}_i(x) = \lambda(x)\mathrm{RS}_i(x) = 1/n(\sum_{j=1}^{i} x_j + (n-i)x_i) = \mathrm{GL}(x,(i/n)) + [((n-i)x_i)/n]$, where $\mathrm{GL}(x,i/n)$ is the ordinate of the generalized Lorenz curve of x at i/n. RS_i and GS_i defined this way may be regarded as indicators of individual well-being. Note that GS_i is continuous, increasing in x_i (assuming that income ranks are unaltered), linear homogeneous, unit translatable, and population replication invariant. For any $x \in D^n$, $x_1 = \mathrm{GS}_1(x) \leq \mathrm{GS}_2(x) \leq \ldots.. \leq \mathrm{GS}_n(x) = \lambda(x)$. If incomes are equally distributed, then RS_i and GS_i become respectively one and the common income itself. [Further discussion along this line can be found in Yitzhaki (1979), Hey and Lambert (1980), Stark and Yitzhaki (1988), Chakravarty (1997b, 2008b), and Chakravarty and Mukherjee (1999).]

For any income distribution x, $\mathrm{RD}_i(x)$ is, in fact, the ordinate $\mathrm{RD}(x,i/n)$ of the RDC corresponding to the cumulative population proportion i/n (*see* Kakwani, 1984a). The RDC of x, $\mathrm{RD}(x,t)$, where $t \in [0,1]$, is completed by assuming $\mathrm{RD}(x,0) = 1$ and by defining

$$\mathrm{RD}\left(x, \frac{i+\tau}{n}\right) = (1-\tau)\mathrm{RD}\left(x, \frac{i}{n}\right) + \tau\mathrm{RD}\left(x, \frac{i+1}{n}\right), \tag{3.5}$$

for all $0 \leq \tau \leq 1$ and $1 \leq i \leq (n-1)$. Clearly, the RDC is downward sloping, which means that for any two persons, the richer person has a lower level of deprivation than the poorer person. If all the incomes are equal, then there is no feeling of deprivation by any person ($\mathrm{RD}(x,t) = 0$ for all t). In this case, the curve coincides with the horizontal axis. In contrast, maximum deprivation arises if the entire income is monopolized by the richest person and the curve coincides with the line BC shown in the Fig. 3.1. Equation (3.3) shows how we can generate the RDC from the Lorenz curve.

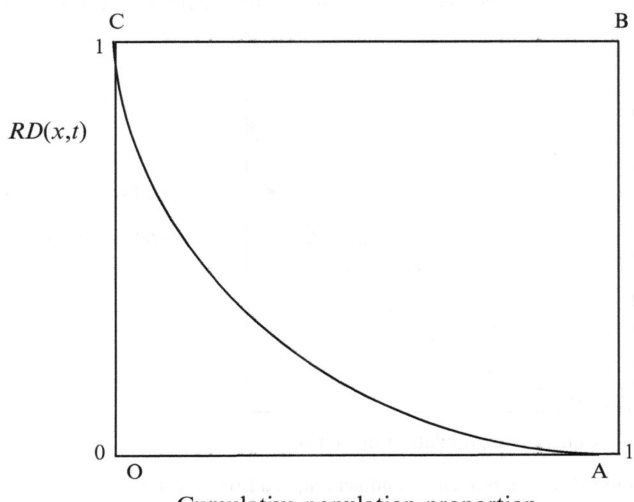

Fig. 3.1 Relative deprivation curve

The absolute deprivation curve (ADC) of x, $\mathrm{AD}(x,t)$, where $t \in [0,1]$, is obtained by multiplying the RDC of x by the mean. Formally, $\mathrm{AD}(x,t) = \lambda(x)\mathrm{RD}(x,t)$, where $t \in [0,1]$. We now define the absolute deprivation dominance (relative deprivation dominance) rule using the ADC (RDC) as follows. Given $x,y \in D^n_+$, we say that y absolute deprivation dominates (relative deprivation dominates) x, what we write $y \geq_{\mathrm{AD}} x (y \geq_{\mathrm{RD}} x)$, if we have $\mathrm{AD}(y,t) \geq \mathrm{AD}(x,t)(\mathrm{RD}(y,t) \geq \mathrm{RD}(x,t))$ for all $t \in [0,1]$, with $>$ for some t.

We can use $\mathrm{RS}_i(x)$ values to define the relative satisfaction curve (RSC), $\mathrm{RS}(x,t)$ associated with x, where $t \in [0,1]$. More precisely, assuming that the ordinate of the curve at the cumulative population proportion i/n is given by $\mathrm{RS}_i(x)$, it is drawn under the assumption that $\mathrm{RS}(x,0) = 0$ and by defining

$$\mathrm{RS}\left(x, \frac{i+\tau}{n}\right) = (1-\tau)\mathrm{RS}\left(x, \frac{i}{n}\right) + \tau\mathrm{RS}\left(x, \frac{i+1}{n}\right), \tag{3.6}$$

for all $0 \leq \tau \leq 1$ and $1 \leq i \leq (n-1)$. This curve is upward sloping. The generalized satisfaction curve (GSC) of the distribution x, $\mathrm{GS}(x,t)$ is produced by scaling up its RSC by the mean. That is, $\mathrm{GS}(x,t) = \lambda(x)\mathrm{RS}(x,t)$, $0 \leq t \leq 1$. It should now be clear the RSC (GSC) of a distribution can be generated by taking complement of the RDC (ADC) from unity (the mean). Given the relationship of GS_i with $\mathrm{GL}(x,i/n)$, we can say that the generalized Lorenz curve of a distribution never lies above its positively sloped GSC. Like the generalized Lorenz curve, the satisfaction curves, which show the levels of satisfactions enjoyed by different fractions of the population, may be interpreted as measures of social welfare. Thus, while deprivation has a negative impact on individual well-being, satisfaction makes a positive contribution to it (Fig. 3.2).

We can define the generalized and relative satisfaction dominance relations $\geq_{\mathrm{GS}}$ and $\geq_{\mathrm{RS}}$ using the GSC and the RSC curves, respectively, in the same way we employed the ADC and the RDC curves to define $\geq_{\mathrm{AD}}$ and $\geq_{\mathrm{RD}}$, respectively.

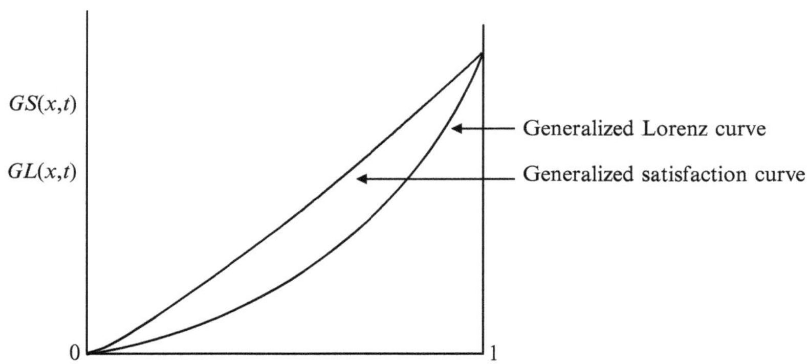

Fig. 3.2 Generalized satisfaction curve and generalized Lorenz curve

The following two theorems, which were established in Hey and Lambert (1980), Chakravarty et al. (1995), Chakravarty (1997b, 2008b), and Chateauneuf and Moyes (2004, 2006), show some implications of the relations $\geq_{AD}$ and $\geq_{GS}$.

Theorem 3.1. *Let $x, y \in D_+^n$, where $\lambda(x) = \lambda(y)$, be arbitrary. Then $y \geq_{RD} x$ implies that x is Lorenz superior to y (that is, $x \geq_{LC} y$). But the converse is not true.*

Proof. $y \geq_{RD} x$ along with $\lambda(x) = \lambda(y)$, in view of (3.3), implies that

$$\sum_{j=1}^{i} x_j + (n-i)x_i \geq \sum_{j=1}^{i} y_j + (n-i)x_i \tag{3.7}$$

for all $1 \leq i \leq n$, with $>$ for some $i < n$. For $i = 1$, the above inequality becomes $nx_1 \geq ny_1$ which gives $x_1 \geq y_1$. Suppose that the result is true for $i = l$, that is, $\sum_{j=1}^{l} x_j \geq \sum_{j=1}^{l} y_j$. We will show that it is true for $i = l+1$ also. Now, for $i = l+1$, inequality (3.7) becomes $\sum_{j=1}^{l+1} x_j + (n-l-1)x_{l+1} \geq \sum_{j=1}^{l+1} y_j + (n-l-1)y_{l+1}$. Adding $(n-l-1)\sum_{j=1}^{l} x_j((n-l-1)\sum_{j=1}^{l} y_j)$ to the left- (right-) hand side of this inequality, we get $(n-l)(\sum_{j=1}^{l} x_j + x_{l+1}) \geq (n-l)(\sum_{j=1}^{l} y_j + y_{l+1})$, from which it follows that $\sum_{j=1}^{l+1} x_j \geq \sum_{j=1}^{l+1} y_j$. This shows that the result is true for $i = l+1$ also. Hence, by the method of mathematical induction, the inequality $\sum_{j=1}^{i} x_j \geq \sum_{j=1}^{i} y_j$ holds for all $1 \leq i \leq n$. Given that there is strict inequality in $\geq_{RD}$ for some $i < n$, there will be similar strict inequality in $\geq_{LC}$ as well. For instance, if the inequality in (3.7) is strict for $i = l+1$, then the corresponding inequality in $\geq_{LC}$ will be strict, that is, we will have $\sum_{j=1}^{l+1} x_j > \sum_{j=1}^{l+1} y_j$. Hence we have $x \geq_{LC} y$.

To demonstrate that the reverse implication does not follow, consider the distribution $y = (5, 10, 15, 20)$. Then $x = (5, 11, 14, 20)$ is derived from y by transferring one unit of income from the person with income 15 to the one with income 10. By the Hardy et al. (1934) theorem, this transfer ensures that $x \geq_{LC} y$ holds, but $y \geq_{RD} x$ does not hold. This completes the proof of the theorem. □

To understand why $y \geq_{RD} x$ does not hold in the example taken above, note that while the RD_i measure for the recipient decreases, that of the donor increases, making the net effect ambiguous. It is evident that in view of the equality of the means, in Theorem 3.1, we can replace $y \geq_{RD} x$ by $y \geq_{AD} x$ or by $x \geq_{RS} y$.

Theorem 3.2. *Let $x, y \in D_+^n$ be arbitrary. Then $x \geq_{GS} y$ implies that x is generalized Lorenz superior to y (i.e., $x \geq_{GL} y$). But the converse is not true.*

Proof. In this case, we compare $\text{GS}_i(x) = 1/n(\sum_{j=1}^{i} x_j + (n-i)x_i)$ with the corresponding expression for $\text{GS}_i(y)$ for all $1 \leq i \leq n$. Since the structure of the proof of the part that $x \geq_{GS} y$ implies $x \geq_{GL} y$ is similar to the demonstration of the claim that $y \geq_{RD} x$ implies $x \geq_{LC} y$, we are omitting the proof. To see that the converse is not true, consider the distributions $y' = (2, 3, 6)$ and $\bar{y} = (1, 4, 5)$. Then we have $y' \geq_{GL} \bar{y}$ but not $y' \geq_{GS} \bar{y}$. □

To understand the reason for not having $y' \geq_{GS} \bar{y}$ in the proof of Theorem 3.2, note that by increasingness of any increasing, strictly S-concave social welfare function W, we get $W(\hat{y}) > W(\bar{y})$, where $\hat{y} = (1,4,6)$. Now, we get y' from $\hat{y}$ by transferring one unit of income from the second richest person to the poorest person. Hence by strict S-concavity of W, $W(y') > W(\hat{y})$, from which it follows that $W(y') > W(\bar{y})$. Thus, by the Shorrocks (1983a) theorem, we have $y' \geq_{GL} \bar{y}$. But while the increase in the richest person's income from 5 to 6 increases his satisfaction, the progressive transfer reduces the satisfaction of the donor and increases that of the recipient, generating an intersection between the GSCs of y' and $\bar{y}$.

Given equivalence of the generalized Lorenz relation with second-order stochastic dominance, it follows from Theorem 3.2 that the generalized satisfaction dominance is a sufficient condition for second-order stochastic dominance as well.

In view of Theorem 3.1, it is clear that we need redistributive principles other than the Pigou-Dalton condition that will be consistent with the dominance principles introduced in this chapter. As a first step, following Chateauneuf and Moyes (2006) and Moyes (2007), we say that for $x, y \in D_+^n$, where $\lambda(x) = \lambda(y)$, x is obtained from y by a T_2-transformation if there exist $\hat{\sigma}, \hat{\rho} > 0$ and two individuals $j, l (1 \leq j < l \leq n)$ such that:

$$
\begin{aligned}
&x_i = y_i \quad \text{for all} \quad i \in \{1,2,\ldots,j-1\} \cup \{j+1,\ldots,l-1\};\\
&x_j = y_j + \hat{\sigma}; \qquad\qquad\qquad\qquad\qquad\qquad\qquad\qquad (3.8)\\
&x_i = y_i - \hat{\rho} \quad \text{for all} \quad i \in \{l,\ldots,n\} \hat{\sigma} = (n-l+1)\hat{\rho}.
\end{aligned}
$$

The essential idea underlying a Chateauneuf-Moyes transformation of type T_2 is that if some amount of income is taken from an individual l, then the same amount of income should be taken from all the persons who are richer than l. The entire rank-preserving transfer is received by person j, who is poorer than l. However, individuals in the set $\{1,2,..j-1\}$ who are poorer than individual j do not benefit from the redistribution.

We can look at the transformation T_2 from a more general perspective. Let us rewrite x as $y+b$, where $b_i = 0$ for all $i \in \{1,2,\ldots,j-1\} \cup \{j+1,\ldots,l-1\}$, $b_j = \hat{\sigma}$, and $b_i = -\hat{\rho}$ for all $i \in \{l,\ldots,n\}$. The condition $\hat{\sigma} = (n-l+1)\hat{\rho}$ shows that $\sum_{i=1}^{n} b_i = 0$. Further, $b_i \geq \sum_{j=i+1}^{n} b_j/(n-i)$ with $>$ for at least one $i < n$. We may verify this claim using the example $x = (10,24,30,38,48)$ and $y = (10,20,30,40,50)$. That is, in going from y to x, if person i has to forgo some amount of money ($b_i < 0$), then this amount should be less than the average net giving up (total giving ups in excess of receiving) of all who are richer than him. Likewise, if the redistribution enables him to get some amount of money ($b_i > 0$), then his receipt should be greater than the average net receipt (total receipt in excess of giving up) of all who are richer than him. One possible way in which such a situation can arise is that a progressive transfer is shared by the recipients, starting from the poorest, in decreasing order of income without destroying incentive preservation. Incentive preservation of a scheme requires that it does not alter rank orders of the individuals. This scheme has a lexicographic flavor in the sense that a person cannot receive his share of the donation unless all persons poorer than him have received their shares. Since the general scheme is a fair way of redistribution, we can refer to it as a "fair redistributive program." We may relate this condition with a balanced fiscal program (y,x) which is minimally progressive and incentive preserving, where y is the pretax income distribution and x is the after tax distribution. Balancedness of the program means that $\sum_{i=1}^{n} x_i = \sum_{i=1}^{n} y_i$, that is, $\sum_{i=1}^{n} b_i = 0$. Since x and y are nondecreasingly ordered, the fiscal program is incentive preserving. Minimal progressivity requires that if $y_i \geq y_j$ then $b_i \geq b_j$. Incentive preservation and minimal progressivity of a tax function are necessary and sufficient for the after tax distribution to be more equally distributed than the pretax distribution by the absolute Lorenz criterion (Moyes, 1988, 1994). Note that fairness does not need $b_1 \geq b_2 \geq \ldots \geq b_n$. Hence, fairness is weaker than minimal progressivity (*see* Chakravarty, 1997b, 2008b; Chakravarty et al., 1995; Moyes, 2007; Zheng, 2007b).

One can see that if we have $y \geq_{\mathrm{RD}} x$ (or $x \geq_{\mathrm{RS}} y$) under the equality of the means, then we can arrive at x from y by a fair redistribution. Conversely, we can start with fairness, that is, $x_i - y_i = b_i \geq \sum_{j=i+1}^{n} b_j/(n-i) = \sum_{j=i+1}^{n} (x_j - y_j)/(n-i)$ with $>$ for some $i < n$. Then we can verify easily that $y \geq_{\mathrm{RD}} x$ holds. The following theorem can now be stated (*see* Chakravarty, 1997b, 2008b).

Theorem 3.3. *Let $x, y \in D_+^n$, where $\lambda(x) = \lambda(y)$, are arbitrary. Then the following conditions are equivalent:*

(i) $y \geq_{\mathrm{RD}} x$ (or $x \geq_{\mathrm{RS}} y$).
(ii) x can be obtained from y by a fair redistributive program.

Essentially Theorem 3.3 says that x has less deprivation than y if and only if the former is obtainable from the latter through a fair redistribution of incomes. Given that the means are the same, we can replace $\geq_{\mathrm{RD}}$ by $\geq_{\mathrm{AD}}$ and $\geq_{\mathrm{RS}}$ by $\geq_{\mathrm{GS}}$ in the theorem. We can also say that if condition (i) in the theorem is satisfied, then x is regarded as less deprived than y by all symmetric deprivation indices whose values reduce under a T_2- transformation/fair redistribution. More precisely, dominance of relative satisfaction of one distribution over that of another distribution is sufficient to guarantee that they can be ranked unambiguously by deprivation indices of the specified type. Furthermore, the converse is also true. If we assume that the means are unequal and population sizes are also not the same, then in addition to population replication invariance and these postulates, we need scale or translation invariance of the indices according as we use $\geq_{\mathrm{RD}}$ or $\geq_{\mathrm{AD}}$. We can develop similar results for relative satisfaction indices using $\geq_{\mathrm{RS}}$.

In addition to the Gini index, the area under the RDC, the following is an example of a deprivation index which corresponds to the relation $\geq_{\mathrm{RD}}$:

$$C_{\bar{\theta}}(x) = \begin{cases} 1 - \dfrac{1}{\lambda(x)} \left(\dfrac{1}{n} \sum\limits_{i=1}^{n} \left(\sum\limits_{j=1}^{i} \dfrac{x_j}{n} + \dfrac{n-i}{n} x_i \right)^{\bar{\theta}} \right)^{1/\bar{\theta}} & , \bar{\theta} \leq 1, \bar{\theta} \neq 0, \\ 1 - \dfrac{1}{\lambda(x)} \prod\limits_{i=1}^{n} \left(\sum\limits_{j=1}^{i} \left(\dfrac{x_j}{n} + \dfrac{n-i}{n} x_i \right) \right)^{1/n} & , \bar{\theta} = 1. \end{cases} \tag{3.9}$$

This index is the shortfall of the ratio between the symmetric mean of order $\bar{\theta}$ of the individual satisfactions and the mean from unity. Since none of the individual satisfaction levels exceeds the mean, the index is bounded between zero and one, where the lower bound is achieved for a perfectly egalitarian distribution. Evidently $(1 - C_{\bar{\theta}})$ can be regarded as a relative satisfaction index. A decrease in the value of $\bar{\theta}$ makes $C_{\bar{\theta}}(1 - C_{\bar{\theta}})$ more sensitive to the deprivation (satisfaction) of the poorer persons. Likewise, one minus the Gini index, the area under the RSC, can also be used as an index of relative satisfaction. An example of an absolute deprivation index is the absolute Gini index, the area under the ADC.

In Theorem 3.3, the RSC makes distributional judgments independently of the size of the distributions, that is, over distributions with a fixed total. Thus, efficiency considerations are absent in RSC comparison. In most circumstances of distributional comparisons, total income is likely to vary. This is likely to be true for intertemporal and intercountry comparisons. For ordering of income distributions with differing totals, we use the GSC.

Note that the area under the GSC is the (abbreviated) Gini welfare function. This is consistent with our observation that GS_i values may be used as indicators of individual well-being. Therefore, it should be clear that the GSC should be helpful in ranking income distributions in terms of welfare. The following theorem may be regarded as a step toward this direction (Chakravarty, 1997b).

Theorem 3.4. *Let $x, y \in D^n_+$ be arbitrary. Then the following conditions are equivalent.*

(i) x is weakly generalized satisfaction dominant over y, that is, $\mathrm{GS}(x,t) \geq \mathrm{GS}(y,t)$ for all $0 \leq t \leq 1$.
(ii) $W(x) \geq W(y)$ for any symmetric social welfare function $W : D^n_+ \to R^1$ which is nondecreasing in individual incomes and also nondecreasing under a fair redistributive program.

Proof. (i) $\Rightarrow$ (ii): Weak generalized satisfaction dominance, which we denote by $x \geq_{\mathrm{WGS}} y$, implies that $\lambda(x) \geq \lambda(y)$. Define the distribution $u \in D^n_+$ by $u_i = y_i$ and $u_n = n(\lambda(x) - \lambda(y)) + y_n$. By nondecreasingness of W, $W(u) \geq W(y)$. Note that $\lambda(u) = \lambda(x)$ and $x \geq_{\mathrm{WGS}} u$. Given the equality $\lambda(u) = \lambda(x)$, and the fact that $\mathrm{GS}(x,t) = \lambda(x)\mathrm{RS}(x,t)$, we can say that x weakly relative satisfaction dominates u. Hence by Theorem 3.3, $W(x) \geq W(u)$, which shows that $W(x) \geq W(y)$. Note that W is symmetric since we have defined it directly on ordered distributions.

(ii) $\Rightarrow$ (i): Consider the social welfare function $W(x) = 1/n(\sum_{j=1}^{i} x_j + (n-i)x_i)$, where $1 \leq i \leq n$. This welfare function satisfies all the assumptions stipulated in condition (ii) of the theorem. Thus, $W(x) = 1/n(\sum_{j=1}^{i} x_j + (n-i)x_i) \geq W(y) = 1/n(\sum_{j=1}^{i} y_j + (n-i)y_i)$ for $1 \leq i \leq n$, which in turn implies that x weakly generalized satisfaction dominates y. □

Theorem 3.4 indicates that an unambiguous ranking of income distributions by all nondecreasing, symmetric, and equity-oriented social welfare functions is achievable if and only if their GSCs do not intersect, where equity orientation is defined involving redistribution of income in a fair way. If we assume that the mean income is the same in the above theorem, then for weak satisfaction dominance to hold the welfare function should only be symmetric and nondecreasing under a fair transformation. This can then be regarded as the satisfaction counterpart to the Dasgupta et al. (1973) theorem, whereas with variable mean, Theorem 3.4 parallels Shorrocks' theorem (1983a) on the generalized Lorenz criterion. Note that the GSC is population replication invariant. Therefore, satisfaction ranking of distributions over differing population sizes using the real valued welfare functions (defined on D_+) that fulfill population replication invariance, along with the requirements specified in condition (ii) of the theorem, can be implemented by seeking GSC dominance. In addition to the Gini welfare function, the abbreviated welfare function $\lambda(1-C_\theta)$ satisfies all these postulates.

Now, if a person feels deprived when comparing himself with a better-off person, he may as well have a feeling of "contentment" when he compares his position with that of a less fortunate person. In other words, he remains contented with the existence of persons who are poorer than him in the society. This specific way of definition of contentment does not take the higher incomes into account. Formally, given the income distribution $x \in D_+^n$, following Zheng (2007b), we define the absolute contentment function of person i as

$$\mathrm{AC}_i(x) = \sum_{j=1}^{i} \frac{(x_i - x_j)}{n}. \tag{3.10}$$

Although both AC_i and GS_i are increasing under rank-preserving increments in x_i, there are important differences between them. While the latter possesses an altruistic flavor in the sense that an order preserving increase in any income less than x_i increases GS_i, the opposite happens for AC_i. AC_i is a focused index, it is based on the distribution $(x_1, x_2, \ldots, x_i)$, which is obtained by truncating x form above at x_i. In contrast, GS_i is defined on the distribution in which all incomes higher than x_i are censored at x_i. Note also that the worst-off person derives some satisfaction if he has a positive income but contentment is not a source of happiness for him even if his income is positive.

We can interpret AC_i from an alternative perspective. Consider the subgroup $\{1, 2, \ldots i\}$ of i persons with i lowest incomes in the society. Any person with income less than x_i may consider the subgroup highest income as his source of envy and, therefore, $1/i \sum_{i=1}^{i} (x_i - x_j)$ may be taken to represent the average level of depression in the subgroup. Thus, AC_i is the product of the proportion i/n of persons in the subgroup and the average depression of this proportion (*see* Chakravarty, 2007). This interpretation is quite similar to the one we have provided for the Kakwani (1984a) index.[1] If x_i is taken as the poverty line for the persons in the subgroup, then $(x_i - x_j)$ is individual j's poverty gap and $\sum_{j=1}^{i} (x_i - x_j)$ gives us the total amount of money necessary to put the persons in the subgroup at the poverty line itself. Then, under the strong definition of the poor, AC_i becomes the

[1] Chateauneuf and Moyes (2006, p. 31) used the term "measure of the absolute satisfaction felt by individual ranked i" for the equation in (3.10). However, we follow Zheng's (2007b) terminology "contentment."

product of two crude poverty indicators, the headcount ratio and the average poverty gap of the poor $1/\sum_{j=1}^{i}(x_i - x_j)/i$.

The society absolute contentment curve (ACC) is a plot of individual contentment functions AC_i 's against the cumulative population proportions i/n. That is, $\mathrm{ACC}(x, i/n) = \mathrm{AC}_i(x)$ and the curve is made smooth throughout assuming that $\mathrm{ACC}(x, (i+\tau)/n) = (1-\tau)\mathrm{ACC}(x, i/n) + \tau\mathrm{ACC}(x, (i+1)/n)$, where $0 \leq \tau \leq 1$, $1 \leq i \leq (n-1)$, and $\mathrm{ACC}(x, 0) = 0$. Clearly, the ACC of a distribution has a positive slope. For $x, y \in D_+^n$, we say that x is absolute contentment inferior to y ($y \geq_{\mathrm{AC}} x$, for short) if $\mathrm{ACC}(x,t) \leq \mathrm{ACC}(y,t)$ for all $0 \leq t \leq 1$ with $<$ for some t. That is, the relation $\geq_{\mathrm{AC}}$ stands for absolute contentment dominance. Now, $\geq_{\mathrm{AD}}$ concentrates on the distribution $(x_i, x_{i+1}, \ldots, x_n)$, which is obtained by truncating x from below at x_i. Therefore, by definition, $\geq_{\mathrm{AC}}$ is different from $\geq_{\mathrm{AD}}$ (*see also* Chateauneuf and Moyes, 2006).

As Chateauneuf and Moyes (2006) and Zheng (2000b) noted, $\geq_{\mathrm{AC}}$ is stronger than $\geq_{\mathrm{LC}}$ (*see also* Chakravarty et al., 2003). Formally,

Theorem 3.5. *Let $x, y \in D_+^n$, where $\lambda(x) = \lambda(y)$, be arbitrary. Then $y \geq_{\mathrm{AC}} x$ implies $x \geq_{\mathrm{LC}} y$ but the converse is not true.*

Proof. The nth inequality in $y \geq_{\mathrm{AC}} x$ can be written more explicitly as $nx_n - \sum_{j=1}^{n} x_j \leq ny_n - \sum_{j=1}^{n} y_j$, which in view of the equality of the means gives $x_n \leq y_n$. Therefore, we must have $\sum_{j=1}^{n-1} x_j \geq \sum_{j=1}^{n-1} y_j$. Thus, the following inequality holds for $i = 1, 2$.

$$\sum_{j=1}^{n-i+1} x_j \geq \sum_{j=1}^{n-i+1} y_j. \tag{3.11}$$

Assume that the inequality is true for $i = l$. We will show that it is true for $i = l+1$ also.

Now, by assumption

$$\sum_{j=1}^{n-l+1} x_j \geq \sum_{j=1}^{n-l+1} y_j, \tag{3.12}$$

which by the equality of the means implies

$$\sum_{j=n-l+2}^{n} x_j \leq \sum_{j=n-l+2}^{n} y_j. \tag{3.13}$$

The $(n-l+1)$th inequality in $y \geq_{\mathrm{AC}} x$ gives $(n-l)x_{n-l+1} - x_{n-l} - \ldots - x_1 \leq (n-l)y_{n-l+1} - y_{n-l} - \ldots - y_1$, which can be rewritten as

$$(n-l+1)x_{n-l+1} + \sum_{j=n-l+2}^{n} x_j - \sum_{j=1}^{n} x_j \leq (n-l+1)y_{n-l+1} + \sum_{j=n-l+2}^{n} y_j - \sum_{j=1}^{n} y_j. \tag{3.14}$$

Given the equality of the means, inequality (3.14) implies that

$$(n-l+1)x_{n-l+1} + \sum_{j=n-l+2}^{n} x_j \leq (n-l+1)y_{n-l+1} + \sum_{j=n-l+2}^{n} y_j. \tag{3.15}$$

Multiplying both sides of (3.13) by $(n–l)$ and then adding the right- (left-) hand side of the resulting expression to the corresponding side of (3.15), we get:

$$(n-l+1) \sum_{j=n-l+1}^{n} x_j \leq (n-l+1) \sum_{j=n-l+1}^{n} y_j. \tag{3.16}$$

Canceling $(n-l+1)$ from both sides of (3.16) and invoking the condition that $\lambda(x) = \lambda(y)$, we deduce that

$$\sum_{j=1}^{n-l} x_j \geq \sum_{j=1}^{n-l} y_j. \tag{3.17}$$

Hence, the inequality (3.11) is true for $i = l+1$ also. Thus, by the method of mathematical induction, (3.11) holds for $1 \leq i \leq n$ and a perfect equality occurs for $i = 1$ (given). The existence of $<$ for some i in $\geq_{AC}$ implies that there will be similar $>$ in $\geq_{LC}$ as well. This demonstrates the claim that $x \geq_{LC} y$ holds. For the numerical income distributions considered in the proof of Theorem 3.1, we have $x \geq_{LC} y$ but not $y \geq_{AC} x$. This completes the proof of the theorem. □

Another implication of $\geq_{AC}$ is Zheng's (2007b) look-down dominance. For $x, y \in D^n_+$, we say that y look-down dominates x, what we write $y \geq_{LD} x$, if $x_i - x_1 \leq y_i - y_1$ holds for $i = 1, 2, \ldots, n$, with $<$ for some i. Thus, look-down dominance compares the excess of each income in a distribution over its minimum with the corresponding excess in another distribution. Evidently, in the dominated distribution, all incomes will be closer to the reference income – the minimum. For this to materialize, the minimum income should be increased. Apart from this, all other incomes can be increased or decreased such that the excesses over the minimum are lower. Formally, we have

Theorem 3.6. *Let $x, y \in D^n_+$ be arbitrary. Then $y \geq_{AC} x$ implies $y \geq_{LD} x$ but the converse is not true.*

Proof. For $i = 2, y \geq_{AC} x$ gives the inequality $x_2 - x_1 \leq y_2 - y_1$. Thus, the result is true for $i = 1, 2$. Assume that it is true for all $i \leq l$. That is, we have $x_i - x_1 \leq y_i - y_1$ for all $i = 1, 2, \ldots, l$. We will show that it is true for $i = l+1$ also. Now, $(l+1)$th inequality in $y \geq_{AC} x$ implies $lx_{l+1} - x_l - \ldots x_1 \leq ly_{l+1} - y_l - \ldots - y_1$. Adding the left- (right-) hand side of the latter inequality with corresponding sides of the inequalities $x_i - x_1 \leq y_i - y_1$ for $i = 1, 2, \ldots, l$, it can be deduced that $x_{l+1} - x_1 \leq y_{l+1} - y_1$. Hence, by the method of induction, the result is true for all $1 \leq i \leq n$. If for some i (say, for $i = j$), strict inequality occurs in $y \geq_{AC} x$, then $x_j - x_1 < y_j - y_1$. To see that the opposite is not true, let $x = (15, 15, 35, 35, 50)$ and $y = (20, 30, 40, 50, 60)$. Then $x_i - x_1 \leq y_i - y_1$ for all i, with three inequalities being strict. But $y \geq_{AC} x$ does not hold. □

It will now be worthwhile to identify a redistributive criterion consistent with the absolute contentment dominance principle. An attempt along this line has been made by Chateauneuf and Moyes (2006). According to these authors, for $x, y \in D^n_+$, where $\lambda(x) = \lambda(y)$, x is obtained from y by a T_3-transformation if there exist $\tilde{\sigma}, \tilde{\rho} > 0$ and two individuals $j, l (1 \leq j < l \leq n)$ such that:

$$\begin{aligned} &x_i = y_i \quad \text{for all} \quad i \in \{j+1, \ldots, l-1\} \cup \{l+1, \ldots, n\}; \\ &x_i = y_i + \tilde{\sigma} \quad \text{for all} \quad i \in \{1, , \ldots, j\}; \\ &x_l = y_l - \tilde{\rho}; \\ &j\tilde{\sigma} = \tilde{\rho}. \end{aligned} \tag{3.18}$$

A Chateauneuf-Moyes transformation of type T_3 demands that if a person receives some amount of income through a rank-preserving progressive transfer, then the transfer should give the same amount of income to all persons poorer than him. This is similar to the lexicographically equitable transfer defined in Chap. 1, this volume. We have stated this here for the sake of completeness and because of its alternative presentation.

Rewriting $x = y + b$, as before, it now appears that if we arrive at x from y by a T_3-transformation, then $b_i \leq \sum_{j=1}^{i-1} b_j/(i-1)$ for all $i = 2, \ldots, n$, with $<$ for some $i > 1$ (*see* Zheng, 2007b). From this, it follows that x has lower contentment than y. The converse is true as well, that is, if we start with an inequality system of the type $b_i \leq \sum_{j=1}^{i-1} b_j/(i-1)$, then we can deduce that $y \geq_{\text{AC}} x$ holds. Hence, we can refer to b as a contentment reducing transformation. The interpretation of the transformation is similar to the one provided for a fair redistributive program. This enables us to state the following:

Theorem 3.7. *Let $x, y \in D^n_+$, where $\lambda(x) = \lambda(y)$, be arbitrary. Then the following conditions are equivalent:*

(i) $y \geq_{\text{AC}} x$.
(ii) x is obtained from y by a contentment reducing transformation.

Note that we can also have an index counterpart to Theorem 3.7, which says that the ranking of two income distributions of a given total, over a given population size, by all symmetric contentment indices that reduce under a transformation defined above is obtainable if and only if their ACCs do not intersect. An example of an index of this type can be the following:

$$C_{\hat{r}}(x) = \left(\frac{1}{n} \sum_{i=1}^{n} \frac{1}{n} \sum_{j=1}^{i} (x_j - x_i)^{\hat{r}} \right)^{1/\hat{r}} \tag{3.19}$$

where $\hat{r} \geq 1$ is a parameter. For $\hat{r} = 1, 2$, $C_{\hat{r}}$ corresponds respectively to the absolute Gini index and the standard deviation. An increase in the value of $\hat{r} > 2$ makes the index more sensitive to the extents of contentment of the poorer persons (Chakravarty et al., 2003).

3.3 Absolute and Relative Income Differentials and Deprivation

Since absolute income differentials are easy to imagine and calculate, they often constitute a natural source of envy for a person when he compares his income with higher incomes. Given $x, y \in D_+^n$, we say that y dominates x by absolute differentials, which we denote by $y \geq_{\mathrm{ADI}} x$, if $x_i - y_i \geq x_{i+1} - y_{i+1}$, for all $i = 1, 2, \ldots, n-1$, with $>$ for some $i < n$. Since we can rewrite $x_i - y_i \geq x_{i+1} - y_{i+1}$ as $y_{i+1} - y_i \geq x_{i+1} - x_i$, $y \geq_{\mathrm{ADI}} x$ simply means that differences between any two consecutive incomes are not lower in y than in x, and will be higher in some case(s). It was first introduced by Marshall et al. (1967) and has been considered as a suitable inequality criterion by Preston (1990) and Moyes (1994, 1999). Marshall and Olkin (1979) showed that for distributions of a given total, absolute differentials dominance implies Lorenz domination. More precisely, for $x, y \in D_+^n$, where $\lambda(x) = \lambda(y)$, $y \geq_{\mathrm{ADI}} x$ implies $x \geq_{\mathrm{LC}} y$. This is intuitively reasonable because nondominant consecutive gaps under x along with the equality of the means will ensure that x has lower inequality. The numerical income distributions x and y taken in the proof of Theorem 3.1 show that $x \geq_{\mathrm{LC}} y$ is true but $y \geq_{\mathrm{ADI}} x$ is not.

If U stands for the identical individual utility function, person i's utility distance from person j can be defined as $U(x_j) - U(x_i)$. Then we say that y utility gap dominates x if $U(x_i) - U(y_i) \geq U(x_{i+1}) - U(y_{i+1})$ holds for all $i = 1, 2, \ldots, n-1$, with $>$ for some $i < n$ (Zheng, 2007b). We can now imagine $\geq_{\mathrm{ADI}}$ as utility gap dominance if $U(x_i) = x_i$. Likewise, if $U(x_i) = \log x_i$, then the utility difference inequality $U(x_i) - U(y_i) \geq U(x_{i+1}) - U(y_{i+1})$ becomes $\log(x_i/y_i) \geq \log(x_{i+1}/y_{i+1})$, which reduces to $x_i/y_i \geq x_{i+1}/y_{i+1}$. This forms the basis of Marshall and Olkin's relative or ratio differentials dominance (Marshall and Olkin, 1979). Formally, y dominates x by ratio differentials, which is denoted by $y \geq_{\mathrm{RDI}} x$, if $x_i/y_i \geq x_{i+1}/y_{i+1}$ for all $i = 1, 2, \ldots, n-1$, with $>$ for some $i < n$. Moyes (1994) showed that the relations $\geq_{\mathrm{ADI}}$ and $\geq_{\mathrm{RDI}}$ are different.

We will now examine some implications of the relations $\geq_{\mathrm{ADI}}$ and $\geq_{\mathrm{RDI}}$. The following theorem shows that the former is sufficient for absolute contentment dominance (*see* Chakravarty et al., 2003; Chateauneuf and Moyes, 2006).

Theorem 3.8. *Let $x, y \in D_+^n$ be arbitrary. Then $y \geq_{\mathrm{ADI}} x$ implies $y \geq_{\mathrm{AC}} x$ but the converse is not true.*

Proof. From $y \geq_{\mathrm{AC}} x$, we have

$$\sum_{j=1}^{i} (y_i - y_j) \geq \sum_{j=1}^{i} (x_i - x_j) \tag{3.20}$$

for all $i = 1, 2, \ldots, n$. Given any i, a sufficient condition for (3.20) to hold is that $(x_i - x_j) \leq (y_i - y_j)$ for $j = 1, 2, \ldots, i-1$. This is same as the condition that $(y_j - x_j) \leq (y_i - x_i)$. We write this more explicitly as $(y_1 - x_1) \leq (y_i - x_i)$, $(y_2 - x_2) \leq (y_i - x_i), \ldots, (y_{i-1} - x_{i-1}) \leq (y_i - x_i)$. A sufficient condition for this inequality to hold is that $(y_1 - x_1) \leq (y_2 - x_2) \leq \ldots .(y_{i-1} - x_{i-1}) \leq (y_i - x_i)$, which follows from $y \geq_{\mathrm{ADI}} x$. Evidently, whenever there is a strict inequality for some i, say, for $i = l$, in $y \geq_{\mathrm{ADI}} x$, there will be strict inequality for $i = l$ in $y \geq_{\mathrm{AC}} x$. Falsity of the converse can be proved using the numerical example $y = (10, 20, 30, 40)$ and $x = (15, 20, 25, 40)$. Here we have $y \geq_{\mathrm{AC}} x$ but not $y \geq_{\mathrm{AD}} x$. □

For two distributions x and y over the population size n, $y \geq_{\mathrm{AD}} x$ implies that $\sum_{j=i+1}^{n}(y_j - y_i) \geq \sum_{j=i+1}^{n}(x_j - x_i)$ for all $i = 1, 2, \ldots, n$, with $>$ for some $i < n$. For any given arbitrary i, a sufficient condition that ensures this inequality system is $(y_{i+1} - y_i) \geq (x_{i+1} - x_i)$, $(y_{i+2} - y_i) \geq (x_{i+2} - x_i), \ldots, (y_n - y_i) \geq (x_n - x_i)$, $1 \leq i \leq n$. We rewrite this latter condition as $(y_{i+1} - x_{i+1}) \geq (y_i - x_i)$, $(y_{i+2} - x_{i+2}) \geq (y_i - x_i), \ldots, (y_n - x_n) \geq (y_i - x_i)$, $1 \leq i \leq n$. This is guaranteed if we assume that $(y_n - x_n) \geq \ldots \geq (y_{i+2} - x_{i+2}) \geq (y_{i+1} - x_{i+1}) \geq (y_i - x_i)$, $1 \leq i \leq n$. But this follows from the condition that $y \geq_{\mathrm{ADI}} x$. Strict inequality for some $i < n$ in $y \geq_{\mathrm{ADI}} x$ generates the corresponding condition in $y \geq_{\mathrm{AD}} x$. Thus, $y \geq_{\mathrm{ADI}} x$ implies $y \geq_{\mathrm{AD}} x$. For $x = (1, 3, 6, 6)$ and $y = (1, 3, 5, 7)$, we have $y \geq_{\mathrm{AD}} x$ but not $y \geq_{\mathrm{ADI}} x$ (Moyes, 2007). These observations are summarized in the following theorem.

Theorem 3.9. *For arbitrary $x, y \in D_{+}^{n}$, $y \geq_{\mathrm{ADI}} x$ implies $y \geq_{\mathrm{AD}} x$ but the converse is not true.*

Chateauneuf and Moyes (2006) defined a T_1-transformation which when applied successively results in distributional improvement according to $\geq_{\mathrm{ADI}}$. For $x, y \in D_{+}^{n}$, where $\lambda(x) = \lambda(y)$, x is obtained from y by a T_1-transformation if there exist $\sigma', \rho' > 0$ and two individuals $j, l (1 \leq j < l \leq n)$ such that:

$$
\begin{aligned}
&x_i = y_i \quad \text{for all} \quad i \in \{j+1, \ldots, l-1\};\\
&x_i = y_i + \sigma' \quad \text{for all} \quad i \in \{1,, \ldots, j\};\\
&x_i = y_i - \rho' \quad \text{for all} \quad i \in \{l,, \ldots, n\};\\
&j\sigma' = (n - l + 1)\rho'.
\end{aligned}
\tag{3.21}
$$

A Chateauneuf-Moyes transformation of type T_1 says that if some amount of income is transferred progressively from a person, then the same amount of income should also be transferred from all those who are not poorer than him. Further, if the progressive transfer gives some amount of income to a person, then all those who are not richer than him are also recipients of the same amount of income. In fact, a T_1-transformation can be regarded as a fiscal program which is balanced, minimally progressive, and incentive preserving (*see* Moyes, 2007). The following theorem of Chateauneuf and Moyes (2006) can now be stated.

Theorem 3.10. *Let $x, y \in D_{+}^{n}$, where $\lambda(x) = \lambda(y)$, be arbitrary. Then the following conditions are equivalent:*

(i) $y \geq_{\mathrm{ADI}} x$.
(ii) x can be obtained from y by a finite sequence of T_1-transformations.

Theorem 3.10 establishes the connection between the absolute differentials dominance relation and the rank-preserving progressive transfers underlying a T_1-transformation.

People often view depression in terms of relative income differentials. Marshall et al. (1967) established that for two distributions x and y of a given total, $y \geq_{\mathrm{RDI}} x$ is sufficient for $x \geq_{\mathrm{LC}} y$ (see also Marshall and Olkin, 1979, p. 129). For the numerical distributions x and y considered in the proof of Theorem 3.1, we have $x \geq_{\mathrm{LC}} y$ and not $y \geq_{\mathrm{RDI}} x$. Hence, $x \geq_{\mathrm{LC}} y$ does not imply $y \geq_{\mathrm{RDI}} x$.

In the following theorem, we identify the relationship between the dominance based on income ratios and the relative contentment dominance relation $\geq_{\mathrm{RC}}$, which relies on the ratios x_i/x_j, $1 \leq j \leq i$. Formally for $x, y \in D_+^n$, $y \geq_{\mathrm{RC}} x$ means that $\sum_{j=1}^{i} (y_i - y_j)/ny_j \geq \sum_{j=1}^{i} (x_i - x_j)/nx_j$ for $1 \leq i \leq n$, with $>$ for some i.

Theorem 3.11. *For all $x, y \in D_+^n$, $y \geq_{\mathrm{RDI}} x$ implies that y relative contentment dominates x, but the converse is not true.*

Proof. By $y \geq_{\mathrm{RC}} x$ we have $\sum_{j=1}^{i} (y_i - y_j)/y_j \geq \sum_{j=1}^{i} (x_i - x_j)/x_j$ for $1 \leq i \leq n$, with $>$ for some i. Given i, a sufficient condition for the above inequality to hold is that $y_i/y_j \geq x_i/x_j$ for $1 \leq j \leq i$. We rewrite this latter inequality as $y_i/x_i \geq y_j/x_j$ for $1 \leq j \leq i$. This requirement is satisfied if we assume that $y_i/x_i \geq y_{i-1}/x_{i-1} \geq \ldots . \geq y_1/x_1$, a condition implied by $y \geq_{\mathrm{RDI}} x$. Whenever there is a strict inequality in $y \geq_{\mathrm{RDI}} x$, there will be a strict inequality in $y \geq_{\mathrm{RC}} x$ also. To check that the converse is not true, consider the numerical distributions x and y taken in the proof of Theorem 3.8. Then we have $y \geq_{\mathrm{RC}} x$ but not $y \geq_{\mathrm{RDI}} x$. □

It may now be worthwhile to make a comparison between $\geq_{\mathrm{RC}}$ and $\geq_{\mathrm{RD}}$. Note that for the distributions $y' = (10, 20, 30, 40)$ and $y'' = (15, 20, 30, 35)$, we have both $y' \geq_{\mathrm{RC}} y''$ and $y' \geq_{\mathrm{RD}} y''$. Next, for the distributions $\bar{y} = (2, 4, 6, 8)$ and $\tilde{y} = (6, 6, 12, 16)$, $\bar{y} \geq_{\mathrm{RC}} \tilde{y}$ holds but $\bar{y} \geq_{\mathrm{RD}} \tilde{y}$ does not hold. To see the converse, consider the distribution $\hat{y} = (4, 8, 14, 14)$. One can check that $\bar{y} \geq_{\mathrm{RD}} \hat{y}$ is true but $\bar{y} \geq_{\mathrm{RC}} \hat{y}$ is not true. Finally, consider the distribution $\ddot{y} = (2, 5, 5, 8)$ and note that neither $\geq_{\mathrm{RD}}$ nor $\geq_{\mathrm{RC}}$ can rank the distributions $\ddot{y}$ and $\bar{y}$. These, observations enable us to conclude that $\geq_{\mathrm{RC}}$ and $\geq_{\mathrm{RD}}$ are different.

One can prove that the relations $\geq_{\mathrm{AC}}$ and $\geq_{\mathrm{RC}}$ are also different. To see this, note that while $\geq_{\mathrm{AC}}$ also cannot rank the distributions $\ddot{y}$ and $\bar{y}$, we have $y' \geq_{\mathrm{AC}} y''$. Next, we can verify that $\bar{y} \geq_{\mathrm{AC}} \tilde{y}$ does not hold. Finally, for the distributions $\dot{y} = (1, 1, 4, 6)$ and $\bar{y}$, we have $\bar{y} \geq_{\mathrm{AC}} \dot{y}$ but not $\bar{y} \geq_{\mathrm{RC}} \dot{y}$. These observations combined with our observations in the earlier paragraph regarding ranking of distributions by $\geq_{\mathrm{RC}}$ demonstrate that $\geq_{\mathrm{AC}}$ and $\geq_{\mathrm{RC}}$ are different (*see* Chakravarty et al., 2003).

3.4 Complaints and Deprivation

The central idea underlying the Temkin (1986, 1993) notion of inequality is individual complaint. Thus, like our earlier treatments in the chapter, the Temkin approach is also an individualistic approach to the assessment of income distributions. Among the various possibilities considered by Temkin (1986, 1993), the one that received principal focus is that the highest income in the society is the reference point and everybody except the richest person has a legitimate complaint. Alternatively, the average income or incomes of all better-off persons can be the reference points of different worse-off individuals (*see* Chakravarty, 1997b). By aggregating the individual complaints in an unambiguous way, we arrive at an overall inequality index. Although there appears to be similarity of this approach with the Runciman (1966) approach, there are differences as well. For instance, reference to the best-off person is one case of difference.

Cowell and Ebert (2004) considered the framework where the highest income x_n is the reference point for all the persons except the richest. Then $\mathrm{SC}_i(x) = (x_n - x_i)$ is the size of complaint of person i. These sizes form the basis of our analysis in this section. The graph of cumulative complaints $1/n\sum_{j=0}^{i}\mathrm{SC}_j(x)$ against the corresponding cumulative population proportions i/n gives us the cumulative complaint contour $\mathrm{CCC}(x,i/n)$ of the distribution x, where $\mathrm{SC}_0(x) = 0$ and $i = 0,1,..,n$. Segments of the curve between any two consecutive population proportions i/n and $(i+1)/n$ is defined by the convex combination $\mathrm{CCC}(x,(i+\tau)/n) = (1-\tau)\mathrm{CCC}(x,i/n) + \tau\mathrm{CCC}(x,(i+1)/n)$, where $0 \le \tau \le 1$. By construction, the CCC of a distribution is upward sloping. We then say that for $x,y \in D_+^n$, y complaint dominates x ($y \ge_{\mathrm{CC}} x$, for brevity) if $\mathrm{CCC}(y,t) \ge \mathrm{CCC}(x,t)$ for all $0 \le t \le 1$, with $>$ for some t.

The following theorem of Cowell and Ebert (2004) shows the relationship between the generalized Lorenz relation $\ge_{GL}$ and the complaint dominance rule $\ge_{\mathrm{CC}}$.

Theorem 3.12. *Let* $x,y \in D_+^n$ *be arbitrary. Then* $y \ge_{\mathrm{CC}} x$ *implies* $(x - x_n 1^n) \ge_{GL} (y - y_n 1^n)$.

Proof. From $y \ge_{\mathrm{CC}} x$, we get $\sum_{j=1}^{i}(x_n - x_j) \le \sum_{j=1}^{i}(y_n - y_j)$ for all $1 \le i \le n-1$, with $<$ for some i. We rewrite this inequality as $\sum_{j=1}^{i}(x_j - x_n 1^n) \ge \sum_{j=1}^{i}(y_j - y_n 1^n)$ for all $1 \le i \le n$, with $>$ for some i. This latter inequality gives $(x - x_n 1^n) \ge_{GL} (y - y_n 1^n)$. □

The next theorem is concerned with the relationship between $\ge_{\mathrm{AC}}$ and $\ge_{\mathrm{CC}}$.

Theorem 3.13. *Let* $x,y \in D_+^n$, *where* $\lambda(x) = \lambda(y)$, *be arbitrary. Then* $y \ge_{\mathrm{AC}} x$ *implies* $y \ge_{\mathrm{CC}} x$, *but the converse is not true.*

Proof. Suppose that we have $y \ge_{CC} x$, which by Theorem 3.12 implies the condition that $(x - x_n 1^n) \ge_{GL} (y - y_n 1^n)$. We can write this latter relation explicitly as:

$$\frac{1}{n}\left(iy_n + \sum_{j=1}^{i} x_j\right) \ge \frac{1}{n}\left(ix_n + \sum_{j=1}^{i} y_j\right), \tag{3.22}$$

for all $i = 1,2,\ldots,n$ with $>$ for at least one i. Given the equality of the total incomes in x and y, two sufficient conditions for (3.22) to hold are $x_n \le y_n$ and $x \ge_{\mathrm{LC}} y$. By Theorem 3.5, under the assumption of the equality of the means, $y \ge_{\mathrm{AC}} x$ implies $x \ge_{\mathrm{LC}} y$. Further, from the proof of Theorem 3.5, we know that under the given assumption $x_n \le y_n$ holds. Hence, $y \ge_{\mathrm{AC}} x$ implies $y \ge_{\mathrm{CC}} x$. Using the example that $y = (10,20,30,40)$ and $x = (10,24,26,40)$, one can check that $y \ge_{\mathrm{CC}} x$ holds but $y \ge_{\mathrm{AC}} x$ does not hold. □

Cowell and Ebert (2004) characterized weighted mean of order $\upsilon \geq 1$ of individual complaints as an index of overall complaint. Formally, the Cowell-Ebert index is given by

$$C_\upsilon(x) = \left[\sum_{i=1}^{n-1} \tilde{w}_i (x_n - x_i)^\upsilon\right]^{1/\upsilon}, \tag{3.23}$$

where the positive weight sequence $\{\tilde{w}_i\}$, satisfying the restriction $\sum_{i=1}^{n-1} \tilde{w}_i = 1$, is nonincreasing if $\upsilon > 1$ and decreasing if $\upsilon = 1$. Members of the class C_υ decrease under a rank-preserving transfer from a person to anyone with lower income. They also demonstrated that $y \geq_{\text{CC}} x$ is equivalent to the condition that $C_\upsilon(y) > C_\upsilon(x)$.

Instead of comparing the aggregated look-up complaints across distributions, we can compare them at individual levels. More precisely, following Zheng (2007b), for $x, y \in D_+^n$, we say that y look-up dominates x, what we write $y \geq_{\text{LU}} x$, if $(x_n - x_i) \leq (y_n - y_i)$ holds for all $1 \leq i \leq n$, with $<$ for some i. Thus, look-up dominance is an alternative dominance implication of Temkin's (1986, 1993) suggestion that the highest income is the reference point. Clearly, $\geq_{\text{LU}}$ requires reduction in the highest income of the dominated distribution because all look-up differences are getting smaller in this distribution. It is easy to see that $\geq_{\text{ADI}}$ implies $\geq_{\text{LU}}$, which in turn implies $\geq_{\text{CC}}$.

Our discussion so far has concentrated on distributions in a particular period. Let us denote the current and previous period income distributions on a set of n persons by x^1 and x^0, respectively, where both $x^1, x^0 \in \Gamma_+^n$. However, they are not assumed to be illfare-ranked. Bossert and D'Ambrosio (2007) suggested the use of

$$\text{BD}_i(x^0, x^1) = \frac{\bar{\alpha}^{|\hat{B}_i(x^1) - \hat{B}_i(x^0)|}}{n} \sum_{j \in \hat{B}_i(x^1)} (x_j^1 - x_i^1) \tag{3.24}$$

as an index of the extent of deprivation felt by person i, where $\bar{\alpha} \geq 1$ is a constant. $\hat{B}_i(x)$ is the set of persons that are better-off than i in the distribution x, the difference $\hat{B}_i(x^1) - \hat{B}_i(x^0)$ gives the set of persons that are in $\hat{B}_i(x^1)$ but not in $\hat{B}_i(x^0)$ and for any set S, $|S|$ is the number of elements in S. If $\bar{\alpha} = 1$, the Bossert-D'Ambrosio index BD_i becomes the Yitzhaki (1979) index of deprivation AD_i. Higher values of $\bar{\alpha}$ assign higher weight to the deprivation suffered from the information that there are people who were not previously richer than i are now richer than him. This information takes into account the dynamic aspect of deprivation. Thus, the dynamic aspect of deprivation depends on the number of persons who were at most as well off as i in the previous period but have now become more well-off than i. If the set of such persons is empty, then also BD_i coincides with AD_i. This implies that if we regard (x^0, x^1) as an incentive preserving fiscal program, then BD_i and AD_i are the same. Bossert and D'Ambrosio (2007) characterized general classes of indices that contain BD_i as special cases.

Our analysis in this chapter reveals that deprivation is a multifaceted phenomenon. There are many ways of incorporating components, such as envy and depression, of individual judgments into distributive justice. Furthermore, we have seen that the required alternative notions of redistributive principles are different from the one based on the Lorenz curve. In each case, our discussion makes the structure and the fundamental properties of the principle quite transparent. It should definitely be clear that the dominance relations we have investigated are incomplete – there may be situations where we have to withhold our judgment concerning superiority of one distribution over another in terms of deprivation.

We may recall here that the "deprivation profile" of Shorrocks (1998) looks at deprivation from a completely different perspective. We may also mention that Satts' (1996) study of relative deprivation in the kibbutz economy uses a completely different structure as well. It explores the equity characteristics of the ideal kibbutz economy which maintains perfect equality as the benchmark. An investigation of the issue has been made in the distributive and productive justice framework of Varian (1974).

Finally, it may be worthwhile to mention that some of the relations discussed in the chapter have also been analyzed from alternative perspectives. For instance, Jewitt (1989), Gilboa and Schmeidler (1994), and Landsberger and Meilijson (1994) used the absolute contentment dominance condition to characterize location-independent riskier prospects. Likewise, Doksum (1969) suggested the use of the absolute differential relations as a tail dominance, whereas Bickel and Lehmann (1979) used it as a dispersion dominance (*see also* Landsberger and Meilijson, 1994; Quiggin, 1993).

Chapter 4
The Measurement of Income Polarization

4.1 Introduction

Over the last 15 years or so, the study of polarization has become quite important for several reasons. Some of the major reasons are its role in analyzing the income distribution evolution, social conflict, and economic growth. Broadly speaking, polarization is concerned with appearance (or disappearance) of groups in a distribution. In politics, it is regarded as a process that leads to division of public opinion and movement of the divided opinion to the extremes. Likewise, one notion of income polarization, which we refer to as bipolarization, is concerned with the decline of the middle class. In this case, the relative frequency of observations associated with the central value of the distribution is low compared to those in the extremes. Polarization in this case is measured by the dispersion of the distribution from the central value toward the extreme points. The principal reason for looking at polarization this way is that a large and wealthy middle class contributes to economic growth in many ways and hence is important to every society. The middle class occupies the intermediate position between the poor and the rich. A person with low income may not be able to become highly rich but may have the expectation of achieving the position enjoyed by a middle-class person. Thus, such a person is likely to work hard to fulfill his expectation and unlikely to revolt against the society. Therefore, a society with thriving middle class contributes significantly to social and political stability as well. In contrast, a society with high degree of polarization may generate social conflicts, rebellions, and tensions (*see* Pressman, 2001). Therefore, in order to avoid or reduce such possible risks, it is necessary to monitor the situation in the society using indices that look at the spread of the distribution from its center. Bipolarization indices have been investigated in details by Foster and Wolfson (1992), Wolfson (1994, 1997), Wang and Tsui (2000), Chakravarty and Majumder (2001), Rodriguez and Salas (2003), Duclos and Echevin (2005), Amiel et al. (2007), Chakravarty et al. (2007), Silber et al. (2007), and others.

Esteban and Ray (1994) developed a more general notion of polarization. They assumed that the society is divided into groups or poles, where the individuals

S.R. Chakravarty, *Inequality, Polarization and Poverty: Advances in Distributional Analysis*, 105
Economic Studies in Inequality, Social Exclusion and Well-Being 6,
DOI: 10.1007/978-0-387-79253-8_4,

belonging to the same group have a feeling of identification and there is a feeling of alienation against individuals in a different group. In other words, individuals in a group share similar characteristics with the other members of the group but in terms of the same characteristics they are different from the members of the other groups. The Esteban and Ray (1994) index regards the concept of polarization as conflict among groups (*see also* Esteban and Ray, 1999). Clearly, high degree of polarization, in terms of presence of conflicting groups, can give rise to instability in a society. Alternatives and variations of the Esteban and Ray (1994) index have been suggested, among others, by Gradin (2000), D'Ambrosio (2001), Zhang and Kanbur (2001), Duclos et al. (2004), and Esteban et al. (2007).

The objective of this chapter is to discuss the two views of polarization, the underlying axioms and the indices rigorously. We also characterize a compromise relative index of bipolarization. A relative index remains invariant under equiproportionate variations in all incomes and is said to possess the compromise property if, when multiplied by the median, becomes an absolute index that does not alter under equal absolute translation of incomes. Clearly, a particular index of bipolarization will rank alternative distributions of income in a complete manner. However, if we use more than one index, there may be different rankings of the distributions. Given the diversity of indices, it will be worthwhile to identify the class of indices that produces a similar ordering of different distributions. Finally, we look at this issue in this chapter.

4.2 Polarization: Two Views, Axioms and Indices

This section begins with a discussion on the postulates for an index of polarization rigorously. We follow Esteban and Ray (1994), Wang and Tsui (2000), Chakravarty and Majumder (2001), and Chakravarty et al. (2007) and present them using uniform notation. For a population of size n, a typical income distribution is given by a pair (p,x), where $x=(x_1,x_2,..x_k)$ and $p=(p_1,p_2,\ldots,p_k)$. Here x_i values indicate different income levels, p_i is the number of individuals with income exactly equal to x_i and $n=\sum_{i=1}^{k} p_i$. Clearly, $p=(p_1,p_2,\ldots,p_k)\in R_+^k$, the nonnegative orthant of the k dimensional Euclidean space R^k. Each x_i is assumed to be drawn from $[\mu,\gamma]$, a nondegenerate interval in the nonnegative part R_+^1 of the real line R^1. The set of income distributions for this population is denoted by S. Thus, we characterize an income distribution as a vector of population masses located on the steps in an income ladder. For any $x_i\in[\mu,\gamma]$, $x\in[\mu,\gamma]^k$, the k-fold Cartesian product of $[\mu,\gamma]$. For the sake of simplicity and convenience, the lower bound of the interval $[\mu,\gamma]$ has been taken to be nonnegative, which in turn implies nonnegativity of all the incomes. Extension of our results to the situation where some of the incomes are negative is quite straightforward.

For any $(p,x)\in S$, the mean and median of (p,x) are denoted, respectively, by $\lambda(p,x)$ and $m(p,x)$ (or, simply by λ and m). If n is odd, the median income is given by

$$m = \left\{ x_j : \sum_{i=1}^{j} p_i = \frac{1}{2} \left(\sum_{i=1}^{k} p_i + 1 \right) \right\}, \tag{4.1}$$

where x_is are illfare-ranked, that is, ordered nondecreasingly and p_is are rearranged accordingly. But if n is even, the arithmetic mean of the $(n/2)$th and the $(n/2+1)$th values is taken as the median (given that the incomes are illfare-ranked and p_i's are permuted accordingly). We will assume throughout the chapter that the mean and the median are positive. For example, let $x = (2,4,10,1)$ and $p = (4,3,9,2)$. The illfare-ranked permutation of x is $(1,2,4,10)$ and the corresponding rearrangement of p is $(2,4,3,9)$. Since $n = 18$ is even here, the median m is the average of the ninth and tenth values, that is, $m = (4+10)/2 = 7$.

Since in the measurement of bipolarization, all incomes are compared with the median, persons with incomes below the median can be regarded as "deprived," where the source of deprivation is the shortfall of their incomes from the median. Likewise, all persons with incomes not below the median can be referred to as "satisfied" (*see* Runciman, 1966).

Some more preliminaries are necessary for the purpose at hand. Assuming that x_i's are illfare-ranked, we denote the vectors of such x_i's that are below the median and of those that are not below the median by x^- and x^+, respectively. The corresponding partition of p, under proper rearrangement, is (p^-, p^+). For the example taken above, $x^- = (1,2,4)$, $x^+ = (10), p^- = (2,4,3)$, and $p^+ = (9)$. The k-coordinated vector of ones is denoted by 1^k. For all $x, y \in [\mu, \gamma]^k$, we write xV_jy to represent the situation that x has been obtained from y by a simple increment in y_j, that is, $x_j > y_j$ for some j and $x_i = y_i$ for all $i \neq j$. Recall from our discussion in Chap. 1 that if income distributions are ordered, the transformation V allows only rank-preserving increments. For $x, y \in [\mu, \gamma]^k$, we write $xT_{\{i,j\}}y$ to denote that x has been obtained from y by a progressive transfer of income from the rich person j to the poor person i. Recall that the transfer does not alter the relative positions of the donor j and the recipient i and for ordered distributions, only rank-preserving transfers are allowed.

A polarization index L is a real valued function defined on S, that is, $L : S \to R^1$. For all $(p,x) \in S$, the functional value $L(p,x)$ indicates the level of polarization associated with the distribution (p,x).

Esteban and Ray (1994) have suggested the following axioms for an index of polarization. All of them are based on an income distribution constituted by three distinct values $x_1 = 0, x_2$, and x_3, and the corresponding population masses p_1, p_2, and p_3, where $x_1 < x_2 < x_3$.

Axiom 1. Let $p_1 > p_2 = p_3 > 0$. Fix $p_1 > 0$ and $x_2 > 0$. There exists $\tilde{c}_1 > 0$ and $\tilde{c}_2 > 0$ (possibly depending on p_1 and x_2) such that if $|x_2 - x_3| < \tilde{c}_1$ and $p_2 < \tilde{c}_2 p_1$, then joining of the masses p_2 and p_3 at their mid-point, $(x_2 + x_3)/2$, increases polarization.

Axiom 2. Let $p_1, p_2, p_3 > 0$; $p_1 > p_3$, and $|x_2 - x_3| < x_2$. There exists $\tilde{c}_3 > 0$ such that if p_2 is moved to the right, toward p_3 by an amount not exceeding $\tilde{c}_3$, polarization increases.

Axiom 3. Let $p_1, p_2, p_3 > 0$; $p_1 = p_3$; and $x_2 = x_3 - x_2 = \tilde{c}_4$. Any new distribution formed by shifting population mass from the central mass p_2 equally to the two lateral masses p_1 and p_3, each $\tilde{c}_4$ units of distance away, must increase polarization.

Before we proceed to state the axioms for a bipolarization index, let us explain the ones proposed by Esteban and Ray (1994). Axiom 1 underlines the idea that lower dispersion inside the groups and higher homogeneity of group's size should augment polarization. The next axiom argues that polarization should go up with heterogeneity among the groups. Finally, according to axiom 3, polarization should increase under a movement of the middle class into higher and lower categories.

The following axioms, for an index of bipolarization, have been suggested by Wang and Tsui (2000), Chakravarty and Majumder (2001), and Chakravarty et al. (2007) or are in common use elsewhere.

Axiom 4. (Normalization): If $(p,x) \in S$ is such that $x = c1^k$, where $c > 0$ is any scalar, then $L(p,x) = 0$.

Axiom 5. (Scale Invariance): For all $(p,x) \in S$ and all scalars $c > 0$, $L(p,x) = L(p,cx)$.

Axiom 6. (Translation Invariance): For all $(p,x) \in S$ and all scalars c such that $x + c1^k \in [\mu, \gamma]^k$, $L(p,x) = L(p, x + c1^k)$.

Axiom 7. (Symmetry): For all $(p,x) \in S$, $L(p,x) = L(p\Pi, x\Pi)$, where Π is any $k \times k$ permutation matrix.

Axiom 8. (Population Principle): For all $(p,x) \in S$, $L(p,x) = L(cp,x)$, where $c > 0$ is any scalar.

Axiom 9. (Increased Spread): If (p,x) and $(p,y) \in S$, where $m(p,x) = m(p,y)$, are related through anyone of the following cases,

(i) yV_jx and $y_j < m(p,y)$, (ii) xV_iy and $y_i > m(p,y)$, and (iii) both (i) and (ii), then $L(p,x) > L(p,y)$.

Axiom 10. (Increased Bipolarity): If (p,x) and $(p,y) \in S$, where $m(p,x) = m(p,y)$, are related through anyone of the following cases,

(i) $xT_{\{i,j\}}y$ and $y_j < m(p,y)$, (ii) $xT_{\{\hat{l},l\}}y$ and $y_{\hat{l}} > m(p,y)$, and (iii) both (i) and (ii), then $L(p,x) > L(p,y)$.

Axiom 11. (Continuity): L is continuous in its income arguments.

Axioms 4–8 and 11 are the bipolarization counterparts to the corresponding inequality axioms. As in the case of inequality indices, only a constant function can fulfill axioms 5 and 6 simultaneously. Note that Symmetry requires the same reordering of incomes and the corresponding population masses. Under the Population Principle, the population masses are changed by a fixed proportion but the incomes are kept unchanged.

Axiom 9, Increased Spread, is a monotonicity condition and close to axiom 3 of Esteban and Ray (1994). Since increments (reductions) in incomes above (below) the median widen the distribution, polarization should go up. That is, greater distancing between the groups below and above the median should make the distribution more polarized. Increased Bipolarity is a bunching or a clustering principle. Since an egalitarian transfer between two individuals on the same side of the median brings the individuals closer to each other, bipolarization should increase. As an egalitarian transfer demands decreasingness of inequality, this axiom explicitly establishes that inequality and polarization are two nonidentical concepts.[1] Thus, bipolarization involves both an inequality-like component, the greater distancing criterion, which increases both inequality and polarization, and an equality-like component, the clustering or bunching principle, which increases polarization, while lowering any inequality index that fulfills the Pigou-Dalton Transfers Principle. This shows that although there is a nice complementarity between the two concepts, there are differences as well.[2]

Using specific subsets of the axioms considered above, we may be able to characterize specific classes of polarization indices. For instance, Esteban and Ray (1994) assumed the quasi-additive structure $\sum_{i=1}^{k}\sum_{j=1}^{k} p_i p_j \tilde{H}[\tilde{g}(p_i), \tilde{A}(|x_i - x_j|)]$; where the continuous identification function $\tilde{g} : R_+^1 \to R_+^1$, satisfying the restriction that $\tilde{g}(p_i) > 0$ whenever $p_i > 0$, gives a sense of identification of an individual with other persons of the same group. The continuous and nondecreasing alienation function $\tilde{A} : R_+^1 \to R_+^1$, with $\tilde{A}(0) = 0$, gives alienation of individual i with individual j, and the continuous effective antagonism function $\tilde{H}$, which is a measure of the extent of antagonism felt by person i toward person j, fulfills the restrictions that $\tilde{H}(\tilde{g}(p_i), 0) = 0$ and increasingness in alienation on the strictly positive part of the domain. They invoked the axioms 1–3 and a population homotheticity axiom which demands that ranking of two distributions by a polarization index remains invariant with respect to the size of the population, to derive the index

$$L_{\text{ER}}(p,x) = \tilde{\Xi} \sum_{i=1}^{k} \sum_{j=1}^{k} p_i^{\tilde{\alpha}+1} p_j |x_i - x_j|, \tag{4.2}$$

where $\tilde{\Xi} > 0$ is a constant and $\tilde{\alpha} \in (0, 1.6]$ (*see* Theorem 1 of the authors). If another axiom [axiom 4 of Esteban and Ray, 1994] which demands that a migration from a very small population mass at a low income to a higher income of moderate size increases polarization is imposed, then $\tilde{\alpha}$ must take on the value in the interval [1,1.6] (*see* Theorem 3 of the authors). The multiplicative constant $\tilde{\Xi}$ is used for population normalization. If the parameter $\tilde{\alpha}$ takes on the value zero, the Esteban-Ray index L_{ER} would correspond to the (absolute) Gini index. The positive value of $\tilde{\alpha}$, and hence the identification function $p_i^{\tilde{\alpha}}$, plays an important role to underline

[1] See Levy and Murname (1992), Collier and Hoeffler (2001), Knack and Keefer (2001), Garcia-Montalvo and Reynal-Querol (2002, 2005), Reynal-Querol (2002), and Bossert and Schworm (2006).

[2] Amiel et al. (2007) investigated whether people's perception about polarization is consistent with different axioms.

the difference between inequality and polarization. As the value of $\tilde{\alpha}$ increases, the greater is the divergence from inequality and consequently, $\tilde{\alpha}$ may be interpreted as a polarization sensitivity parameter. Given income classes and total population, the index achieves its maximum value when half the population is concentrated in the lowest income class and the remainder is in the highest income class. On the other hand, it attains its minimum value if the entire population mass is concentrated at one value, which coincides with the mean and the median.

Duclos et al. (2004) developed an axiomatic characterization of the index

$$L_{\mathrm{DER}}(f) = \int_0^{\infty}\int_0^{\infty} (f(v'))^{1+\tilde{\alpha}} f(v)|v-v'|\mathrm{d}v\mathrm{d}v', \tag{4.3}$$

for income distributions defined in the continuum with a normalized mean of unity, where f is the income density function and $\tilde{\alpha} \in [.25, 1]$. The Duclos et al. index $L_{\mathrm{DER}}(f)$ can be regarded as the continuous analogue to the index L_{ER} in (4.2). It overcomes the limitation of the original index L_{ER} that requires a population to be bunched into relevant groups. They also constructed estimators for their index to use in the case of disaggregated data.

Clustering of the population into groups such that individuals feel identified inside a group and alienated outside it looses important information about income disparity within each group. Esteban et al. (2007) proposed an index that corrects L_{ER} in (4.2) from this perspective. Consider an income distribution with density f and the mean normalized at unity. For an income distribution with J income classes, let $\pi_i = \int_{x_{i-1}}^{x_i} f(v)\mathrm{d}v$ and $\lambda_i = 1/\pi_i \int_{x_{i-1}}^{x_i} vf(v)\mathrm{d}v$, respectively, be the population frequency and mean income of the income class $[x_{i-1}, x_i]$, $i = 1, 2, \ldots, J$. The corresponding vectors are given by $\underline{\pi}$ and $\underline{\lambda}$. Then the index L_{ER} applied to the discrete grouping considered here, with a correction for within-group inequality, is given by

$$L_{\mathrm{EGR}}(\underline{\pi}, \underline{\lambda}) = \sum_{i=1}^{J}\sum_{j=1}^{J} \pi_i^{1+\tilde{\alpha}}\pi_j|\lambda_i - \lambda_j| - c_5\mathrm{er}(\underline{\pi}, \underline{\lambda}), \tag{4.4}$$

where the error $\mathrm{er}(\underline{\pi}, \underline{\lambda})$ corresponds "to the implicit fuzziness of group identification" (Esteban et al., 2007, p. 5) and $c_5 \geq 0$ is the weight assigned to the error. The presence of the error term ensures that the Esteban et al. index $L_{\mathrm{EGR}}(\underline{\pi}, \underline{\lambda})$ is decreasing in within-group and increasing in between-group disparities. They also considered the problem of grouping the population such that the error function, which has been chosen as the average of income distances within all groups, is minimized. The modified index can be applied to all kinds of income distributions.[3] If in (4.4), the term under double summation is multiplied by $(1 - I_{\mathrm{G}}^i)^{\tilde{\mu}}$ and the second term $-c_5\mathrm{er}(\underline{\pi}, \underline{\lambda})$ is dropped, then the resulting index becomes the variant of $L_{\mathrm{EGR}}(\underline{\pi}, \underline{\lambda})$ suggested by Lasso de la Vega and Urrutia (2006), where I_{G}^i is the Gini index of group i and $\tilde{\mu} \geq 0$ is a constant. Formally, their index is given by

[3] Gradin (2000) extended the index in (4.3) to the case when groups are defined according to attributes other than income, for example, education level, health.

$L_{\mathrm{LU}}(\underline{\pi},\underline{\lambda}) = \sum_{i=1}^{J}\sum_{j=1}^{J}\pi_i^{1+\tilde{\alpha}}\pi_j(1-I_{\mathrm{G}}^i)^{\tilde{\mu}}|\lambda_i-\lambda_j|$. The constant $\tilde{\mu}\geq 0$ represents the degree of sensitivity toward group cohesion. The sense of identification of each member of group i is now given by $\pi_i^{\tilde{\alpha}}(1-I_{\mathrm{G}}^i)^{\tilde{\mu}}$. Multiplication by the increasing function $(1-I_{\mathrm{G}}^i)^{\tilde{\mu}}$ of the Gini index of equity $(1-I_{\mathrm{G}}^i)$ makes the polarization index L_{LU} a decreasing function of within-group dispersion. It is evidently increasing in between-group inequality. It should be clear that Esteban et al. index and its variant L_{LU} have several common properties.

D'Ambrosio (2001) proposed a modification of L_{ER} in (4.2) using the Kolomogorov measure of distance as the alienation function instead of the simple distance function $|x_i - x_j|$ for taking into account the intergroup measure of disparity. The D'Ambrosio index is then given by

$$L_{\mathrm{D}}(\underline{\pi},\underline{f}) = \frac{1}{2}\sum_{i=1}^{J}\sum_{j=1}^{J}\pi_i^{\tilde{\alpha}+1}\pi_j\int_0^{\infty}|f_i(v)-f_j(v)|\mathrm{d}v, \tag{4.5}$$

where π_is are population frequencies; $1/2\int_0^{\infty}|f_i(v)-f_j(v)|\mathrm{d}v$ is the Kolomogorov measure of distance between groups i and j; f_i and f_j, are respectively, the densities of income distributions corresponding to these groups and $\underline{f}=(f_1,f_2,\ldots,f_J)$. An advantage of the use of this alternative alienation function is that the disparity between groups are now compared using their income distributions, not by their means, as is done in (4.2).

Milanovic (2000) suggested an index with the objective that it (1) achieves the minimal value zero for a distribution with population mass concentrated at a single point; (2) takes on the maximal value one for a society subdivided into two extreme groups of equal size, where all the incomes in the first group are zero and all the incomes in the other group are twice the mean; (3) increases if the difference between the incomes of the two groups increases, keeping the population masses in the groups fixed; and (4) satisfies scale invariance but decreases under equal absolute augmentation in all incomes. Postulates (1) and (2) are similar to the corresponding properties of L_{ER} in (4.2). Postulate (3) is analogous to the alienation function of Esteban and Ray (1994). The Milanovic index, which incorporates the idea of alienation in its formulation, has a Gini-type structure and measures the divergence of incomes from the situation of minimum polarization.

Zhang and Kanbur (2001) employed the ratio between the between-group and within-group components of the Shorrocks (1980) weighted generalized entropy index of inequality for measuring polarization. Formally, the Zhang-Kanbur index is defined as

$$L_{\mathrm{ZK}}(p,x) = \frac{I(p;\lambda_1 1^{n_1},\lambda_2 1^{n_2},\ldots..,\lambda_J 1^{n_J})}{\sum_{i=1}^{J} w_i(\underline{\lambda},\underline{n})I(p^i,x^i)}, \tag{4.6}$$

where for any partitioning of the population into J groups with respect to some homogeneous characteristic (say, age, sex, region, etc.), n^i is the population size of group i whose income distribution and mean income are respectively (p^i,x^i) and λ_i, $\underline{\lambda}=(\lambda^1,\lambda^2,\ldots..,\lambda^J)$, $\underline{n}=(n^1,n^2,\ldots\ldots,n^J)$, $w_i(\underline{\lambda},\underline{n})$ is the positive weight attached to inequality in (p^i,x^i), assumed to depend on the vectors $\underline{n}$ and $\underline{\lambda}$, and

$p = (p^1, p^2, \ldots.., p^J)$, $x = (x^1, x^2, \ldots.., x^J)$. Although the Zhang-Kanbur approach is different from that of Esteban and Ray (1994), there is a similarity in interpretation. The within-group term may be interpreted as an inverse indicator of feelings of identification between similar individuals – L_{ZK} increases if the groups become more concentrated, that is, if within-group inequality reduces. Also, the further apart are the means, the greater is the degree of polarization. Thus, the between-group term is an indicator of feelings of alienation between dissimilar individuals. The weighted generalized entropy family, which forms the basis of the index L_{ZK} and can be expressed as the sum of the between-group and within-group components considered in (4.6), is defined as

$$I_S(p,x) = \begin{cases} \frac{1}{n\bar{c}(\bar{c}-1)} \sum\limits_{i=1}^{k} p_i \left[\left(\frac{x_i}{\lambda}\right)^{\bar{c}} - 1 \right], \bar{c} \neq 0, 1, \\ \frac{1}{n} \sum\limits_{i=1}^{k} p_i \left[\log\left(\frac{\lambda}{x_i}\right) \right], \bar{c} = 0, \\ \frac{1}{n} \sum\limits_{i=1}^{k} p_i \left[\left(\frac{x_i}{\lambda}\right) \log\left(\frac{x_i}{\lambda}\right) \right], \bar{c} = 1, \end{cases} \tag{4.7}$$

where positivity of the lower bound μ of the income interval $[\mu, \gamma]$ is necessary for the index I_S to be well-defined in all cases. The real number $\bar{c}$ is a transfer sensitivity parameter – a transfer of income from a person to anyone who has a lower income decreases I_S by a larger amount, the lower is the value of $\bar{c}$ (*see* Shorrocks, 1980).

In the remainder of this section, we will discuss polarization indices that are concerned with the decline of the middle class, more precisely, with bipolarization. Several attempts considered some income interval around the median and defined the decline of the middle class in terms of reduction in population/income share corresponding to the interval. (*See*, e.g., Beach, 1989; Beach et al., 1997; Blackburn and Bloom, 1985; Horrigan and Haugen, 1988; Ilg and Haugen, 2000; McMahon and Tsechetter, 1986; Rosenthal, 1985; Wolfson, 1997).

Rigorous attempts to study the decline of the middle class have first been made by Foster and Wolfson (1992) and Wolfson (1994, 1997). Given any income distribution, they defined its (relative) bipolarization curve that shows for any population proportion, how far a normalized value of the share of the total income enjoyed by that proportion is from the corresponding share that it would receive under the hypothetical situation where everybody enjoys the median income (*see* Sect. 4.4). The area under the curve, which is popularly known as the Wolfson polarization index, is given by

$$L_W(p,x) = \frac{2\lambda(2Q - I_G(p,x))}{m}, \tag{4.8}$$

where $Q = (\lambda(p^+, x^+) - \lambda(p^-, x^-))/2\lambda$ and $I_G(p,x) = 1/2n^2\lambda \sum_{i=1}^{k} \sum_{j=1}^{k} p_i p_j |x_i - x_j|$ is the (relative) Gini index of the income distribution (p,x). L_W fulfills all the postulates for a bipolarization index. For bipartitioning of the population into deprived and satisfied groups, L_W can be rewritten as

$$L_{\mathrm{W}}(p,x) = \frac{2\lambda(I_{\mathrm{G}}^{\mathrm{BI}}(p,x) - I_{\mathrm{G}}^{\mathrm{WI}}(p,x))}{m}, \tag{4.9}$$

where $I_{\mathrm{G}}^{\mathrm{BI}}(I_{\mathrm{G}}^{\mathrm{WI}})$ is the corresponding between-group(within-group) component of the Gini index (*see* Rodriguez and Salas, 2003). Under ceteris paribus assumptions, L_{W} is increasing in $I_{\mathrm{G}}^{\mathrm{BI}}$, the alienation component, and decreasing in $I_{\mathrm{G}}^{\mathrm{WI}}$, an inverse indicator of identification.

Rodriguez and Salas (2003) also suggested the use of the difference

$$L_{\mathrm{RS}}(F) = I_{\mathrm{DWW}}^{\mathrm{BI}}(F) - I_{\mathrm{DWW}}^{\mathrm{WI}}(F) \tag{4.10}$$

as a bipolarization index and referred to this as the extended Wolfson index, where F is the income distribution function. $I_{\mathrm{DWW}}^{\mathrm{BI}}(F)(I_{\mathrm{DWW}}^{\mathrm{WI}}(F))$ is the between-group (within-group) component associated with the Donaldson and Weymark (1980, 1983) welfare ranked S-Gini inequality index, given that the population is bipartitioned using the median as the reference point. The boundedness condition $2 \leq \delta \leq 3$ is necessary for the extended index to satisfy the postulate Increased Bipolarity. The higher is the value of δ, the higher is the weight assigned by the Rodriguez-Salas index to the identification and alienation terms.

If we employ the Gini index in (4.6) under the bipartitioning of the population using the median, then L_{ZK} will be $L_{\mathrm{ZK}}^{I_{\mathrm{G}}}(p,x) = I_{\mathrm{G}}^{\mathrm{BI}}/I_{\mathrm{G}}^{\mathrm{WI}}$. The increasing transformation

$$L_{\mathrm{SDH}}(p,x) = \frac{L_{\mathrm{ZK}}^{I_{\mathrm{G}}} - 1}{L_{\mathrm{ZK}}^{I_{\mathrm{G}}} + 1} \tag{4.11}$$

of $L_{\mathrm{ZK}}^{I_{\mathrm{G}}}(p,x)$ was suggested as an index of bipolarization by Silber et al. (2007). Since the Silber et al. index L_{SDH} is increasingly related to $L_{\mathrm{ZK}}(p,x)$, applied to the Gini index, it shares the properties of the latter. As Silber et al. (2007) noted $1 - L_{\mathrm{SDH}}$ is an indicator of kurtosis of the income distribution (Berrebi and Silber, 1989). A measure of kurtosis indicates the degree of steepness or peakedness of the distribution.

In an interesting paper, Wang and Tsui (2000) suggested the use of

$$L_{\mathrm{WT}}^{\phi}(p,x) = \frac{1}{n}\sum_{i=1}^{k} p_i \phi\left(\left|\frac{x_i - m}{m}\right|\right) \tag{4.12}$$

and

$$L_{\mathrm{WT}}^{\varphi}(p,x) = \frac{1}{n}\sum_{i=1}^{k} p_i \varphi(|x_i - m|), \tag{4.13}$$

as relative and absolute indices of bipolarization. The Wang-Tsui indices aggregate the deviations of individual incomes from the median through the continuous transformations ϕ and φ, respectively. They are easy to understand and quite reasonable intuitively. Wang and Tsui (2000) also showed that they satisfy Increased Spread and Increased Bipolarityif and only ϕ and φ are increasing and strictly concave.

Alesina and Spolaore (1997) proposed a median-based index L_{AS}, which is implicitly defined by

$$F(m+L_{\mathrm{AS}})-F(m-L_{\mathrm{AS}})=\frac{1}{2}. \tag{4.14}$$

Since $F(v)$ gives the cumulative proportion of the population with income less than or equal to v, we can interpret the Alesina-Spolaore index I_{AS} as follows. It is that level of income which when added to and subtracted from the median makes the difference between the resulting cumulative population proportions equal to half. Since L_{AS} identifies a symmetric income interval around the median, it has some similarity with the interval-based indices we have discussed earlier.

So far the indices we have considered are descriptive; they are derived without using any concept of welfare. Such indices contrast with ethical indices that are designed from explicit social welfare functions. Needless to say, neither type of indices is meant to supplant the other type. Chakravarty and Majumder (2001) and Chakravarty et al. (2007) suggested relative and absolute indices of bipolarization using explicit forms of social welfare function. In their framework, bipolarization is measured in terms of welfare related to the given distribution. The relative index proposed by Chakravarty and Majumder (2001) is defined as

$$\begin{aligned} L_{\mathrm{CM}}(p,x) = & \frac{\Xi(\lambda(p^+,x^+),I(p^+,x^+))+2\lambda(p^+,x^+)}{2m} \\ & + \frac{\Xi(\lambda(p^-,x^-),I(p^-,x^-))-B_1(m)\lambda(p^-,x^-)}{2m}+B_2(m) \end{aligned} \tag{4.15}$$

where the reduced form social welfare function Ξ is increasing in efficiency (λ) and decreasing in relative inequality (I). The continuous normalization coefficients $B_1(m)$ and $B_2(m)$ have to be chosen such that different postulates for a bipolarization index are satisfied.

To illustrate the Chakravarty-Majumder index in (4.15), suppose that $\mu > 0$ and welfare evaluation is done with the weighted mean of order $\theta < 1$, the Atkinson (1970) abbreviated welfare function for (p,x), that is,

$$\Xi_{\mathrm{A}}(\lambda(p,x),I_{\mathrm{A}}(p,x)) = \begin{cases} \left(\frac{1}{n}\sum\limits_{i=1}^{k} p_i x_i^{\theta}\right)^{1/\theta}, \theta<1, \theta\neq 0, \\ \prod\limits_{i=1}^{k} (x_i)^{p_i/n}, \theta = 0, \end{cases} \tag{4.16}$$

and $B_1(m) = (m/\mu)^{1-\theta}$, $B_2(m) = 1/2(m/\mu)^{1-\theta} - 2$. Then L_{CM} becomes a fairly natural translation of the Atkinson (1970) index of inequality into bipolarization measurement. Under a progressive income transfer on the either side of the median, a reduction in the value of θ increases polarization by a larger amount, the lower is the value of θ. As $\theta \to -\infty$, Ξ_{A} approaches the Rawls (1971) maximin welfare function and I_{CM} becomes the relative maximin index of bipolarization. Next, if $\Xi(p,x) = \lambda(1-I_{\mathrm{G}})$, the Gini welfare function, $B_1(m) = 4$ and $B_2(m) = 0$, then L_{CM} becomes the Wolfson index (for even values of n). Thus, given any relative inequality index (or its associated welfare function), we can generate a corresponding relative bipolarization index using (4.15).

The absolute counterpart to L_{CM} suggested by Chakravarty et al. (2007) is given by

$$L_{\mathrm{CMR}}(p,x) = \frac{\Xi(\lambda(p^+,x^+),I(p^+,x^+)) + 2\lambda(p^+,x^+)}{2} + \frac{\Xi(\lambda(p^-,x^-),I(p^-,x^-)) - B_3(m)\lambda(p^-,x^-)}{2} + B_4(m), \quad (4.17)$$

where the continuous normalization coefficients $B_3(m)$ and $B_4(m)$ serve the same purpose as $B_1(m)$ and $B_2(m)$ in (4.15), and the abbreviated welfare function Ξ retains all the assumptions, except relativity of I. In this case, we assume that I is an absolute index. For the purpose of illustration, assuming that n is even, $B_3(m) = 4$ and $B_4(m) = 0$, we can use the absolute Gini index in (4.17). The resulting Chakravarty et al. index L_{CMR} may be referred to as the absolute Gini index of bipolarization. Alternatively, we may employ the weighted Kolm (1976a)-Pollak (1971) welfare function

$$\Xi_{\mathrm{KP}}(\lambda(p,x),I_{\mathrm{KP}}(p,x)) = -\frac{1}{\beta}\log\frac{1}{n}\sum_{i=1}^{k} p_i(\exp(-\beta x_i)) \quad (4.18)$$

in (4.17) to get the corresponding form of the bipolarization index, where the free parameter $\beta > 0$ determines the curvature of the social indifference surfaces. An increase in the value of β makes the social indifference curve more convex to the origin. The normalization coefficients chosen in this case are $B_3(m) = \exp(-\beta(\mu - m))$ and $B_4(m) = m\exp(-\beta(\mu - m))/2 - 2m$. Thus, given any absolute inequality index, we have a corresponding index of bipolarization. These indices will differ in the way we make welfare evaluation.[4]

4.3 A New Compromise Bipolarization Index, its Properties, and Characterization

In bipolarization measurement, we are concerned with deviations of incomes from the median. This motivates us to construct a compromise index of polarization based on transformed values of such deviations. Formally, for any income distribution (p,x), we consider the transformed deviations $\psi(|m - x_i|)$, where ψ is continuous, increasing and $\psi(0) = 0$. A median-based deviation function ψ satisfying these

[4] Some of these studies and several other studies have examined the extent of polarization in different countries over different periods. See, for example, Thurow (1984), Kosters and Ross (1988), Morris et al. (1994), Jenkins (1995), Kovacevic and Binder (1997), Quah (1997), Wolfson (1997), Gradin (2000, 2002), Chakravarty and Majumder (2001), Zhang and Kanbur (2001), Anderson (2004a,b), Duclos and Echevin (2005), Gigliarano (2006), Chakravarty et al. (2007), and Esteban et al. (2007).

conditions will be called regular. Given any income distribution, let d_e be the associated representative deviation, that is, d_e is that level of deviation which, if assigned to each individual, will make the resulting distribution median-based deviation indifferent to the existing distribution. Formally, given the income distribution (p,x) and a regular ψ, the corresponding d_e is implicitly defined by,

$$\sum_{i=1}^{k} p_i \psi(d_e) = \sum_{i=1}^{k} p_i \psi(|m - x_i|). \tag{4.19}$$

As an index of bipolarization, we now suggest the use of

$$L_\psi(p,x) = \frac{d_e}{m}. \tag{4.20}$$

The index L_ψ simply is an average of income deviations from the median as a fraction of the median itself.

The following theorem summarizes some properties of L_ψ.

Theorem 4.1. *Assume that ψ is regular.*

(i) Then L_ψ satisfies Normalization, Symmetry, the Population Principle, Increased Spread, and Continuity.
(ii) L_ψ satisfies Increased Bipolarity if and only if ψ is strictly concave.

Proof (i). From (4.19), we note that we can write d_e explicitly as $d_e(p,x) = \psi^{-1}[(1/n)\sum_{i=1}^{k} p_i \psi(|m - x_i|)]$. Since each x_i is drawn from the compact set $[\mu, \gamma]$ and the deviations $|m - x_i|$ are nonnegative, they will also take values in a compact set of the form $[0, \gamma']$. Thus, the domain of the function $\psi(|m - x_i|)$ is $[0, \gamma']$. Now, since ψ is increasing and the continuous image of a compact set is compact (Rudin, 1976, p. 89), $\psi(|m - x_i|)$ takes values in the compact set $[\psi(0), \psi(\gamma')]$, which, in view of the fact that $\psi(0) = 0$, can be rewritten as $[0, \psi(\gamma')]$. For a given p, continuity and increasingness of the function ψ implies that the average function $(1/n)\sum_{i=1}^{k} p_i \psi(|m - x_i|)$ is continuous and takes values in $[0, \psi(\gamma')]$. Observe that increasingness of ψ ensures the existence of ψ^{-1}. Continuity and increasingness of ψ^{-1} on $[0, \psi(\gamma')]$ now follows from Theorem 4.53 of Apostol (1975, p. 95). This in turn demonstrates continuity of L_ψ.

Since $\psi(0) = 0$ and ψ is increasing, $\psi^{-1}(0) = 0$. This establishes that L_ψ satisfies Normalization. It is easy to check that L_ψ satisfies Symmetry and the Population Principle. Given that ψ^{-1} is increasing, the proof of satisfaction of Increased Spread by L_ψ follows from Proposition 5 of Wang and Tsui (2000).

Proof (ii). Using the fact that ψ^{-1} is increasing and Proposition 5 of Wang and Tsui (2000) again, we can show that L_ψ satisfies Increased Bipolarity if and only if ψ is strictly concave. This completes the proof of the theorem. □

Since the index in (4.20) has been expressed in a ratio form, it is reasonable to expect that it will be a relative index. However, Theorem 4.1 does not say anything about this. There can be many regular ψ functions for which the theorem holds. Examples of such functions are: $\psi_1(v) = \eta_1 v^{\varepsilon}, 0 < \varepsilon < 1, \eta_1 > 0$; $\psi_2(v) = 1 - e^{-\eta_2 v}, \eta_2 > 0$; and $\psi_3(v) = (v/1+v)$. The following theorem shows that ψ_1 is the only regular ψ function for which L_{ψ} is a relative index.

Theorem 4.2. *Assume that ψ is regular and strictly concave. Then L_{ψ} in (4.20) is a relative index if and only if $\psi(v) = \eta_1 v^{\varepsilon}$, where $0 < \varepsilon < 1$ and $\eta_1 > 0$ are constants.*

Proof. Since the denominator of (4.20) is linear homogeneous, for L_{ψ} to be a relative index, we need linear homogeneity of the numerator as well. Note that $d_e(p,x) = \psi^{-1}[(1/n)\sum_{i=1}^{k} p_i \psi(|m - x_i|)]$ is a quasi-linear mean of income deviations and, given continuity of ψ, it satisfies linear homogeneity if and only if $\psi(v) = \eta_1 v^{\varepsilon} + \tilde{\eta}_1$, where η, ε, and v_1 are constants (Aczel, 1966, p.153). Since ψ is increasing and strictly concave, we must have $0 < \varepsilon < 1$ and $\eta > 0$. Next, $\psi(0) = 0$ ensures that $\tilde{\eta}_1 = 0$. This establishes the necessity part of the theorem. The sufficiency is easy to check. □

Substitution of the form of ψ, identified in Theorem 4.2, in (4.20) yields the following form of the bipolarization index:

$$L_{\varepsilon}(p,x) = \frac{(1/n\sum_{i=1}^{k} |m - x_i|^{\varepsilon})^{1/\varepsilon}}{m}, \quad 0 < \varepsilon < 1. \tag{4.21}$$

L_{ε} in (4.21) is the ratio between the weighted mean of order ε of deviations of individual incomes from the median and the median. Given (p,x), an increase in the value of ε increases L_{ε}. A progressive transfer of income on the either side of the median increases L_{ε} by a larger amount, the lower is the value of ε. As $\varepsilon \to 1$, L_{ε} approaches the simple average of the relative deviations of individual incomes from the median. In this particular case, L_{ε} satisfies Increased Spread but not Increased Bipolarity.

The absolute version $L_{A\varepsilon}$ of L_{ε} is given by mL_{ε}, that is,

$$L_{A\varepsilon}(p,x) = \left(\frac{1}{n} \sum_{i=1}^{k} p_i |m - x_i|^{\varepsilon} \right)^{1/\varepsilon}, \quad 0 < \varepsilon < 1. \tag{4.22}$$

Conversely, we can start with the absolute index $L_{A\varepsilon}$ and translate it into its relative counterpart L_{ε} by dividing by the median. This compromise property is shared by the Wolfson index also.

4.4 Bipolarization Dominance

Evidently, different indices of bipolarization may rank alternative distributions of income in different directions. To avoid such different directional rankings, this section attempts to develop criteria for ordering income distributions in the same direction using bipolarization indices. Since median is the reference income in the measurement of bipolarization, our orderings rely on deviations of incomes from the median. For simplicity of exposition, we assume that the population mass vector is given by $p = 1^k$, that is, the frequency of each income is 1. Therefore, we now write $L(x)$ instead of $L(p,x)$ to denote the level of bipolarization of the distribution (p,x). Further, all income distributions are assumed to be illfare-ranked and let $\hat{k} = (k+1)/2$.

For any $x \in [\mu, \gamma]^k$, the normalized aggregate deviation $\mathrm{RB}(x, j/k) = 1/km \sum_{j \leq i < \hat{k}} (m - x_i)$ is the shortfall of the total income of the population proportion j/k from the corresponding total that it would enjoy under the hypothetical distribution where everybody possesses the median income, as a fraction of the factor km, where $1 \leq j < \hat{k}$. This is, in fact, the ordinate corresponding to the population proportion j/k of the relative bipolarization curve (RBC) of x, where $1 \leq j < \hat{k}$. For incomes not below the median, the corresponding ordinate is $(1/km) \sum_{\hat{k} \leq i \leq j} (x_i - m), \hat{k} \leq j \leq k$. If k is odd, the RBC of x, $\mathrm{RB}(x,t)$, where $t \in [0,1]$, is completed by assuming $\mathrm{RB}(x,0) = 1$ and by defining

$$\mathrm{RB}\left(x, \frac{j+\tau}{k}\right) = (1-\tau)\mathrm{RB}\left(x, \frac{j}{k}\right) + \tau\mathrm{RB}\left(x, \frac{j+1}{k}\right) \tag{4.23}$$

for all $0 \leq \tau \leq 1$ and $1 \leq j \leq (k-1)$. Recall that if k is odd, then $m = x_{\hat{k}}$ is the middle most income of the distribution and the ordinate at $\hat{k}/k$ is well-defined.

If k is even, the curve is completed by setting $\mathrm{RB}(x,0) = 1$ and by defining

$$\mathrm{RB}\left(x, \frac{j+\tau}{k}\right) = (1-\tau)\mathrm{RB}\left(x, \frac{j}{k}\right) + \tau\mathrm{RB}\left(x, \frac{j+1}{k}\right),$$
$$\text{for all } 0 \leq \tau \leq 1 \text{ and } 1 \leq j \leq (k-1), \quad j \neq \hat{k}, \tag{4.24}$$

and

$$\mathrm{RB}\left(x, \frac{\hat{k}-.5+\tau}{k}\right) = (1-\tau)\mathrm{RB}\left(x, \frac{\hat{k}-.5}{k}\right) + \tau\mathrm{RB}\left(x, \frac{\hat{k}+.5}{k}\right), \quad \text{for all } 0 \leq \tau \leq 1.$$

Note that when k is even, $x_{\hat{k}}$ is not in x. However, the ordinate corresponding to the proportion $\hat{k}/k$ is defined (*see* Chakravarty et al., 2007).

If the income distribution is perfectly equal, the RBC coincides with the horizontal axis. For a typical unequal income distribution, the curve decreases until we reach the midpoint, where it coincides with the horizontal axis and then increases monotonically (Fig. 4.1).

Given any two income distributions $x, y \in [\mu, \gamma]^k$, x is said to dominate y with respect to relative bipolarization ($x \geq_{\mathrm{RB}} y$, for short) if

$$\mathrm{RB}(x,t) \geq \mathrm{RB}(y,t) \tag{4.25}$$

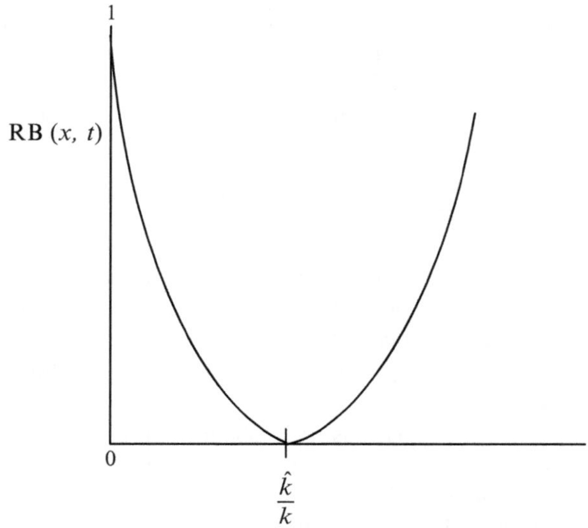

Fig. 4.1 Relative bipolarization curve

for all $t \in [0,1]$, with strict inequality for some t. That is, $x \geq_{\text{RB}} y$ means that the RBC of x lies nowhere below that of y and at some places (at least), the former lies above. Clearly, the relative bipolarization dominance relation $\geq_{\text{RB}}$ is transitive, that is, for any $x, y, u \in [\mu, \gamma]^k$ if $x \geq_{\text{RB}} y$ and $y \geq_{\text{RB}} u$ hold, then we must have $x \geq_{\text{RB}} u$. However, it is not complete, that is, we may be able to find $x, y \in [\mu, \gamma]^k$ such that neither $x \geq_{\text{RB}} y$ nor $y \geq_{\text{RB}} x$ holds. Obviously, this is a consequence of intersection of the two curves. Thus, like its Lorenz counterpart, $\geq_{\text{RB}}$ is a quasi-ordering.

To illustrate the construction of the RBC, consider the distribution $x = (1,2,5,6,10)$. Here $m = 5, \hat{k} = 3, x^- = (1,2)$, and $x^+ = (5,6,10)$. Then the ordinates of the RBC of x corresponding to the population proportions $j/5$, where $j = 1,2,\ldots.,5$, are given, respectively, by $7/25, 3/25, 0, 1/25$, and $6/25$.

The following result is an implication of the dominance relation $\geq_{\text{RB}}$ for income distributions with the same population size and arbitrary medians.

Theorem 4.3. *Let $x, y \in [\mu, \gamma]^k$ be arbitrary. Then the following conditions are equivalent:*

(i) $x \geq_{RB} y$.
(ii) $L(x) > L(y)$ for all relative bipolarization indices $L : [\mu, \gamma]^k \to R^1$ that satisfy Increased Spread, Increased Bipolarity, and Symmetry.

Proof. The idea of the proof is taken from Foster and Shorrocks (1988b) and Chakravarty et al. (2007). In proving the theorem, we assume for simplicity that n is odd. A similar proof will hold when n is even.

(i) $\Rightarrow$ (ii): Define $u = m(x)/m(y)y$. Since RBC is scale invariant, we have $\mathrm{RB}(y,t) = \mathrm{RB}(u,t)$, which in turn says that $x \geq_{\mathrm{RB}} y$ is same as $x \geq_{\mathrm{RB}} u$. Observe also that $m(x) = m(u)$. Assume that the curves do not coincide for the subvectors x^+ and y^+ (hence u^+). Then $x \geq_{\mathrm{RB}} u$ along with $m(x) = m(u)$ implies

$$\sum_{i=\hat{k}}^{j} x_i \geq \sum_{i=\hat{k}}^{j} u_i, \hat{k} \leq j \leq k, \quad \text{with} > \text{ for some } j. \tag{4.26}$$

This gives rise to one of following two possibilities: (iii) $\lambda(u^+) = \lambda(x^+)$ and (iv) $\lambda(u^+) \neq \lambda(x^+)$. If the former holds then we have $x^+ \geq_{\mathrm{LC}} u^+$ and x^+ is obtained from u^+ by a finite sequence of rank-preserving progressive income transfers among persons above the median (Hardy et al., 1934). If condition (iv) holds then we note from (4.26) that $\lambda(u^+) < \lambda(x^+)$. Define $\tilde{u}_i = u_i^+$ for $\hat{k} \leq i < k$ and $\tilde{u}_k = u_k^+ + (k - \hat{k} - 1)(\lambda(x^+) - \lambda(u^+))$. That is, $\tilde{u}$ is obtained from u^+ by a simple increment. Then (4.26) implies either $x^+ = \tilde{u}$ or $x^+ \geq_{\mathrm{LC}} \tilde{u}$, in which case we can obtain x^+ from $\tilde{u}$ by a finite sequence of rank-preserving progressive transfers as before.

Likewise, if we assume that the two curves do not coincide for subvectors x^- and y^- (hence u^-), then x^- is obtained from u^- by reducing some incomes and/or by some equalizing transfers below the median. This means that the overall distribution x can be derived from the distribution u through the transformations specified in Increased Spread and/or Increased Bipolarity.

Since L satisfies Increased Spread and Increased Bipolarity, we have $L(x) > L(u)$. Symmetry of L follows from the fact that it has been defined on ordered distributions. As L is a relative index, $L(y) = L(u)$. This implies that $L(x) > L(y)$.

(ii) $\Rightarrow$ (i): Our demonstration above shows that the deduction of x from u by a sequence of spread increasing movements and/or egalitarian transfers on the same side of the median is equivalent to relative bipolarization dominance on that side. This in turn proves the implication (ii) $\Rightarrow$ (i) of the theorem. (See Theorem 1.4.) This completes the proof of the theorem. □

Theorem 4.3 shows that a unanimous ranking of income distributions over a given population size by all symmetric, relative bipolarization indices satisfying Increased Spread and Increased Bipolarity can be obtained if and only if relative bipolarization dominance holds. But if the two curves cross, we can get two different indices with these properties that will rank the underlying income distributions in opposite directions. Note that in the proof of the theorem, if condition (iv) holds, then x^+ second order stochastic dominates u^+. Equivalently, we can say that $x^+ \geq_{\mathrm{GL}} u^+$ holds.

Comparisons of polarization across populations generally involve different population sizes. For polarization ranking of distributions with differing population sizes, we have the following result.

Theorem 4.4. *Let $x \in [\mu, \gamma]^k, y \in [\mu, \gamma]^l$ be arbitrary. Then the following conditions are equivalent:*

(i) $x \geq_{\mathrm{RB}} y$.
(ii) $L(x) > L(y)$ *for all relative bipolarization indices* $L : \Psi \to R^1$ *that satisfy Increased Spread, Increased Bipolarity, Symmetry, and the Population Principle, where* $\Psi = \bigcup_{k \in N} [\mu, \gamma]^k$ *and N is the set of positive integers.*

Proof. (i) ⇒ (ii): Let u^1 and u^2 be l- and k-fold replications of x and y, respectively. Since RBC is population replication invariant, we have $\mathrm{RB}(x,t) = \mathrm{RB}(u^1,t)$ and $\mathrm{RB}(y,t) = \mathrm{RB}(u^2,t)$. Therefore, $x \geq_{\mathrm{RB}} y$ is same as $u^1 \geq_{\mathrm{RB}} u^2$. As u^1 and u^2 are two distributions over the population size kl, using Theorem 4.3, we have $L(u^1) > L(u^2)$ for all relative bipolarization indices L that meet the properties stated in condition (ii) of Theorem 4.3. By the Population Principle, we have $L(u^1) = L(x)$ and $L(u^2) = L(y)$. Hence, $L(x) > L(y)$. A similar argument will demonstrate that the reverse implication is also true. □

Theorem 4.4 states that an unambiguous ranking of two arbitrary income distributions by relative bipolarization indices can be achieved through pairwise comparisons of their RBCs. Since we do not assume equality of the medians and the population sizes, this is the most general result we can have along this direction.

We can also focus our attention on the fixed median arbitrary population size case. In this case, the domain of definition of bipolarization indices is $\Psi_{\bar{m}} = \{x \in \Psi | m(x) = \bar{m}\}$. For all indices defined on $\Psi_{\bar{m}}$, we now have the following equivalence theorem, whose proof is similar to those of Theorems 4.3 and 4.4.

Theorem 4.5. *Let* $x, y \in \Psi_{\bar{m}}$ *be arbitrary. Then the following conditions are equivalent:*

(i) $x \geq_{\mathrm{RB}} y$.
(ii) $L(x) > L(y)$ *for all bipolarization indices* $L : \Psi_{\bar{m}} \to R^1$ *that fulfill Increased Spread, Increased Bipolarity, Symmetry, and the Population Principle.*

Given the median, relative bipolarization dominance becomes a sufficient condition for all relative and absolute (hence compromise) bipolarization indices, satisfying the axioms stated in condition (ii) of Theorem 4.5, to rank different income distributions in the same way.

Finally, if both mean income and median are fixed, the postulates we need for the indices to be consistent with the relation $\geq_{\mathrm{RB}}$ are Increased Bipolarity, Symmetry, and the Population Principle. There can also be situations where mean is fixed, median is different, and population size is equal/unequal. For consistency with $\geq_{\mathrm{RB}}$, while in the former case, the relative indices should be symmetric and increasing under the permissible egalitarian transfers; in the latter case, they should be population replication invariant as well.

For ranking income distributions by absolute bipolarization indices, Chakravarty et al. (2007) scaled up the RBC by the median to generate the absolute bipolarization curve (ABC). Formally, we have $\mathrm{AB}(x,t) = m\mathrm{RB}(x,t)$ for $0 \leq t \leq 1$. The area under this curve turns out to be mL_{W}, the absolute version of the Wolfson index. Thus, the Wolfson index can be converted into an absolute index by multiplying with the median.

Clearly, we can have absolute counterparts to Theorems 4.3–4.4 if we replace relative indices by absolute indices and $\geq_{\mathrm{RB}}$ by $\geq_{\mathrm{AB}}$, the absolute bipolarization dominance relation, defined in the same way as $\geq_{\mathrm{RB}}$. In fact, in some cases, ambiguous comparison under $\geq_{\mathrm{RB}}$ can be unambiguous under $\geq_{\mathrm{AB}}$. For example, consider two distributions x and y, where $m(x) > m(y)$ and the RBC of the former lies below that of the latter up to a point t_0 below the midpoint of the horizontal axis. But after that the RBC of x does not lie below that of y. Given that we have $m(x) > m(y)$, multiplication of these RBCs by the corresponding medians may give rise to an upward shift in the ABC of x at the left of the point of intersection t_0 such that $x \geq_{\mathrm{AB}} y$ holds. Thus, the higher median has a scaling effect for pushing the lower curve upward to guarantee absolute bipolarization dominance.

Chapter 5
The Measurement of Multidimensional Inequality

5.1 Introduction

In our treatment of the earlier chapters, income has been taken as the only indicator of well-being. But often this is inappropriate. Well-being of a population is a multidimensional phenomenon; income is just one of its many dimensions. It is certainly true that with high income a person may be able to improve the buying capacity of some of his nonincome dimensions of well-being. But for some dimensions, markets may not exist. An example is pollution control program in a community. This, therefore, shows inappropriateness of the use of prices as relative weights for the dimensions to arrive at a single measure of well-being or income. Further, the assumption of adequacy of prices for normative purposes is questionable (Tsui, 2002).

In the basic-needs approach, an improvement in an array of certain fundamental needs, such as housing, food, clothing, education, health, various other social and political activities, and freedom is taken as an indication of development, not just growth of income alone (Streeten, 1981). Sen (1992) argued that the proper space for social evaluation is that of "functionings," the different things, such as essential services, adequate nourishment, having self-respect, environmental factors, and communing with friends, etc., a person may value doing, having (or being). While the sets of realized functionings of different persons constitute an important part of social evaluation, more is required to get a complete picture of well-being. "Capability set" of an individual provides information on the set of functionings that he could achieve. The set of alternative functioning vectors from which a person has the freedom to choose, when the resource allocation is given, gives his capability set. Thus, capabilities represent real opportunities related to living conditions. The determination of living standard then relies on the opportunity set of the available basic capabilities of the person to function. Thus, the freedom to choose becomes an important component of the standard of living. This shows that well-being is intrinsically multidimensional from the capability-functioning perspective.

Since the direct method of calculating welfare "is not based on particular assumptions of consumer behavior which may or may not be accurate," "it is superior

S.R. Chakravarty, *Inequality, Polarization and Poverty: Advances in Distributional Analysis,* Economic Studies in Inequality, Social Exclusion and Well-Being 6,
DOI: 10.1007/978-0-387-79253-8_5,

to the income method" (Sen, 1981, p. 26). In case of unavailability of direct information on different dimensions, one can certainly adopt the income method, "so that the income method is at most a second best" (Sen, 1981, p. 26).

An example of a multidimensional indicator of well-being of a population is the human development index suggested by the UNDP (1990). It aggregates country level achievements in three basic functionings of human life, namely, a decent living standard measured by the per capita gross domestic product, a long and healthy life measured by life expectancy at birth, and knowledge measured by the educational attainment rate. However, by focusing on country-level attainments, the human development index and its alternatives and variants fail to provide any information on how achievements are distributed at individual levels.

The purpose of this chapter is to make an analytical presentation of alternative approaches to the measurement of multidimensional inequality by taking into account the individual level of information on different attributes of well-being. Contributions along this line have been made by Kolm (1977), Atkinson and Bourguignon (1982), Maasoumi (1986, 1989a,b, 1999), Maasoumi and Nickelsburg (1988), Dardanoni (1995), Koshevoy (1995, 1998), Tsui (1995, 1999), Koshevoy and Mosler (1996), Bourguignon (1999), List (1999), Lugo (2005), Gajdos and Weymark (2005), Savaglio (2006a,b), Weymark (2006), and Diez et al. (2007). We also explore the possibility of transporting and adapting the methodology used for constructing multidimensional indices of inequality to the appraisal of employment segregation indices by sex (Chakravarty and Silber, 2007). An occupational segregation index by sex is concerned with inequality between male and female employees across occupational groups.[1]

5.2 Postulates for an Index of Multidimensional Inequality

The number of persons in the society is denoted by $n \geq 2$ and let $d \geq 2$ be the number of attributes of well-being. We will often use the term "dimension" or "functioning" for an attribute. Attributes may or may not vary in kind. For instance, earnings in two different time periods can be two attributes. For the simplicity of exposition, we assume that n is fixed. The results can be extended to the variable population setup under appropriate assumptions.

It is assumed that each dimension is represented by a variable which is measurable on a ratio scale. This means that it has a natural zero and is unique up to a multiplication by a positive constant. Income is an example of a variable of this type. Let x_{ij} be the quantity of attribute j possessed by person i. It is possible to vary these quantities in a continuous manner. Thus, our framework rules out the possibility of including a functioning that is categorical or an ordinal in nature. A categorical variable has one or more categories or types. For example, gender is a categorical variable with two categories – male and female. An ordinal variable

[1] In presenting some parts of the chapter, we follow Weymark (2006).

is similar to a categorical variable but there is a well-defined ordering rule. For example, we can order the educational achievement levels starting from elementary school education to university education by assigning some numbers in increasing order. Another ordinal dimension can be self-reported health status of an individual (*see also* Sect. 1.8). (Formulations based on dimensions that are represented by categorical and ordinal variables are discussed and analyzed in Sects. 5.6 and 6.3, respectively).

The quantity x_{ij} is the (i, j)th entry of an $n \times d$ distribution matrix X. The distribution of attribute j among n-persons is denoted by the column vector $x_{.j}$, the jth column of X. Similarly, the row vector $x_{i.}$, the ith row of X, represents the quantities of d attributes possessed by person i. For any vector $x_{.j}$, we write $x^0_{.j}$ for its welfare-ranked permutation, that is, $x^0_{1j} \geq x^0_{2j} \geq \cdots \geq x^0_{nj}$.

Let $\mathbf{M}$ be the set of three different sets of distribution matrices. More precisely, $\mathbf{M} = \{M_1, M_2, M_3\}$, where M_1 is the set of all possible distribution matrices. Next, M_2 is the set of all distribution matrices such that $x_{ij} \geq 0$ for all pairs $(i, j) \in \{1,2,\ldots,n\} \times \{1,2,..,d\}$ and $\lambda(x_{.j}) > 0$ for all $1 \leq j \leq d$. Finally, M_3 is the set of all distribution matrices such that $x_{ij} > 0$ for all pairs $(i, j) \in \{1,2,\ldots,n\} \times \{1,2,..,d\}$. Thus, for matrices in the sets M_2 and M_3, the mean of each attribute is positive. An arbitrary element of the set $\mathbf{M}$ is denoted by M, that is, M can be anyone of the three M_i's. A multidimensional inequality index I is a real valued function defined on M.That is, $I : M \rightarrow R^1$. For any $X \in M$, $I(X)$ determines the extent of inequality associated with the distribution matrix X.

As in the single-dimensional case, an inequality index can be of relative or absolute variety. Formally, an inequality index $I : M \rightarrow R^1$ is of relative type if

$$I(X\Omega) = I(X), \tag{5.1}$$

where $\Omega = \text{diag }(\omega_1, \omega_2, \ldots, \omega_d)$ and $\omega_i > 0$ for all i.

Condition (5.1) is a ratio scale invariance assumption. It says that inequality remains invariant under any change in the units of measurement of attributes. However, this condition is inappropriate if some of the dimensions are measured in the same unit. For example, there is a relationship between units of incomes in two different states of the world. An alternative form of the ratio scale invariance condition (5.1) can be $I(X) = I(cX)$, where $c > 0$ is a scalar (*see* Weymark, 2006). In contrast, an index will be of absolute variety if addition of a constant to the quantities of a given attribute does not alter the level of inequality. Technically, I is an absolute index if

$$I(X + \hat{A}) = I(X), \tag{5.2}$$

where $\hat{A}$ is any $n \times d$ matrix with identical rows such that $X + \hat{A} \in M$.

A multidimensional index of inequality, whether of relative or absolute type, should satisfy the following postulates.

Continuity: I is a continuous function on X.
Normalization: For any $X \in M$, if X has identical rows, then $I(X) = 0$.

Symmetry: For any $X \in M$, $I(\Pi X) = I(X)$, where Π is any $n \times n$ permutation matrix.

Uniform Majorization Principle: For all $X, Y \in M$, if $X = AY$ for some $n \times n$ bistochastic matrix A that is not a permutation matrix, then $I(X) < I(Y)$.

Continuity ensures that the inequality index is not oversensitive to errors in the measurement of the attribute distributions. According to Normalization, if each person has the same quantities of different attributes, then the level of inequality is zero. Symmetry, as in the single-dimensional case, demands that the individuals are not distinguished by anything other than the attributes. The Uniform Majorization Principle is the multidimensional analogue to the Pigou-Dalton Transfers Principle. This principle ensures that I is symmetric.

Recall the discussion on equivalence between progressive transfers and T-transformation. The following desideratum can be regarded as the multidimensional analogue to this condition.

Uniform Pigou-Dalton Transfers Principle: For all $X, Y \in M$, if $X = \hat{A}Y$, where $\hat{A}$ is the product of a finite number of $n \times n$ T-transformations, then $I(X) < I(Y)$.

The product of T-transformations is a nonpermutation bistochastic matrix. For $d = 1$ or $n = 2$, the converse is also true. However, for $d \geq 2$ and $n \geq 3$, there exist nonpermutation bistochastic matrices that are not products of $T-$transformations (Marshall and Olkin, 1979, p. 431).Thus, except in the special situations noted above, the condition is less restrictive than the Uniform Majorization Principle.

The central idea underlying the redistributive criteria Uniform Majorization Principle and Uniform Pigou-Dalton Transfers Principle is that X has less dispersion than Y. Further, the mean value of each attribute is the same in both the matrices. That is why they are quite appropriate for incorporating egalitarian bias into distributional judgments. However, Fleurbaey and Trannoy (2003) demonstrated that in a society with heterogeneous individual preferences, multidimensional versions of the Pigou-Dalton Transfers Principle may come into conflict with the Pareto Principle, which requires that for $X, Y \in M$, if $X \neq Y$ and $x_{ij} \geq y_{ij}$ for all (i, j), then X has higher level of welfare than Y. This shows inappropriateness of applications of multidimensional forms of the Pigou-Dalton Condition in heterogeneous populations.

5.3 Normative Multidimensional Inequality Indices

In this section, we will analyze multidimensional counterparts to the normative indices presented in Chap. 1. We begin by assuming the existence of a social welfare function $W : M \to R^1$ which satisfies Continuity, the Pareto Principle, and Strict Uniform S-concavity. Continuity is similar to the corresponding property of an inequality index I. Strict Uniform S-concavity of W demands that $W(X) > W(Y)$, where X and Y are the same as specified in the postulate Uniform Majorization Principle. A strictly uniform S-concave function satisfies Symmetry. Since Strict Uniform S-concavity ensures that W is egalitarian, we may call it a welfare majorization condition (*see* Kolm, 1977). These three assumptions are multidimensional counterparts to the basic assumptions made for an income distribution-based welfare function. For the utilitarian social welfare function with identical individual utility function U, the majorization condition holds if U is strictly concave (Kolm, 1977).

The Kolm (1977) multidimensional counterpart to the Atkinson-Kolm-Sen inequality index measures the inequality of a distribution matrix by the fraction of the total amount of each attribute that could be saved if the distribution of each attribute across the individuals is perfectly equalized and the resulting distribution becomes socially indifferent to the original distribution according to W. To define the index in a formal way, we assume that $M \in \mathbf{M} - \{M_1\}$. For any $X \in M$, let X_λ be the distribution matrix each of whose jth column entries is $\lambda(x_{.j})$ for all $1 \leq j \leq d$. Now, define $\Lambda(X)$ implicitly by $W(X_\lambda \Lambda(X)) = W(X)$. The Pareto Principle and Continuity ensure that $\Lambda(X)$ is well-defined.

The multidimensional Kolm (1977) inequality index $I_{\mathrm{KM}} : M \to R^1$ is then defined as

$$I_{\mathrm{KM}}(X) = 1 - \Lambda(X). \tag{5.3}$$

For $d = 1$, I_{KM} reduces to I_{AKS} defined in Chap. 1. For $X, Y \in M$, if $X_\lambda = Y_\lambda$, then by the Pareto Principle, $\Lambda(X) \geq \Lambda(X)$ if and only if $W(X) \geq W(Y)$. Given assumptions about W, I_{KM} satisfies Continuity, Symmetry, and the Uniform Majorization Principle. Since $X_\lambda = AX$ for the bistochastic matrix A in which all entries are $1/n$, the Uniform Majorization Principle and the Pareto Principle imply positivity of I_{KM} whenever $X \neq X_\lambda$ (Weymark, 2006). If $X = X_\lambda$, then $I_{\mathrm{KM}} = 0$. It is evident that I_{KM} is bounded above by one. Thus, I_{KM} is bounded between zero and one, where the lower bound is achieved if $X = X_\lambda$.

For characterizing the multidimensional Atkinson index, we concentrate on the distribution matrices in M_3. In addition to the three basic assumptions made about W, Tsui (1995) imposed two more conditions on W. The first is a separability axiom, which shows how we can calculate overall welfare when the population is subdivided into two subgroups. More precisely, $W(X) = W(\tilde{h}(X^1), X^2)$, where $\tilde{h}$ is some continuous function, X^1 is the submatrix of X including the vectors of persons in the subgroup containing some, say n_1, persons and X^2 is the complement of X^1.The second axiom is a scale consistency condition, which requires that the ranking of any two distribution matrices remains unaltered if the dimensions are rescaled according to their respective ratio scales. That is, for $X, Y \in M_3$, $W(X) = W(Y) \Leftrightarrow W(X\Omega) = W(Y\Omega)$, where Ω is a $d \times d$ diagonal matrix with positive entries in the diagonal. Given that $n \geq 3$, Tsui (1995) showed that these conditions hold together if and only if W is ordinally equivalent to $\sum_{i=1}^{n} U(x_{i.})$, where

$$U(x_{i.}) = a' + b' \prod_{j=1}^{d} x_{ij}^{\theta_j} \quad \text{or} \quad U(x_{i.}) = a' + \sum_{j=1}^{d} c_j \log x_{ij}, \tag{5.4}$$

where $c_j > 0$ for all $1 \leq j \leq d$, a' is any real number and the real numbers b' and $\theta_j, 1 \leq j \leq d$, are chosen so that U in (5.4) is increasing and strictly concave (*see* Theorem 1 of Tsui, 1995).

Using this particular form of W, one can calculate the corresponding form of $\Lambda(X)$, which when substituted in (5.3) generates the following form of the inequality index:

$$I_{\mathrm{AM}}(X) = 1 - \left[\frac{1}{n}\sum_{i=1}^{n}\prod_{j=1}^{d}\left(\frac{x_{ij}}{\lambda(x_{.j})}\right)^{\theta_j}\right]^{1/\sum_{j=1}^{d}\theta_j}$$

or

$$I_{\mathrm{AM}}(X) = 1 - \left[\frac{1}{n}\prod_{i=1}^{n}\prod_{j=1}^{d}\left(\frac{x_{ij}}{\lambda(x_{.j})}\right)^{c_j/\sum_{j=1}^{d}c_j}\right]^{1/n}, \tag{5.5}$$

where $X \in M_3$, $c_j > 0$ for all j, and θ_j is appropriately restricted. For instance, if $d = 2$, $0 < \theta_1 < 1$ and $\theta_2 < (1-\theta_1)$. I_{AM} in (5.5) is the multidimensional Atkinson index of inequality. For $d = 1$, the formula coincides with the single-dimensional Atkinson (1970) index.

We now present the Tsui (1995) generalization of Kolm's (1976a) univariate absolute index. For any $X \in M$, define the scalar $\overline{K}(X)$ implicitly by

$$W(X_\lambda - \overline{K}(X)\mathbf{1}) = W(X), \tag{5.6}$$

where $\mathbf{1}$ is the $n \times d$ distribution matrix, all of whose entries are one. Continuity and the Pareto Principle guarantee that $\overline{K}$ is well-defined.

Then the multidimensional Tsui inequality index $I_{\mathrm{TM}} : M \to R^1$ is defined as

$$I_{\mathrm{TM}}(X) = \overline{K}(X). \tag{5.7}$$

I_{TM} measures inequality by the amount of each attribute that can be taken from each individual in order to obtain a distribution matrix which is socially indifferent to the existing distribution matrix, given that the distribution of each attribute is equalized across persons. For the polar case $d = 1$, I_{TM} coincides with I_{KP}. It can be checked that I_{TM} is nonnegative and equals zero if $X = X_\lambda$.

To derive the multidimensional Kolm-Pollak index, we assume that the domain of the social welfare function and hence of the inequality index is M_1. Suppose we replace the scale consistency condition by a translation scale invariance axiom and retain the basic and the separability assumptions on W. Translation scale invariance requires invariance of ranking of two distribution matrices under a constant addition to quantities of each attribute. That is, $W(X) = W(Y) \Leftrightarrow W(X+\hat{A}) = W(Y+\hat{A})$, where $\hat{A}$ is an $n \times d$ matrix with identical rows. Then given that $n \geq 3$, all these assumptions hold together if and only if W is ordinally equivalent to $\sum_{i=1}^{n} U(x_{i.})$, where

$$U(x_{i.}) = a'' + b''\prod_{j=1}^{d}\exp(\beta_j x_{ij}), \tag{5.8}$$

where a'' is an arbitrary constant and the parameter b'' and $\beta_j, 1 \leq j \leq d$, are chosen so that U in (5.8) is increasing and strictly concave (*see* Theorem 2 of Tsui, 1995).

The corresponding form of the Tsui (1995) multidimensional absolute inequality index is given by

$$I_{\mathrm{KPM}}(X) = \frac{1}{\sum_{j=1}^{d} \beta_j} \log \left[\frac{1}{n} \sum_{i=1}^{n} \exp \left(\sum_{j=1}^{d} \beta_j (\lambda(x_{.j}) - x_{ij}) \right) \right], \tag{5.9}$$

where $X \in M_1$ and the parameters satisfy the appropriate restrictions. This index is the multidimensional analogue to the Kolm (1976a)-Pollak (1971) index. It reduces to the single dimensional Kolm-Pollak family if $d = 1$.

Since the Gini index is the most commonly used index of relative inequality, it will be worthwhile to discuss the multidimensional analogues to this index or its generalized forms. Gajdos and Weymark (2005) developed interesting characterization of multidimensional generalized Gini welfare functions using multidimensional counterparts to the axioms used by Weymark (1981) to axiomatize the single-dimensional generalized Gini welfare functions and two other axioms, Strong Attribute Separability and Weak Comonotonic Additivity. According to the first of these two latter axioms, any subset of the attributes is separable from the set of remaining attributes.

A distribution matrix $X \in M$ is called nonincreasing comonotonic if the entries for each dimension, that is, in each column, are welfare-ranked. More precisely, $x_{1j} \geq x_{2j} \geq \ldots \geq x_{nj}$ and $1 \leq j \leq d$. That is, in the nonincreasing comonotonic distribution matrix X, person $(i-1)$ receives at least as much of each attribute as person i, where $i = 1, 2, \ldots n$. Let M^{CM} be the set of nonincreasing comonotonic matrices in M. Then Weak Comonotonic Additivity says that for all $X, Y \in M^{\mathrm{CM}}$ and $X' \in M_1^{\mathrm{CM}}$ for which there exists a j_0, $1 \leq j_0 \leq d$, such that (i) $x_{.j} = y_{.j}$ for all $j \neq j_0$, (ii) $x'_{ij} = 0$ for all $1 \leq i \leq n$ and all $j \neq j_0$, and (iii) $X + X' \in M^{\mathrm{CM}}$ and $Y + X' \in M^{\mathrm{CM}}$, $W(X) \geq W(Y)$ if and only if $W(X + X') \geq W(Y + X')$. Note that the distribution matrices $X, Y, X + X'$, and $Y + X'$ are all nonincreasing comonotonic and have identical distributions in all the attributes except j_0. The matrices $X + X'$ and $Y + X'$ are obtained, respectively, from X and Y by adding a common distribution of attribute j_0 to both $x_{.j_0}$ and $y_{.j_0}$. Then the axiom requires that social ordering of two comonotonic distribution matrices remains invariant under this kind of change. [Gajdos and Weymark (2005) also suggested a stronger version of the axiom.]

Assuming that $M = M_2$ and $d \geq 3$, the Gajdos and Weymark (2005) homogeneous form of the multidimensional generalized Gini welfare function $W_{\mathrm{GWM}} : M_2 \to R^1$ is a weighted mean of order ω, where ω is a scalar. More precisely,

$$\begin{aligned} W_{\mathrm{GWM}}(X) &= \left[\sum_{j=1}^{d} \tilde{a}_j \left(\sum_{i=1}^{n} b_{ij} x_{ij}^{0} \right)^{\omega} \right]^{1/\omega}, \quad \text{if } \omega \neq 0 \quad \text{and} \\ W_{\mathrm{GWM}}(X) &= \prod_{j=1}^{d} \left(\sum_{i=1}^{n} b_{ij} x_{ij}^{0} \right)^{\tilde{a}_j}, \quad \text{if } \omega = 0, \end{aligned} \tag{5.10}$$

where for each attribute j, the coefficients b_{ij} satisfying the restrictions $\sum_{i=1}^{n} b_{ij} = 1$ and increasingness of $b_{.j}$, are positive and the positive sequence $\{\tilde{a}_j\}$ fulfils the condition $\sum_{j=1}^{d} \tilde{a}_j = 1$. Thus, given any attribute j, W_{GWM} first employs a linear weighted aggregation over the corresponding quantities possessed by different persons, and then a mean of order ω type aggregation is taken over all the attributes.

The corresponding class of multidimensional Kolm (1977) relative inequality indices is given by

$$I_{\text{GWR}}(X) = 1 - \frac{\left[\sum\limits_{j=1}^{d} \tilde{a}_j \left(\sum\limits_{i=1}^{n} b_{ij} x_{ij}^0\right)^{\omega}\right]^{1/\omega}}{\left[\sum\limits_{j=1}^{d} \tilde{a}_j (\lambda(x_{.j}))^{\omega}\right]^{1/\omega}}, \quad \text{if } \omega \neq 0 \quad \text{and}$$

$$I_{\text{GWR}}(X) = 1 - \frac{\prod_{j=1}^{d} \left(\sum_{i=1}^{n} b_{ij} x_{ij}^0\right)^{\tilde{a}_j}}{\prod_{j=1}^{d} \lambda(x_{.j})^{\tilde{a}_j}}, \quad \text{if} \quad \omega = 0 \tag{5.11}$$

where $X \in M_2$. This is a multidimensional generalized Gini relative inequality index.

To derive the absolute sister of I_{GWR}, Gajdos and Weymark (2005) first characterized a welfare function on M_1 using a Kolm (1976a)-Pollak (1971) type aggregation involving a parameter ω, where ω is a scalar. The explicit functional form is given by

$$W_{\text{GWA}}(X) = \frac{1}{\omega} \log\left[\sum_{j=1}^{d} \tilde{a}_j \exp\left(\omega \sum_{i=1}^{n} b_{ij} x_{ij}^0\right)\right], \quad \text{if} \quad \omega \neq 0 \quad \text{and}$$

$$W_{\text{GWA}}(X) = \left[\sum_{j=1}^{d} \tilde{a}_j \left(\sum_{i=1}^{n} b_{ij} x_{ij}^0\right)\right], \quad \text{if} \quad \omega = 0 \tag{5.12}$$

where the coefficients b_{ij} satisfying the restrictions $\sum_{i=1}^{n} b_{ij} = 1$ and increasingness of $b_{.j}$ are positive. However, the sequence $\{\tilde{a}_j\}$ needs to be positive only. So, if $\omega \neq 0$, first an exponential type aggregation is employed over quantities of an attribute of different individuals and then a logarithmic aggregation is used over the attributes. Note that if $\omega = 0$, we have linear aggregation at each stage.

The corresponding class of multidimensional Tsui (1995) absolute inequality indices is given by

$$I_{\text{GWA}}(X) = \frac{1}{\omega} \log\left[\frac{\sum_{j=1}^{d} \tilde{a}_j \exp(\omega \lambda(x_{.j}))}{\sum_{j=1}^{d} \tilde{a}_j \exp\left(\omega \sum\limits_{i=1}^{n} b_{ij} x_{ij}^0\right)}\right], \quad \text{if} \quad \omega \neq 0 \quad \text{and}$$

$$I_{\text{GWA}}(X) = \left[\sum_{j=1}^{d} \tilde{a}_j \left(\lambda(x_{.j}) - \sum_{i=1}^{n} b_{ij} x_{ij}^0\right)\right], \quad \text{if} \quad \omega = 0, \tag{5.13}$$

where $X \in M_1$. This index is a multidimensional generalized Gini absolute inequality index.

5.4 Multidimensional Generalized Entropy Indices of Inequality

Throughout the section, we assume that the domain of the inequality index is M_3, the set of all distribution matrices with positive entries. The social welfare functions underlying the multidimensional Atkinson (1970) and Kolm (1976a)-Pollak (1971) indices first aggregate an individual's allocation of different attributes into an indicator of well-being. These individual utilities are then summed up to arrive at a measure of social utility. Maasoumi (1986) suggested a multidimensional inequality index by directly employing a two-stage aggregation procedure. He used a utility function in the first stage to aggregate individual allocations. Formally, the attribute quantities of person i are aggregated using a constant elasticity type rule: $\sigma_i = \left(\Sigma_{j=1}^{d} a''_j x_{ij}^{-\hat{\delta}}\right)^{-\hat{\delta}}$, where the nonnegative sequence $\{a''_j\}$ fulfills the restriction that $\Sigma_{j=1}^{d} a''_j = 1$ and $\hat{\delta} \geq -1$ is a parameter that reflects the elasticity of substitution between attributes. Note that the constant elasticity of substitution between any two attributes is given by $1/(1+\hat{\delta})$. For $\hat{\delta} = -1$, the aggregation is linear and there is perfect substitutability between the attributes. On the other hand, for $\hat{\delta} = 0$, we get the Cobb-Douglas utility function. An increase in the value of $\hat{\delta}$ decreases the scope for substitution.

Maasoumi's (1986) second stage aggregation is Shorrocks' generalized entropy type aggregation on σ_is (Shorrocks, 1980). Formally, the index of multidimensional inequality proposed by Maasoumi (1986, 1999) is

$$I_{\text{MM}}(X) = \begin{cases} \frac{1}{nc(c-1)} \sum_{i=1}^{n} \left[\left(\frac{\sigma_i}{\lambda(\sigma)} \right)^{\bar{c}} - 1 \right], \bar{c} \neq 0, 1, \\ \frac{1}{n} \sum_{i=1}^{n} \left[\log \left(\frac{\lambda(\sigma)}{\sigma_i} \right) \right], \bar{c} = 0, \\ \frac{1}{n} \sum_{i=1}^{n} \left[\left(\frac{\sigma_i}{\lambda(\sigma)} \right) \log \left(\frac{\sigma_i}{\lambda(\sigma)} \right) \right], \bar{c} = 1, \end{cases} \tag{5.14}$$

where $\lambda(\sigma)$ is the mean of the utility vector $\sigma = (\sigma_1, \sigma_2, \ldots, \sigma_n)$ and the parameter $\bar{c}$ has the same interpretation as in Shorrocks' (1980) case, now in terms of σ_is. The index I_{MM} is additively decomposable. We may also establish a relationship between the Atkinson (1970) index defined on σ_is and I_{MM}. (*See* our discussion in Chap. 1 on the generalized entropy family.) Note here that I_{AM} and I_{KPM} do not involve two-stage aggregation in the sense of Maasoumi.

Dardanoni (1995) claimed that multidimensional inequality indices that rely on Maasoumi's two-stage procedure may not satisfy the Uniform Majorization Principle. To prove this, he considered the following example:

Let

$$Y = \begin{bmatrix} 10 & 10 & 10 \\ 10 & 90 & 10 \\ 90 & 10 & 10 \end{bmatrix} \quad \text{and} \quad A = \begin{bmatrix} 1 & 0 & 0 \\ 0 & 0.5 & 0.5 \\ 0 & 0.5 & 0.5 \end{bmatrix}$$

We then have

$$X = AY = \begin{bmatrix} 10 & 10 & 10 \\ 50 & 50 & 10 \\ 50 & 50 & 10 \end{bmatrix}.$$

Since A is a bistochastic matrix, by the majorization criterion we should have $I(X) < I(Y)$. Assume that the relative inequality index I at the second stage is strictly S-convex. Suppose also that the utility function U employed at the first stage is symmetric, increasing, and concave. This in turn gives $U(y_{1.}) = U(x_{1.}) < U(y_{2.}) = U(y_{3.}) \leq U(x_{2.}) = U(x_{3.})$. If the weak inequality reduces to equality, then I remains unchanged. If the weak inequality is strict, the I regards X as more unequal than Y. Thus, in either case, I becomes a violator of the majorization criterion. As Weymark (2006) argued, this raises question about the two-stage aggregation procedure of Maasoumi (1986).

An alternative extension of the generalized entropy index to the multivariate setup was suggested by Tsui (1999). The corresponding functional form is given by

$$I_{\text{TME}}(X) = \frac{\hat{e}}{n}\sum_{i=1}^{n}\left(\prod_{j=1}^{d}\left(\frac{x_{ij}}{\lambda(x_{.j})}\right)^{\hat{c}_j} - 1\right), \qquad (5.15)$$

where the constants $\hat{e}$ and $\hat{c}_1, \hat{c}_2, .., \hat{c}_d$ are required to satisfy some restrictions for verification of different postulates. For instance, if $d = 2$, then $\hat{e}\hat{c}_1(\hat{c}_1 - 1) > 0, \hat{c}_1\hat{c}_2(1 - \hat{c}_1 - \hat{c}_2) > 0$, and $\hat{e}\hat{c}_1\hat{c}_2 > 0$, which imply that $\hat{e} > 0, \hat{c}_1, \hat{c}_2 < 0$. This index attains its lower bound zero whenever attribute distributions are equal and it is additively decomposable.

Diez et al. (2007) derived a family of unit consistent multidimensional inequality indices which has similarity with I_{TME}. A multidimensional inequality index $I : M_3 \to R^1$ is called unit consistent if for $X, Y \in M_3$, $I(X) < I(Y)$ implies $I(X\Omega) < I(Y\Omega)$, where Ω is same as in (5.1). The functional form of this index is given by

$$I_{\text{DVU}}(X) = \frac{\hat{e}}{n\prod_{j=1}^{d}(\lambda(x_{.j}))^{\hat{c}_j - \delta'}}\sum_{i=1}^{n}\left(\prod_{j=1}^{d}(x_{ij})^{\hat{c}_j} - \prod_{j=1}^{d}(\lambda(x_{.j}))^{\hat{c}_j}\right), \qquad (5.16)$$

where δ' is a real number. If $\delta' = 0$, then I_{DVU} coincides with I_{TME}. In fact, I_{DVU} is a relative index if and only if $\delta' = 0$. No member of this family is an absolute index. For $\delta' > (<)0$, an equiproportionate increase in the quantities of an attribute for different individuals increases (decreases) inequality.

5.5 Correlation Increasing Switch and Multidimensional Inequality

The subject of this section is an issue which is of very much practical importance. It is that of correlation between attributes and the way it affects multidimensional inequality. Atkinson and Bourguignon (1982) argued that multidimensional inequality should take into account the correlation between attribute distributions. Tsui (1999) has suggested one way in which an inequality index can be made sensitive to such a switch. His axiom requires that inequality should increase under a switch of this type.

To understand the issue explicitly, for $x, y \in R^d$, define $x \vee y = (\max\{x_1, y_1\}, \ldots, \max\{x_d, y_d\})$ and $x \wedge y = (\min\{x_1, y_1\}, \ldots, \min\{x_d, y_d\})$. For $X, Y \in M$, we say that Y is obtained from X by a correlation increasing switch if $X \neq Y$ and there exist $1 \leq i, l \leq n$ such that (i) $y_{i.} = x_{i.} \wedge x_{l.}$, (ii) $y_{i.} = x_{i.} \vee x_{l.}$, and (iii) $x_{i_1.} = y_{i_1.}$ for all $i_1 \notin \{i, l\}$. That is, under a correlation increasing switch, the allocations of two individuals are rearranged so that one of them receives at least as much of every attribute as the other and more of at least one attribute. For instance, suppose that in the 2×2 distribution matrix X, $x_{11} > x_{21}$ but $x_{22} > x_{12}$. Now if we make a switch of attribute 2 between the two individuals, in the postswitch distribution matrix Y person 1's vector of attribute quantities is given by (x_{11}, x_{22}), whereas person 2 now possesses the vector (x_{21}, x_{12}). Since person 1, who had more of attribute 1, has more of attribute 2 as well after the switch, the correlation between the attributes has gone up. Note that a correlation increasing switch keeps the mean of each attribute constant.

A function $\hat{h} : R^d \to R^1$ is called $L-$ superadditive if for all $x, y \in R^d$, $\hat{h}(x \wedge y) + \hat{h}(x \vee y) \geq \hat{h}(x) + \hat{h}(y)$. For strict $L-$ superadditivity, the weak inequality is replaced by a strict inequality, whenever $x \wedge y \neq x$ and $x \vee y \neq y$ (*see* Marshall and Olkin, 1979, Chap. 6). A function $\hat{h} : R^d \to R^1$ is called $L-$ subadditive (strictly $L-$ subadditive) if $-\hat{h}$ is $L-$ superadditive (strictly $L-$ superadditive). If $\hat{h}$ is twice differentiable, then it is $L-$ superadditive (respectively strictly $L-$ superadditive; $L-$ subadditive; strictly $L-$ subadditive) if and only if for all distinct $1 \leq j, l \leq d$ and all $x \in R^d$, $\hat{h}_{jl} = (\partial^2 \hat{h}(x))/(\partial x_j \partial x_l) \geq 0$ (respectively $> 0, \leq 0$, and < 0).

The utilitarian social welfare function $W = \sum_{i=1}^{n} U(x_{i.})$ decreases under a correlation increasing switch if U is increasing and strictly $L-$ subadditive. Furthermore, if Y is obtained from X by such a switch and U is strictly $L-$ subadditive then $(U(x_{1.}), \ldots, U(x_{n.})) \geq_{\mathrm{GL}} (U(y_{1.}), \ldots, U(y_{n.}))$ (*see* Tsui, 1999).

Tsui's (1999) axiom on correlation increasing switch can now be stated as:

Correlation Increasing Majorization: For $X, Y \in M$, if Y is obtained from X by a correlation increasing switch, then $I(X) < I(Y)$.

The indices I_{TME} and I_{DVU} discussed in the earlier section satisfy this axiom. List (1999) suggested a generalization of the Atkinson (1970) index that satisfies this axiom. For all $X \in M_2$, define $X_C = X\Lambda_C$, where Λ_C is the $d \times d$ diagonal matrix diag $(1/\lambda(x_{.1}), \ldots, 1/\lambda(x_{.d}))$. The mean value of each attribute in the matrix X_C is 1. The generalized Atkinson index of List relies on the real valued function LI defined on M_2, by the implicit relation,

$$W(LI(X)\mathbf{1}) = W(X_C). \tag{5.17}$$

The List multidimensional relative inequality index is then defined as

$$I_{\mathrm{LM}}(X) = 1 - LI(X), \tag{5.18}$$

where $X \in M_2$. The multidimensional Atkinson index suggested by List is defined using a specific functional form of A. Note that I_{LM} is an alternative to the Kolm (1977) multidimensional inequality index.

It may be mentioned here that the Gajdos and Weymark (2005) multidimensional generalized Gini indices are not correctly responsive to Tsui's (1999) axiom on correlation increasing switch. The reason behind this is inconsistency of separability across attributes with the correlation of the distributions.

For the two-attribute case, Atkinson and Bourguignon 1982) studied implications of correlation increasing switch for the utilitarian social welfare function. The two attributes are substitutes if the utility function U is strictly $L-$ subadditive (the cross-partial derivative $U_{12} < 0$) and they are complements if U is strictly $L-$ superadditive ($U_{12} > 0$). The value of a utilitarian social welfare function increases under a correlation increasing switch if the two attributes are complements. That is why, Bourguignon and Chakravarty (2003) argued that inequality should increase or decrease in response to a correlation increasing switch between two attributes according as the attributes are substitutes or complements.

Finally, we present a discussion made along this line made by Bourguignon (1999). Assuming that $d = 2$, he considered the following form of the individual utility function

$$U(x_{i.}) = (a_1'' x_{i1}^{-\hat{\delta}} + a_2'' x_{i2}^{-\hat{\delta}})^{-(1+\bar{c})/\hat{\delta}}, \tag{5.19}$$

where $-1 < \bar{c} < 0$ is the inequality sensitivity parameter and $\hat{\delta} \geq -1$ represents the degree of substitutability between the two attributes and a_i'' is the weight assigned to the ith attribute. [See the discussion related to (5.14).] The following may then be regarded as an extension of the Dalton inequality index to the multidimensional setup:

$$I_{\mathrm{BDM}}(X) = 1 - \frac{\sum_{i=1}^{n} \left(a_1'' x_{i1}^{-\hat{\delta}} + a_2'' x_{i2}^{-\hat{\delta}}\right)^{-(1+\bar{c})/\hat{\delta}}}{n(a_1''(\lambda(x_{.1}))^{-\hat{\delta}} + a_2''(\lambda(x_{.2}))^{-\hat{\delta}})^{-(1+\bar{c})/\hat{\delta}}}. \tag{5.20}$$

This Bourguignon-Dalton index is continuous, normalized, symmetric, and uniformly majorized. However, it is not scale invariant. Further, it is quite close to I_{MM}. The main difference between them arises from normalization of individual welfare. In the latter, each individual aggregator is normalized by the mean aggregator and inequality as expressed as a $\bar{c}$-power mean of these normalized values. In the former, normalization is done using the welfare level of a person who enjoys the mean levels of the two attributes. The two indices differ by the simple transformation given below:

$$T_{\mathrm{BM}}(X) = \frac{\sum_{i=1}^{n} \left(a_1'' x_{i1}^{-\hat{\delta}} + a_2'' x_{i2}^{-\hat{\delta}}\right)^{-1/\hat{\delta}}}{n(a_1''(\lambda(x_{.1}))^{-\hat{\delta}} + a_2''(\lambda(x_{.2}))^{-\hat{\delta}})^{-1/\hat{\delta}}}. \tag{5.21}$$

It may be noted that this ratio itself can be regarded as an index of equality.

The condition for the cross derivative U_{12} to be positive and, therefore, for higher correlation to lead to less inequality becomes $\hat{\delta} + \bar{c} + 1 > 0$. By strict quasiconcavity of U, we have $\hat{\delta} > -1$ and $\bar{c} < 0$. Values of these parameters can be chosen appropriately to ensure increasing or decreasing inequality under a correlation increasing switch. More correlation corresponds to less inequality only when the substitutability between the attributes, as measured by the elasticity of substitution $1/(1+\hat{\delta})$, is below some level. However, it is unclear whether I_{MM} possesses this property.

5.6 Multidimensional Inequality and the Measurement of Occupational Segregation

This section shows how the methodology used for constructing multidimensional inequality indices can be transported to the measurement of occupational segregation which refers to inequality in the distribution of types of workers across occupational groups. In contrast, equality in the occupational distribution across groups is known as integration (*see* Duncan and Duncan, 1955; Hutchens, 2004; Chakravarty and Silber, 2007). Complete or perfect integration refers to the ideal situation where employees are allocated to different occupations in proportions to their shares in the population. Segregation arises if this condition for allocation of employees does not hold. Thus, segregation is concerned with comparison of actual distributions of types of workers across occupations with the ideal distribution that would arise if types had been allocated in proportions to their shares in the total population. Under given assumptions, an increase in the value of a segregation index will correspond to a reduction in the associated integration index and vice versa.

Consider a society with $T \geq 2$ types of people distributed over $H > 1$ groups or occupations. Examples of different types of workers are male, female, Asian, European etc. If $T = 2$, we may assume that the two types of employees are male and female. Let n_{ij} be the number of employees of type i in occupation $j(i = 1,2,\ldots,T; j = 1,2,\ldots,H)$. We may as well regard n_{ij} as the number of working hours of type i employees in occupation j. Each n_{ij} is a nonnegative real number. Our formulation allows noninteger values of n_{ij} because part-time workers can be treated as fractional workers. We denote the number of type$i$ people by n_i, that is, $n_i = \sum_{j=1}^{H} n_{ij} > 0, i = 1,2,\ldots\text{T}$. Thus, for each i, the number of type i people is assumed to be positive. An occupation distribution matrix X is a $T \times H$ matrix whose entries are n_{ij} values. We write M for the set of all $T \times H$ occupation distribution matrices.

An occupational segregation index O is a real valued function defined on M, that is, $O : M \to R^1$, where R^1 is the real line. For any $X \in M, O(X)$ indicates the extent of segregation that exists in X between T types of employees in H different occupations.

Following Hutchens (2004) and Chakravarty and Silber (2007), we now propose some axioms for an index of segregation.

Normalization: If $X \in M$ such that $n_{1l}/n_1 = n_{2l}/n_2 = \ldots = n_{\text{T}l}/n_{\text{T}}$ for all $l \in \{1,2,..,H\}$, then $O(X) = 0$.

Continuity: O is a continuous function on M.

Scale Invariance: For any $X \in M, O(X) = O(\Omega X)$, where Ω is the $T \times T$ diagonal matrix $\Omega = diag\,(\omega_1, \omega_2, \ldots, \omega_T)$ and $\omega_i > 0$ for all i.

Symmetry in Occupations: For any $X \in M$ if $Y \in M$ is obtained from by a permutation of columns of X, then $O(X) = O(Y)$.

Symmetry in Types: For any $X \in M, O(X) = O(\Pi X)$, where Π is any $T \times T$ permutation matrix.

Before we state the sixth axiom, let us explain the ones already proposed. Normalization says that there is zero segregation if employees are distributed across occupations in proportion to their shares in the working populations. By Continuity, the segregation index is not oversensitive to minor changes in the numbers of employees in different occupations. According to Scale Invariance if different types have different ratio scales, then any rescaling of the types will not change the level of segregation. Thus, if the total numbers of employees of different types are multiplied by a positive scalar and the shares of different types of workers in all the occupations remain the same then segregation does not change. Clearly, by this axiom, the segregation index remains unaltered under an l^i-fold replication of the ith type of workers, where $l^i \geq 2, i = 1, 2, \ldots, T$. The next axiom says that segregation is independent of the labeling of occupations. For instance, the level of segregation when we assign the number 1 to legal occupation and the number 2 to management occupation is the same as that when the assignment of numbers to these occupations is done in the opposite way. Symmetry in Types makes the types anonymous the way Symmetry in Occupations makes the occupations anonymous.

The two notions of symmetry clearly bring out the distinguishing features between the measurement of inequality and segregation. While in the former, only anonymity among individuals is assumed; in the latter, we assume anonymity in both types and occupations. As we have seen the reason for this is that no particular meaning is attached to the ways of arrangements of occupations and types. Therefore, the variables considered in the case of segregation are purely categorical, whereas in the case of inequality, the variables are not of this type.

The next axiom is regarding the movement of individuals between occupations. For any $X \in M$, we say that $X' \in M$ is obtained from X by a disequalizing movement of type l_1 people if, for j_1 and j_2, (i) $n_{lj_1} = n_{lj_2} = n'_{lj_1} = n'_{lj_2} > 0$, (ii) $(n_{l_1 j_1}/n_{lj_1}) < (n_{l_1 j_2}/n_{lj_2})$, (iii) $n'_{l_1 j_1} = n_{l_1 j_1} - c$ and $n'_{l_1 j_2} = n_{l_1 j_2} + c$ for $0 < c \leq n_{l_1 j_1}$, and (iv) $n_{ij} = n'_{ij}$, $i = 1, 2, \ldots, T; j \neq j_1, j_2$ and $l \neq l_1$. To understand this, let us consider the following occupation distribution matrix. Here we have $n_{22} = n_{23} = 3$, $(n_{12}/n_{22}) = (2/3) < (7/3) = (n_{13}/n_{23})$. If one woman moves from the second occupation to the third occupation, then occupation 3 will have eight women and occupation 2 will have one woman. This shift increases the proportion of female workers in the female dominant occupation 3 and the proportion of male in the male dominant occupation 2.

$$\begin{array}{r} \\ \\ \text{Women} \\ \text{Men} \end{array} \begin{array}{c} \text{Occupation} \\ \begin{array}{ccc} 1 & 2 & 3 \end{array} \\ \begin{bmatrix} 3 & 2 & 7 \\ 7 & 3 & 3 \end{bmatrix} \end{array}$$

This movement should increase segregation because of higher concentration in the occupation-wise distribution of women and men. This discussion enables us to state the following axiom of Hutchens (1991):

Movement Between Occupations: For any $X \in M$, if $X' \in M$ is obtained by a disequalizing movement from X, then $O(X) < O(X')$.

Assuming that there are only two types of workers, Chakravarty and Silber (2007) characterized the following segregation indices on the set of occupation distribution matrices with positive entries:

$$O_{AS}(X) = 1 - \left[\frac{1}{T}\sum_{i=1}^{T}\prod_{j=1}^{2}\left(\frac{n_{ij}}{n_i}\right)^{\hat{\alpha}}\right]^{1/2\hat{\alpha}}, \text{ where } 0 < \hat{\alpha} < 1 \text{ and}$$
$$\mathrm{O}_{AS}(X) = 1 - \prod_{i=1}^{T}\left[\prod_{j=1}^{2}\left(\frac{n_{ij}}{n_i}\right)^{1/2}\right]^{1/T}. \quad (5.22)$$

Since these indices employ Atkinson (1970) type aggregation to the products of proportions of employees of two types in different occupations, they may be referred to as the segregation counterparts to the multidimensional Atkinson indices. Thus, these indices are appropriate transformations of the multidimensional Atkinson indices to the measurement of segregation. A disequalizing movement between the occupations will increase segregation (as measured by the first index) by a higher amount as the value of $\hat{\alpha}$ decreases. For $\hat{\alpha} = 1/2$, the first member of the family becomes increasingly related to the Hutchens (2004) square root index O_{HUT}, a member of a family related to the generalized entropy indices of income inequality, as follows: $O_{HUT} = 1 - \mathrm{T}(1 - O_{AS})$.

In addition to satisfying all the axioms stated above, the indices given by (5.22) are also insensitive to the proportional division of occupations (Hutchens, 1991). For instance, if a large occupation with 120 women and 120 men are split into five suboccupations, each containing 24 women and 24 men, then segregation does not change. When there are only two types, Hutchens (1991) defined the segregation curve as the graph of cumulative proportions of type 1 employees against the corresponding proportions of type 2 employees, given that both proportions are arranged in nondecreasing order of (n_{1i}/n_{2i}). For any $X, Y \in M$, if Y segregation dominates X, where segregation dominance is defined in the same way as $\geq_{LC}$, then $O(X) < O(Y)$ for all segregation indices $O : M \to R^1$ that are symmetric in occupations, scale invariant, increasing under a disequalizing movement, and insensitive to proportional divisions of occupations. The converse is also true (Hutchens, 1991). The family of indices defined in (5.22) is consistent with the segregation dominance relation.

Chapter 6
The Measurement of Multidimensional Poverty

6.1 Introduction

In Chap. 2, we have presented a detailed and analytical discussion on the measurement of poverty using income as the only attribute of well-being. But as we have argued in Chap. 5, income is simply one of the many dimensions of well-being Therefore, poverty being a manifestation of insufficient well-being, should as well be regarded as a multidimensional phenomenon. In fact, there are many reasons for viewing poverty from a multidimensional perspective. The basic-needs approach regards poverty as lack of basic needs, and hence poverty is intrinsically multidimensional from this perspective. The importance of low income as a determinant of undernutrition is a debatable issue. (*See* Behrman and Deolikar, 1988; Dasgupta, 1993; Lipton and Ravallion, 1995; Ravallion, 1990, 1992.)

In the capability-functioning approach, poverty is regarded as a problem of capability failure. As Sen (1999) argued, capability failure captures the notion of poverty that people experience in day-to-day living condition. This approach constitutes a very sensible way of conceptualizing poverty since capability failure is generated from inability of possession of a wide range of characteristics related to the living standard rather than simply from the lowness of income. (*See also* Lewis and Ulph, 1988; Sen, 1985a, 1992; Townsend, 1979.)

An alternative way of looking at multidimensional poverty is in terms of social exclusion, which refers to exclusion of individuals from standard way of living and basic social activities (Townsend, 1979). A frequently used definition of social exclusion is "the process through which individuals or groups are wholly or partially excluded from full participation in society in which they live" (European Foundation, 1995, p. 4). According to Atkinson (1998), it is a relative concept, in order to say whether a person is socially excluded or not, it is necessary to look at the positions of the others in the society as well. It is a dynamic process in which exclusion of individuals from full participation can be taken as the end product. Since social exclusion refers to exclusion of individuals from economic and social activities, it is a multidimensional phenomenon. We may, therefore, say that it incorporates the process aspect of capability failure (Sen, 2002). As Sen (2000) argued, if capability

S.R. Chakravarty, *Inequality, Polarization and Poverty: Advances in Distributional Analysis,* 139
Economic Studies in Inequality, Social Exclusion and Well-Being 6,
DOI: 10.1007/978-0-387-79253-8_6, © Springer Science+Business Media, LLC 2009

poverty is a consequence of lack of freedom, social exclusion curtails the freedom additionally. Thus, there is a close relationship between the two notions of poverty.

The human poverty index suggested by the UNDP (1997) can be regarded as a multidimensional index of poverty in the capability-failure framework. It is a summary indicator of the country level deprivations in the living standard of a population in the three basic dimensions of life, namely, decent living standard, life expectancy at birth, and educational attainment rate. Since an index of this type aggregates failures at the national level, it does not take into account the individual failures.

In this chapter, we assume that each person possesses a vector of attributes of well-being and a direct way of identification of the poor checks whether he has "minimally acceptable levels" (Sen, 1992 p. 139) of different attributes. These minimally acceptable quantities of the attributes represent their threshold levels that are necessary for maintaining a subsistence living standard. Indices of multidimensional poverty that are based on individual failures or shortfalls of attribute quantities from respective thresholds have been suggested, among others, by Chakravarty et al. (1998), Bourguignon and Chakravarty (1999, 2003), Tsui (2002), Alkire and Foster (2007), and Lugo and Maasoumi (2008a, b). Bourguignon and Chakravarty (2008) also investigated the issue whether one distribution of multidimensional attributes exhibits less poverty than another for all multidimensional poverty indices satisfying certain postulates (*see also* Duclos et al., 2006a, b).

In different sections of this chapter, we discuss a set of desirable axioms for multidimensional poverty indices, analyze their implications, and examine alternative multidimensional poverty indices and the poverty dominance criteria.

6.2 Postulates for an Index of Multidimensional Poverty

We follow the notation adopted in Chap.5. The number of attributes of well-being is d and the number of persons in the society is n. Each attribute is assumed to be measurable on a ratio scale. Thus, we rule out the possibility of including a variable of the type that says whether a person is ill or not (*see* Sect. 5.2). The matrix $X = (x_{ij})_{n\times d}$ is a typical distribution matrix whose (i, j)th entry x_{ij} shows the quantity of attribute j possessed by person i, $1 \le i \le n, 1 \le j \le d$. We assume that $X \in M \in \{M_1', M_2, M_3\}$ is arbitrary, where M_1' is the set of all $n \times d$ matrices with nonnegative entries and, M_2 andM_3 are the same as in Chap. 5 (*see* Sect. 5.2).

In the present multivariate setup, a poverty threshold or cutoff is defined for each attribute. These cutoffs represent the minimal quantities of the d attributes necessary for maintaining a subsistence standard of living. Let $\underline{z} = (z_1, z_2, \ldots, z_d) \in Z$ be the vector of poverty thresholds, where Z is a nonempty subset of Γ_+^d, the strictly positive part of the d dimensional Euclidean space. The censored distribution matrix associated with X is denoted by X^*, where the (i, j)th entry x_{ij}^* of X^* is defined as $x_{ij}^* = \min\{x_{ij}, z_j\}$.

In this framework, person i is regarded as poor or deprived with respect to attribute j if $x_{ij} < z_j$. Otherwise, he is called nonpoor in attribute j. Thus, we are using the weak definition to identify a poor person in a dimension. The deprivation score of a person is the total number of dimensions in which he is poor. If a person is poor in a dimension then we say that it is a meager dimension for him. Person i is called rich if $x_{ij} \geq z_j$ holds for all $1 \leq j \leq d$. Each individual is regarded as either poor or nonpoor in a dimension. But there can be a wide range of cutoffs for the attributes that coexist in a reasonable harmony (*see* Thorbecke, 2006). The possibility that the relevant information is missing may lead to an ambiguity in the concept of poverty. This may as well arise from insufficiency of information on consumption quantities of the attributes. With a view to tackling problems of this type in which indefiniteness arises from ambiguity, the fuzzy set approach appears to be quite justifiable.[1]

In this chapter, we assume that there is complete information on quantities of the attributes and thresholds. Let $\text{SP}_j(X)$ (or SP_j) be the set of persons who are poor with respect to attribute j in any given $X \in M$. Bourguignon and Chakravarty (2003) argued that a very simple way of counting the number of poor in the multiattribute structure is to define the poverty indicator variable $\text{ID}(x_{i.}, \underline{z})$ which takes on the value one if there is at least one dimension j in which person i is poor, where the row vector $x_{i.}$, the ith row of X, shows the quantities of d attributes possessed by person i. Otherwise, it takes on the value zero. Formally,

$$\text{ID}(x_{i.}, \underline{z}) = \begin{cases} 1 & \text{if } \exists\ j \in \{1, 2, \ldots, d\} : x_{ij} < z_j \\ 0, & \text{otherwise.} \end{cases} \tag{6.1}$$

Then the total number of poor in the multidimensional framework is given by $n_p(X) = \sum_{i=1}^{n} \text{ID}(x_{i.}, \underline{z})$. Hence, the multidimensional headcount ratio is given by n_p/n. This method of identifying the set of multidimensional poor persons is referred to as the union method of identification. An alternative identification approach is the intersection method which says that a person is poor if he is poor in all dimensions and this leads us to identify the number of poor as the total number of persons who are poor in all dimensions. But if a person is poor in one dimension and nonpoor in another, then trade-off between these dimensions may not be possible, which in turn rules out the possibility that he becomes nonpoor in both the dimensions. An example is an old beggar who cannot trade-off his high age for low income to become rich in both income and life expectancy. Such a person cannot be regarded as rich simply because of his high longevity. Therefore, this definition does not appear to be appropriate. Alkire and Foster (2007) defined person i as multidimensionally poor if $x_{ij} < z_j$ holds for $\bar{l}$ many values of j, where $\bar{l}$ is some integer between 1 and d. Clearly, this intermediate identification method coincides with the union or the intersection method as $\bar{l} = 1$ or d (*see also* Gordon et al., 2003; Mack and Lindsay, 1985).

A multidimensional poverty index P is a nonconstant real-valued function defined on the Cartesian product $M \times Z$. For any $X \in M$ and $\underline{z} \in Z$, $P(X, \underline{z})$ determines the intensity of poverty associated with the attribute matrix X and the threshold vector $\underline{z}$.

---

[1] See Cerioli and Zani (1990), Cheli and Lemmi (1995), Chiappero Martinetti (1996, 2006), Balestrino (1998), Qizilbash (2003, 2006), Deutsch and Silber (2005), Betti et al. (2006, 2008) and Chakravarty (2006).

Most of the postulates we consider below for an arbitrary P are generalizations of income-based poverty axioms. They are stated in terms of an arbitrary population size n. In presenting these axioms, we follow Chakravarty et al. (1998), Bourguignon and Chakravarty (1999, 2003, 2008), Tsui (2002), and Chakravarty and Silber (2008).

Focus Axiom: For any $(X,\underline{z}) \in M \times Z$ and for any person i and attribute j such that $x_{ij} \geq z_j$, an increase in x_{ij}, such that all other attribute quantities in X remain unchanged, does not change the extent of poverty $P(X,\underline{z})$.

Normalization Axiom: For any $(X,\underline{z}) \in M \times Z$ if $x_{ij} \geq z_j$ for all i and j, then $P(X,\underline{z}) = 0$.

Monotonicity Axiom: For any $(X,\underline{z}) \in M \times Z$, any person i and attribute j such that $x_{ij} < z_j$, an increase in x_{ij}, given that other attribute levels in X remain unaltered, decreases the poverty value $P(X,\underline{z})$.

Population Replication Invariance Axiom: For any $(X,\underline{z}) \in M \times Z$, $P(X,\underline{z}) = P(X^{(l)},\underline{z})$, where $X^{(l)}$ is the l-fold replication of X, that is, $X^{(l)} = (X^1, X^2, \ldots X^l)$ with each $X^i = X$, and $l \geq 2$ is arbitrary.

Symmetry Axiom: For any $(X,\underline{z}) \in M \times Z$, $P(X,\underline{z}) = P(\Pi X,\underline{z})$, where Π is any $n \times n$ permutation matrix.

Continuity Axiom: $P(X,\underline{z})$ is continuous in $(X,\underline{z})$.

Subgroup Decomposability Axiom: Let $X^1, X^2, \ldots, X^J$ are J distribution matrices of d attributes over population sizes $n_1, n_2, \ldots, n_J$ such that $\sum_{i=1}^{J} n_i = n$. Then for $\underline{z} \in Z, P(X,\underline{z}) = \sum_{i=1}^{J} \frac{n_i}{n} P(X^i,\underline{z})$, where $X = (X^1, \ldots, X^J) \in M$.

Transfer Axiom: For any $\underline{z} \in Z$, $X,Y \in M$ if X is obtained from Y by the Uniform Majorization Principle or the Uniform Pigou-Dalton Transfers Principle, where the transfers are among the poor, then $P(X,\underline{z}) \leq P(Y,\underline{z})$.

Increasing Threshold Levels Axiom: For any $X \in M$, $P(X,\underline{z})$ is increasing in z_j for all j.

Nonpoverty Growth Axiom: For any $(Y,\underline{z}) \in M \times Z$, if X is obtained from Y by adding a rich person to the society, then $P(X,\underline{z}) \leq P(Y,\underline{z})$.

Scale Invariance Axiom: For all $(X^1,\underline{z}^1) \in M \times Z$, $P(X^1,\underline{z}^1) = P(X^2,\underline{z}^2)$, where $X^2 = X^1\Omega$, $\underline{z}^2 = \underline{z}^1\Omega$, and $\Omega = \text{diag}(\omega_1, \omega_2, \ldots, \omega_d)$, $\omega_i > 0$ for all i.

The Normalization, Population Replication Invariance, Continuity, Subgroup Decomposability, Increasing Threshold Levels, Nonpoverty Growth, and Scale Invariance Axioms are multidimensional versions of the corresponding income-based poverty axioms. The Monotonicity Axiom says that poverty decreases if the condition of a person who is poor in a dimension improves. It parallels the Strong Monotonicity Axiom discussed in Chap. 2 and implies the *Dimensional Monotonicity Axiom* of Alkire and Foster (2007) which demands that poverty should fall if improvement makes the person rich in the attribute. The Transfer Axiom is the poverty counterpart to the majorization criteria of multidimensional inequality indices. According to the Focus Axiom, if a person is nonpoor with respect to an attribute, then improving his position in the attribute does not change the level of poverty, even if he/she is poor in the other attributes. That is, poverty is independent of quantities of attributes that are above thresholds. If one views poverty in terms of shortfalls of attribute quantities from thresholds then this axiom is quite sensible. It rules out trade-off between two attributes of a person who is in poverty with respect to one but not in poverty with respect to the other. For instance, if education and a composite good are two attributes, more education above the threshold cannot be traded off to compensate the lack of composite good whose quantity is below its threshold. Equivalently, we say that above the threshold level of an attribute, the isopoverty contour of an individual becomes parallel to the axis that represents the quantities of the attribute. This, however, does not exclude the possibility of a trade-off between the attributes if a person is poor with respect to both of them. We can also consider a weak version of the axiom which says that the poverty index is independent of attribute quantities of rich persons only. Clearly, in this case the trade-off of the type we have discussed above is permissible because we do not assume that the poverty index is independent of the quantities of attributes in which a person is non-poor. But although trade-off is allowed, poverty is never eliminated. This means that there is a positive lower bound of the poverty index. Consequently, the isopoverty contour becomes a line asymptotically.

The next axiom, suggested by Bourguignon and Chakravarty (2003), is concerned with poverty change under a correlation increasing switch (*see* Chap. 5). If the two attributes involved in the correlation increasing switch are close to each other, that is, they are substitutes, then one can compensate the smallness of the other in the definition of individual poverty. Then increasing correlation between the attributes will not reduce poverty. The reason behind this is that because of closeness between the attributes, the switch can be regarded as a regressive rearrangement in the sense that the richer poor is becoming even better-off after the switch. This in turn makes the poorer poor worse-off. Assuming that the poverty index is subgroup decomposable, the following Bourguignon-Chakravarty axiom can be stated:

Nondecreasing Poverty Under Correlation Increasing Switch Axiom: For any $(X,\underline{z}) \in M \times Z$, if $Y \in M$ is obtained from X by a correlation increasing switch between two poor persons who are poor in the two concerned attributes, then $P(X,\underline{z}) \le P(Y,\underline{z})$ if the two attributes are substitutes.

The corresponding property, when the attributes are complements, demands that poverty should not increase under such a switch. Note that for these two properties to be well defined, the two persons should be poor in both the attributes involved in the switch. If the poverty index is insensitive to a correlation increasing switch, then the underlying attributes are independent.

6.3 Indices of Multidimensional Poverty

The objective of this section is to discuss some important indicators for multidimensional poverty and analyze their properties. We begin with the observation that by repeated application of the Subgroup Decomposability Axiom, the poverty index can be written as

$$P(X,\underline{z}) = \frac{1}{n}\sum_{i=1}^{n}\zeta(x_{i.},\underline{z}), \tag{6.2}$$

where $\zeta(x_{i.},\underline{z}) = P(x_{i.},\underline{z})$ is the individual multidimensional poverty function (*see* 2.2). Thus, the symmetric and population replication invariant index P in (6.2) is simply the average of individual poverty levels.

While the Subgroup Decomposability Axiom deals with nonoverlapping subgroups of the population, we can have an analogous postulate for attributes, which we refer to as Factor Decomposability Axiom. According to the Factor Decomposability Axiom, overall poverty is a weighted average of poverty levels for individual attributes. Formally,

Factor Decomposability Axiom: For any $(X,\underline{z}) \in M \times Z$,

$$P(X,\underline{z}) = \sum_{j=1}^{d} \hat{b}_j P(x_{.j}, z_j), \tag{6.3}$$

where the nonnegative sequence $\{\hat{b}_j\}$ satisfies the restriction that $\sum_{j=1}^{d} \hat{b}_j = 1$ and $x_{.j}$ is the jth column of the distribution matrix X. That is, $x_{.j}$ gives the distribution of attribute j among n persons. The weight $\hat{b}_j \geq 0$ assigned to attribute j reflects the importance of this attribute in the aggregation defined in (6.3). It may also be interpreted as the priority that the government assigns for removing poverty from the jth dimension of well-being. The contribution of dimension j to overall poverty is given by the amount $\hat{b}_j P(x_{.j}, z_j)$. Complete elimination of poverty from dimension j will reduce total poverty exactly by this quantity. Thus, the percentage contribution of dimension j to overall poverty becomes $100(\hat{b}_j P((x_{.j}, z_j))/P(X,z)$ (*see* Alkire and Foster, 2007; Chakravarty and Silber, 2008; Chakravarty et al., 1998).

If the two decomposition postulates are employed simultaneously, we can calculate each subgroup's contribution for each dimension. To see this, suppose that there are only two subgroups with population sizes n_1 and n_2, and the corresponding components of the distribution matrix X are X^1 and X^2 so that $X = (X^1, X^2)$. Then by the Subgroup Decomposability Axiom $P(X,\underline{z}) = (n_1/n)P(X^1,\underline{z}) + (n_1/n)(X^2,\underline{z})$, which in view of (6.3), for $d = 2$, becomes

$$P(X,\underline{z}) = \frac{n_1}{n}[\hat{b}_1 P(x^1_{.1}, z_1) + \hat{b}_2 P(x^1_{.2}, z_2)] + \frac{n_2}{n}[\hat{b}_1 P(x^2_{.1}, z_1) + \hat{b}_2 P(x^2_{.2}, z_2)], \tag{6.4}$$

where $x^i_{.j}$ is the jth column of the matrix X^i and $P(x^i_{.j}, z_j)$ is the poverty level in subgroup i for dimension $j, i, j = 1, 2$. By looking at the individual components of the micro-breakdown of poverty, as shown in (6.4), we can identify simultaneously the population subgroup(s) as well as dimensions(s) for which poverty levels are very high. For instance, suppose we first note that between the two subgroups, the poverty level for subgroup 1 is higher. Next, it is observed that this subgroup's poverty for dimension 2 is more, that is, $\hat{b}_2 P(x^1_{.2}, z_2) > \hat{b}_1 \mathrm{P}(x^1_{.1}, z_1)$. Therefore, the subgroup-attribute combination (1,2) of the population should get maximum attention from antipoverty perspective. This type of two-way splitting of poverty becomes especially helpful when the limited resources of the society may not be sufficient for removal of poverty from one entire subgroup or for one dimension of the entire population (*see* Chakravarty and Silber, 2008; Chakravarty et al., 1998).

The general form of the poverty index fulfilling the two decomposability postulates is given by

$$P(X,\underline{z}) = \frac{1}{n}\sum_{j=1}^{d} \hat{b}_j \sum_{i\in SP_j} \zeta(x_{ij}, z_j). \tag{6.5}$$

Under the Scale Invariance, Focus, Normalization, Monotonicity, and Transfer Axioms, we can rewrite $\zeta(x_{ij}, z_j)$ as $h(x_{ij}/z_j)$, where $h : R^1_+ \to R^1$ is continuous, decreasing, convex, and $h(x_{ij}/z_j) = 0$ for all $x_{ij} \geq z_j$ (*see* 2.19). In view of the assumption that $h(x_{ij}/z_j) = 0$ for all $x_{ij} \geq z_j$, we can restrict attention on the censored matrix X^*. By assumptions on $h, P(X,\underline{z})$ in (6.5) is increasing in threshold limits and satisfies the Nonpoverty Growth Axiom. However, the entire family of indices given by (6.5) is insensitive to a correlation increasing switch.

To illustrate the formula (6.5), let $h(x^*_{ij}/z_j) = -\log(x^*_{ij}/z_j)$, where $x^*_{ij} > 0$. Then the resulting index becomes the multidimensional Watts index of poverty

$$P_{\mathrm{WM}}(X,\underline{z}) = \frac{1}{n}\sum_{i=1}^{n}\sum_{j=1}^{d} \hat{b}_j \log\left(\frac{z_j}{x^*_{ij}}\right), \tag{6.6}$$

where $X \in M_3$. Tsui (2002) and Chakravarty and Silber (2008) characterized a more general form of P_{WM} which requires that $\hat{b}_j \geq 0$, with $>$ for some j, without the restriction $\sum_{j=1}^{d} \hat{b}_j = 1$. It is a normalized version of the Lugo and Maasoumi (2008a) first class of IT poverty indices based on the "aggregate poverty line approach." Chakravarty et al. (2008) employed this index to investigate different causal factors of poverty. The transfer sensitivity property of P_{WM} is similar to its single-dimensional sister.

Next, suppose that $h(x^*_{ij}/z_j) = (1 - x^*_{ij}/z_j)^{\alpha_j}$, where $\alpha_j \geq 1$ is a parameter. Then the resulting index is a multidimensional generalization of the Foster et al. index (Foster et al., 1984):

$$P_{\mathrm{FGTM}}(X,\underline{z}) = \frac{1}{n}\sum_{i=1}^{n}\sum_{j=1}^{d} \hat{b}_j \left(1 - \frac{x^*_{ij}}{z_j}\right)^{\alpha_j}. \tag{6.7}$$

If $\alpha_j = 1$ for all j, then P_{FGTM} becomes a weighted average of the product of $\mathrm{PD}_j = q_j/n$, the proportion of population in poverty in dimension j, and the average of the relative gaps $\mathrm{RG}_j = \sum_{i\in SP_j}(1 - x^*_{ij})/q_j z_j$, across all dimensions. If $\alpha_j = 2$ for all j, then the formula can be written as

$$P_{\mathrm{FGTM}}(X,\underline{z}) = \frac{1}{n}\sum_{j=1}^{d} \hat{b}_j \mathrm{PD}_j(\mathrm{RG}^2_j + (1 - \mathrm{RG}^2_j)(I^j_{\mathrm{CV}})^2), \tag{6.8}$$

where I^j_{CV} is the coefficient of variation of the distribution of attribute j among the associated deprived persons. Given other things, an increase in I^j_{CV}, say through a rank-preserving regressive transfer between two persons for whom dimension j is meager, increases the poverty index. Thus, the decomposition in (6.8) shows that the poverty index is increasingly related to the dimension-wise inequality levels of the poor.

Finally, for the specification $1-(x^*_{ij}/z_j)^{e_j}$, where $0 < e_j \leq 1$, the associated poverty index turns out to be

$$P_{\text{CM}}(X,\underline{z}) = \frac{1}{n}\sum_{i=1}^{n}\sum_{j=1}^{d}\hat{b}_j\left(1-\left(\frac{x^*_{ij}}{z_j}\right)^{e_j}\right). \tag{6.9}$$

This form of the multidimensional Chakravarty index was considered by Chakravarty et al. (1998). Given other things, the index is increasing in e_j for all j. For $e_j = 1$, it coincides with the particular case of P_{FGTM} when $\alpha_j = 1, 1 \leq j \leq d$. On the other hand, as $e_j \to 0$ for all j, P_{CM} approaches its lower bound, zero. As the value of e_j decreases over the interval $(0,1]$, P_{CM} shows greater sensitivity to transfers at lower down the scale of the distribution of attribute j.

We derive formula (6.5) from (6.2) assuming that $\zeta(x_{i.},\underline{z})$ satisfies an additivity condition across dimensions. A more general representation of subgroup decomposable indices can be made by defining transformations (not necessarily additive) of dimension-wise poverty gaps of the individuals in different subgroups. The Bourguignon-Chakravarty general form of the multidimensional poverty index is based on this type of aggregation:

$$P_{\text{BC}}(X,\underline{z}) = \frac{1}{n}\sum_{i=1}^{n}\bar{h}\left(\left(\sum_{j=1}^{d}\left(\bar{b}_j\left(1-\frac{x^*_{ij}}{z_j}\right)\right)^{\bar{\eta}}\right)^{1/\bar{\eta}}\right), \tag{6.10}$$

where $\bar{h}$ is increasing, convex, and $\bar{h}(0) = 0$, $\bar{b}_j$ is the positive weight assigned to poverty gaps in dimension j and $\bar{\eta} > 1$ is a parameter that enables us to parameterize the elasticity of substitution between relative shortfalls in different dimensions. If $\bar{h}$ is the identity function then for $\bar{\eta} = 1$, at the first stage P_{BC} adds the dimension-wise relative gaps $(1-x^*_{ij}/z_j)$ weighted by the sequence $\{\bar{b}_j\}$ and then these weighted gaps are averaged across individuals. In this case, we have straight-line individual isopoverty contours and the relative gaps are perfectly substitutable.

If $\bar{\eta} \to \infty$, then the corresponding limiting form of P_{BC} is given by

$$P_{\text{BC}}(X,\underline{z}) = \frac{1}{n}\sum_{i=1}^{n}\bar{h}\left(\max_j\left\{1-\frac{x^*_{ij}}{z_j}\right\}\right). \tag{6.11}$$

Since the two-dimensional individual isopoverty curves associated with the functional form (6.11) are of rectangular shape, there is no scope for substitutability between the two relative shortfalls in this case. The informational requirement of this index is minimal, we only need information on the relative shortfalls $(1-x^*_{ij}/z_j)$ and a functional form for $\bar{h}$ to perform the aggregation. This index is nonincreasing under a correlation increasing switch. [*See* Bourguignon and Chakravarty (1999), for further discussion.]

An alternative of interest arises from the Foster et al. (1984) type specification $\bar{h}(v) = v^{\alpha}$, where $\alpha > 0$. The corresponding member of the family P_{BC} in (6.10) is given by

$$P_{\mathrm{BC}}(X, \underline{z}) = \frac{1}{n}\sum_{i=1}^{n}\left[\sum_{j=1}^{d}\bar{b}_j\left(1 - \frac{x_{ij}^{*}}{z_j}\right)^{\bar{\eta}}\right]^{\alpha/\bar{\eta}}. \tag{6.12}$$

The stages of aggregation employed in (6.12) are as follows. We first aggregate the transformed relative poverty shortfalls $(1-(x_{ij}^{*}/z_j)^{\bar{\eta}})$ of each person across dimensions into an aggregate relative shortfall using the coefficients $\bar{b}_j$. At the second stage, we take the average of such shortfalls, raised to the power α, over the whole population, to define multidimensional poverty. The index in (6.12) is the symmetric mean of power α of aggregated transformed relative poverty shortfalls of individuals in different dimensions. Therefore, it may be regarded as an alternative multidimensional generalization of the Foster et al. (1984) index. As the value of α increases, it becomes more sensitive toward extreme poverty. It is nondecreasing or nonincreasing under a correlation increasing switch depending on whether α is greater or less than $\bar{\eta}$.

Tsui (2002) characterized a family of multidimensional poverty indices using the multidimensional version of the Subgroup Consistency Axiom. This family turns out to be a generalization of the Chakravarty (1983c) index. The functional form of the Tsui family of indices is given by

$$P_{\mathrm{TCM}}(X, \underline{z}) = \frac{1}{n}\sum_{i=1}^{n}\left[\prod_{j=1}^{d}\left(\frac{z_j}{x_{ij}^{*}}\right)^{\bar{e}_j} - 1\right], \tag{6.13}$$

where $X \in M_3$ and the nonnegative parameters $\bar{e}_j$'s have to be chosen such that different postulates are satisfied. For instance, if $d = 2$, the restrictions $\bar{e}_1(\bar{e}_1+1) \geq 0$ and $\bar{e}_1\bar{e}_2(\bar{e}_1\bar{e}_2+1) \geq 0$ are necessary for fulfillment of the Transfers Axiom. These two conditions are guaranteed by nonnegativity of $\bar{e}_1$ and $\bar{e}_2$. Nonnegativity of $\bar{e}_1\bar{e}_2$ ensures that P_{TCM} is nondecreasing under a correlation increasing switch.

Lugo and Maasoumi (2008b) employed an information theory-based approach to the design of multidimensional poverty indices. Their index is subgroup decomposable and the individual poverty function relies on the same aggregation rule, as employed in Maasoumi (1986), for aggregating the attributes of a person (*see* Sect. 5.4). Then a Foster et al. (1984) type transformation is used to aggregate the individual indices into an overall index. More precisely, the Lugo-Maasoumi index of poverty is given by

$$P_{\mathrm{LMM}}(X, \underline{z}) = \begin{cases} \frac{1}{n}\sum_{i=1}^{n}\left(1 - \frac{\left(\sum_{j=1}^{d} a_j''(x_{ij}^{*})^{-\hat{\delta}}\right)^{-1/\hat{\delta}}}{\left(\sum_{j=1}^{d} a_j''(z_j)^{-\hat{\delta}}\right)^{-1/\hat{\delta}}}\right)^{\alpha}, \hat{\delta} \neq 0, \\ \frac{1}{n}\sum_{i=1}^{n}\left(1 - \frac{\prod_{j=1}^{d}(x_{ij}^{*})^{a_j''}}{\prod_{j=1}^{d}(z_j)^{a_j''}}\right)^{\alpha}, \hat{\delta} = 0, \end{cases} \tag{6.14}$$

where $X \in M_3$, a''_j and $\hat{\delta}$ are the same as in σ_i used in (5.14) and $\alpha > 0$. Note that in this case, the poverty thresholds are also aggregated using the same transformation. By construction, this index is independent of the attribute quantities that are above the corresponding thresholds and hence it is focused. Lugo and Maasoumi (2008b) also considered a variant of the index that meets the weak version of the Focus Axiom.

Alkire and Foster (2007) suggested an index that relies on the intermediate identification method. For any distribution matrix X, they defined the deprivation function of person i in dimension j as $d_{ij}^{\alpha} = (1 - x_{ij}/z_j)^{\alpha}$ if $x_{ij} < z_j$ while $d_{ij}^{\alpha} = 0$ if $x_{ij} \geq z_j$ and $\alpha > 0$. This function is then used to identify the poor persons in their framework as follows: define $d_{ij}^{\alpha}(\bar{l}) = d_{ij}^{\alpha}$ if the deprivation score of person i is at least $\bar{l}$, while $d_{ij}^{\alpha}(\bar{l}) = 0$ if the deprivation score is less than $\bar{l}$. That is, we consider the transformed relative shortfalls $(1 - x_{ij}/z_j)^{\alpha}$ of persons i in different dimensions and check if he has positive shortfalls in at least $\bar{l}$ dimensions, in which case he is treated as multidimensionally poor. Equivalently, we say that person i is deprived in the Alkire-Foster sense if his deprivation score is at least $\bar{l}$. The Alkire-Foster multidimensional poverty index is then defined as

$$P_{\mathrm{AFM}}(X, \underline{z}) = \frac{1}{nd} \sum_{i=1}^{n} \sum_{j=1}^{d} d_{ij}^{\alpha}(\bar{l}). \tag{6.15}$$

P_{AFM} is the sum of α powers of the relative poverty gaps of the poor divided by the maximum possible value that the sum can take. Note that in (6.7), if we assume that $\hat{b}_j = 1/d$, $\alpha_j = \alpha$ for all $1 \leq j \leq d$ and adopt the intermediate notion of identification, then it coincides with P_{AFM}.

As we have mentioned in Chap. 5, some of the dimensions of well-being may be of ordinal type. Therefore, each variable representing a dimension can be transformed using an increasing function which need not be identical across dimensions. Let $\mathrm{TR}_j : R_+^1 \to R_+^1$ be an arbitrary increasing function. Thus, for each j, x_{ij} gets transformed into $\mathrm{TR}_j(x_{ij})$. Likewise, for each j, z_j becomes $\mathrm{TR}_j(z_j)$. Now, measurability information invariance requires that the poverty level based on x_{ij} and z_j values should be same as that calculated using $\mathrm{TR}_j(x_{ij})$ and $\mathrm{TR}_j(z_j)$ values, where $1 \leq i \leq n$ and $1 \leq j \leq d$. Clearly, the indices based on shortfalls of the type $(1 - x_{ij}/z_j)$ may not fulfill the required information invariance assumption. The reason is that $(1 - \mathrm{TR}_j(x_{ij})/\mathrm{TR}_j(z_j))$ may not be equal to $(1 - x_{ij}/z_j)$, $1 \leq i \leq n$, and $1 \leq j \leq d$. However, the headcount ratio remains unaltered under this type of transformations. Thus, if some of the dimensions are ordinally measurable and the remaining dimensions are measurable on ratio scales, then the headcount ratio is a suitable index of poverty. Another index that survives this requirement is the Alkire and Foster (2007) dimension adjusted headcount ratio. It is given by the total number of deprivation scores of the poor in the Alkire-Foster sense divided by nd, the maximum deprivation score that could be experienced by all people. This index is obtained as the limiting case of P_{AFM} as $\alpha \to 0$. It satisfies the Dimensional Monotonicity Axiom, that is, a reduction in the deprivation score of a person decreases the index. However, the headcount ratio does not fulfill this axiom.

6.4 Multidimensional Poverty Orderings

In this section, we are concerned with the ranking of distribution matrices by a given set of poverty indices assuming that the threshold limits are the same. For the sake of simplicity, we assume that there are only two attributes of well-being. That is, our objective is to deal with two-dimensional poverty-measure ordering.

In order to simplify the exposition, a continuous representation of the bivariate distribution is considered. The cumulative distribution function $G(x_1,x_2)$ is defined on the range $[0,\hat{v}_1]\times[0,\hat{v}_2]$. (Since the formulation involves a continuum of population, the suffix i in $x_{i.}$ is dropped.) The marginal distribution function for attribute i is denoted by G_i, $i=1,2$. Our objective now is to compare two distributions represented by the distribution functions G and G^*. The difference $G(x_1,x_2)-G^*(x_1,x_2)$ will be denoted by $\Delta G(x_1,x_2)$. Assuming that the poverty index is subgroup decomposable, we can write it as

$$P(G,\underline{z})=\int_0^{\hat{v}_1}\int_0^{\hat{v}_2}\zeta(x_1,x_2,z_1,z_2)\mathrm{d}G. \tag{6.16}$$

If ζ is twice differentiable then positivity of ζ_{12}, the cross partial derivative of ζ with respect to attribute quantities, means that the two attributes are substitutes. If ζ_{12} is negative, then the attributes are complements. The intermediate situation $\zeta_{12}=0$ means that they are independent. We write $\Delta\mathrm{PG}(G,G^*,\underline{z})$ for the poverty difference $P(G,\underline{z})-P(G^*,\underline{z})$.

The following theorem of Bourguignon and Chakravarty (2008) can now be stated:

Theorem 6.1. *Let G and G^* be two bivariate distribution functions on the same range $[0,\hat{v}_1]\times[0,\hat{v}_2]$.*

Assume that the poverty index is twice differentiable. Then the following conditions are equivalent:

(i) $\Delta P(G,G^*,\underline{z})\leq 0$ for all poverty indices that satisfy the Focus, Symmetry, Population Replication Invariance, Subgroup Decomposability, Monotonicity, and Nondecreasingness of Poverty under Correlation Increasing Switch Axioms.

(ii) $\Delta G_i(x_i)\leq 0$ for all $x_i<z_i$ for $i=1,2$, and $\Delta G(x_1,x_2)\leq 0$ for all $x_1<z_1$ and $x_2<z_2$.

Theorem 6.1 demands that poverty dominance under properties stated in condition (i) requires the headcount ratio in each dimension not to be higher for all threshold limits below the thresholds z_i and the headcount ratio in the two-dimensional space, defined by any combination of poverty lines below the threshold values (z_1,z_2), not to be higher. That is, weak single dimensional dominance in each dimension and weak two dimensional dominance on the set of poor persons are required simultaneously. This two-dimensional dominance simply means that the headcount ratio should not be higher in the intersection of the two sets in which the individuals are poor attribute-wise. Note that this situation arises when the two attributes are substitutes.

If in condition (i) of Theorem 6.1 we replace nondecreasingness of poverty under correlation increasing switch by its nonincreasingness counterpart and retain all other assumptions, then the corresponding equivalent condition becomes $\Delta G(x_1)+\Delta G_2(x_2)-\Delta G(x_1,x_2)\leq 0$, for all $x_1<z_1$ and/or $x_2<z_2$. When evaluated at $x_1=0$ and $x_2=0$, this condition implies weak single-dimensional headcount ratio dominances. Dominance in the two-dimensional space thus requires weak single-dimensional dominances. The additional condition that the headcount ratio should not be higher in the union of the two sets in which people are poor dimension-wise has to be fulfilled. In this case, the two attributes are complements.

If the two attributes are neither substitutes nor complements, then instead of nondecreasingness of poverty under a correlation increasing switch, we assume in condition (i) of Theorem 6.1 that poverty does not change with respect to such a switch and maintain other assumptions. The equivalent dominance condition becomes $\Delta G_i(x_i)\leq 0$ for all $x_i<z_i$ for $i=1,2$. This means that the individual poverty function is additive across components. In this case, we simply have weak single-dimensional headcount ratio dominances. Equivalently weak first-order stochastic dominance for each marginal distribution is required. The reason behind this is that because of independence between the attributes we simply need to check attribute-wise dominance. Since in the case of independence, the dominance condition reduces to the single-dimensional ordering, the attribute-wise second-order stochastic dominance can also be employed. Duclos et al. (2006a) considered bivariate poverty orderings using an alternative set of assumptions. Their framework treats the attributes only as substitutes. There is a major difference between the Bourguignon-Chakravarty and the Duclos et al. frameworks because the latter assumes the dependence of the threshold limit of one dimension on that of the other and vice versa.

Extended Bibliography

Aaberge R (2000) Characterizations of Lorenz curves and income distributions. Social Choice and Welfare 17.

Aaberge R (2001) Axiomatic characterization of the Gini coefficient and Lorenz curve orderings. Journal of Economic Theory 101.

Aaberge R (2007) Gini's nuclear family. Journal of Economic Inequality 5.

Aboudi R, Thon D (2003) Transfer principles and relative inequality aversion: a majorization approach. Mathematical Social Sciences 45.

Aboudi R, Thon D (2006) Refinements of Muirheads's lemma and income inequality. Mathematical Social Sciences 51.

Aboudi R, Thon D (2008) Second degree Pareto dominance. Social Choice and Welfare 30.

Aczel J (1966) Lectures on functional equations and their applications. Academic Press, London.

Adelman I, Levy A (1986) Decomposing Theil's index of inequality: a reply. Review of Income and Wealth 32.

Aigner DJ, Heins AJ (1967) A social welfare view of the measurement of income inequality. Review of Income and Wealth 13.

Alesina A, Spolaore E (1997) On the number and size of nations. Quarterly Journal of Economics 113.

Alkire S, Foster JE (2007) Counting and multidimensional poverty measurement. OPHI Working Paper.

Allingham MG (1972) The measurement of inequality. Journal of Economic Theory 5.

Allison PD (1978) Measures of inequality. American Sociological Review 43.

Allison RA, Foster JE (2004) Measuring health inequality using qualitative data. Journal of Health Economics 23.

Amiel Y, Cowell FA (1992) Measurement of income inequality: experimental test by questionnaire. Journal of Public Economics 17.

Amiel Y, Cowell FA (1994) Inequality changes and income growth. In: Eichhorn W (ed.) Models and measurement of welfare and inequality. Springer-Verlag, New York.

Amiel Y, Cowell FA (1997) The measurement of poverty: an experimental questionnaire investigation. Empirical Economics 22.

Amiel Y, Cowell FA (1998) Distributional orderings and the transfer principle: a re-examination. Research on Economic Inequality 8.

Amiel Y, Cowell FA (1999) Thinking about inequality. Cambridge University Press, Cambridge.

Amiel Y, Cowell FA (2003) Inequality, welfare and monotonicity. Research on Economic Inequality 9.

Amiel Y, Creedy J, Hurn S (1999) Measuring attitude towards inequality. Scandinavian Journal of Economics 101.

Amiel Y, Cowell FA, Slottje D (2003) Why do people violate the transfer principle? Evidence from educational sample surveys. Research on Economic Inequality 11.
Amiel Y, Cowell FA, Ramos X (2007) On the measurement polarization: a questionnaire study. Mimeograph.
Anand S (1977) Aspects of poverty in Malaysia. Review of Income and Wealth 23.
Anand S (1983) Inequality and poverty in Malaysia. Oxford University Press, London.
Anand S, Sen AK (1996) Notes on the measurement of inequality in general spaces. Harvard University Press, Cambridge, MA.
Anderson G (2004a) Making inferences about polarization, welfare and poverty of nations: a study of 101 countries 1970–1995. Journal of Applied Econometrics 19.
Anderson G (2004b) Towards an empirical analysis of polarization. Journal of Econometrics 122.
Apostol TM (1975) Mathematical analysis. Addison-Wesley, London.
Araar A, Duclos JY (2003) An Atkinson-Gini family of social evaluation functions. Economics Bulletin 3.
Arnold BC (1987) Majorization and the Lorenz order. Springer-Verlag, New York.
Arriaga EE (1970) A new approach to the measurement of urbanization. Economic Development and Cultural Change 18.
Arrow KJ (1971) Essays in the theory of risk bearing. North-Holland, Amsterdam.
Atkinson AB (1970) On the measurement of inequality. Journal of Economic Theory 2.
Atkinson AB (1983a) The economics of inequality, 2nd edn. Oxford University Press, London.
Atkinson AB (1983b) Social justice and public policy. MIT Press, Cambridge.
Atkinson AB (1987) On the measurement of poverty. Econometrica 55.
Atkinson AB (1989) Poverty and social security. Wheatsheaf, New York.
Atkinson AB (1992) Measuring poverty and difference in family composition. Economica 59.
Atkinson AB (1998) Social exclusion, poverty and unemployment. In: Atkinson AB, Hills J (eds.) Exclusion, employment and opportunity. CASE Paper No. 4, Centre for the Analysis of Social Exclusion, London School of Economics.
Atkinson AB (2003) Multidimensional deprivation: contrasting social welfare and counting approaches. Journal of Economic Inequality 1.
Atkinson AB (2008) More on the measurement of inequality. Journal of Economic Inequality 6.
Atkinson AB, Bourguignon F (1982) The comparison of multidimensioned distributions of economic status. Review of Economic Studies 49.
Atkinson AB, Bourguignon F (1987) Income distributions and differences in needs. In: Feiwell GR (ed.) Arrow and the foundation of the theory of economic policy. Macmillan, New York.
Balestrino A (1998) Counting the poor in a fuzzy way: the headcount ratio and the monotonicity and transfer axioms. Notizie di Politeia 14.
Ballano CJ, Ruiz-Castillo J (1993) Searching by questionnaire for the meaning of income inequality. Revista Esponala de Economia 10.
Baluch B, Masset E (2003) Do monetary and non-monetary indicators tell the same story about chronic poverty? A study of Vietnam in the 1990s. World Development 31.
Bane M, Ellwood D (1986) Slipping into and out of poverty. Journal of Human Resources 21.
Bardahan P, Mookherjee D (2006) Relative capture of local and central governments: an essay in the political economy. University of California, Berkeley.
Barrett CR, Salles M (1995) On a generalization of the Gini coefficient. Mathematical Social Sciences 30.
Basmann RL, Rhodes GF (eds.) (1984) Advances in econometrics – 3. JAI Press, Connecticut.
Basmann RL, Slottje DJ, Hayes K (1994) Some new methods for measuring and describing economic inequality. JAI Press, Connecticut.
Basu K (1985) Poverty measurement: a decomposition of the normalization axiom. Econometrica 53.
Basu K (1987) Axioms for a fuzzy measure of inequality. Mathematical Social Sciences 14.
Baumol W (1986) Review of on economic inequality. Economica 42.
Beach C (1989) Dollars and dreams: a reduced middle class? Alternative explanations. Journal of Human Resources 24.

Beach C, Chaykowski R, Slotsve G (1997) Inequality and polarization of male earnings in the United States: 1968–1990. North American Journal of Economics and Finance 8.

Beach C, Davidson R (1983) Distribution free statistical inference with Lorenz curves and income shares. Review of Economic Studies 50.

Behrman J, Deolikar AB (1988) Health and nutrition. In: Chenery H, Srinivasan TN (eds.) Handbook of development economics. Elsevier Science, Amsterdam.

Ben Porath E, Gilboa I (1994) Linear measures, the Gini index, and the income-equality tradeoff. Journal of Economic Theory 64.

Berrebi ZM, Silber J (1981) Weighting income ranks and levels: a multiple-parameter generalization for relative and absolute indices. Economics Letters 7.

Berrebi ZM, Silber J (1985) Income inequality indices and deprivation: a generalization. Quarterly Journal of Economics 100.

Berrebi ZM, Silber J (1987a) Interquantile differences, income inequality measurement and the Gini concentration index. Mathematical Social Sciences 13.

Berrebi ZM, Silber J (1987b) Dispersion, asymmetry and the Gini index of inequality. International Economic Review 28.

Berrebi ZM, Silber J (1989) Deprivation, the Gini index of inequality and the flatness of an income distribution. Mathematical Social Sciences 18.

Berry A, Bourguignon F, Morrisson C (1983) The level of world inequality: how much can we say? Review of Income and Wealth 29.

Besley T, Preston I (1988) Invariance and the axiomatics of income tax progressivity: a comment. Bulletin of Economic Research 40.

Betti G, Cheli B, Lemmi A, Verma V (2006) Multidimensional and longitudinal poverty: an integrated fuzzy approach. In: Lemmi A, Betti G (eds.) Fuzzy set approach to multidimensional poverty measurement. Springer Science and Business Media, New York.

Betti G, Cheli B, Lemmi A, Verma V (2008) The fuzzy approach to multidimensional poverty. In: Kakwani NC, Silber J (eds) Quantitative approaches to multidimensional poverty measurement. Palgrave MacMillan, London.

Bhattracharya N, Mahalanobis B (1967) Regional disparities in household consumption in India. Journal of the American Statistical Association 62.

Bhide S, Mehta AK (2004) Chronic poverty in rural India: issues and findings from panel data. Journal of Human Development 5.

Bickel PJ, Lehmann EL (1979) Descriptive statistics for nonparametric models IV: spread. In: Jureckova J (ed.) Contributions to statistics. J. Hajek Memorial Volume, Reidel, Dordrecht.

Bishop JA, Formby JP, Thistle PD (1989) Statistical inference, income distribution and social welfare. Research on Economic Inequality 1.

Bishop JA, Formby JP, Zheng B (1996) Regional income inequality and welfare in China: a dominance analysis. Asian Economic Journal 10.

Bishop JA, Formby JP, Zheng B (1997) Statistical inference and the Sen index of poverty. International Economic Review 38.

Blackburn M (1989) Poverty measurement: an index related to a Theil measure of inequality. Journal of Business and Economic Statistics 7.

Balkburn M (1994) International comparisons of poverty. American Economic Review 84.

Blackburn M, Bloom DE (1985) What is happening to the middle class? American Demographics 7.

Blackorby C, Bossert W, Donaldson D (1999) Income inequality measurement: the normative approach. In: Silber J (1999) Handbook on income inequality measurement. Kluwer, Dordrecht.

Blackorby C, Bossert W, Donaldson D (2005) Population issues in social choice theory, welfare economics and ethics. Cambridge University Press, Cambridge.

Blackorby C, Donaldson D (1977) Utility versus equity: some plausible quasiorderings. Journal of Public Economics 7.

Blackorby C, Donaldson D (1978) Measures of relative equality and their meaning in terms of social welfare. Journal of Economic Theory 18.

Blackorby C, Donaldson D (1980a) A theoretical treatment of indices of absolute inequality. International Economic Review 21.
Blackorby C, Donaldson D (1980b) Ethical indices for the measurement of poverty. Econometrica 48.
Blackorby C, Donaldson D (1984a) Social criteria for evaluating population change. Journal of Public Economics 25.
Blackorby C, Donaldson D (1984b) Ethically significant ordinal indexes of relative inequality. Advances in Econometrics 3.
Blackorby C, Donaldson D, Auersperg M (1981) A new procedure for the measurement of inequality within and among population subgroups. Canadian Journal of Economics 14.
Bonferroni C (1930) Elemente di statistica generale. Libreria Seber, Firenze.
Bos D, Rose M, Seidl C (eds.) (1988) Welfare and efficiency in public economics. Springer-Verlag, New York.
Bosmans K (2006) Income inequality, quasi-concavity and gradual population shifts. Mathematical Social Sciences 53.
Bossert W (1990a) An axiomatization of the single-series Ginis. Journal of Economic Theory 50.
Bossert W (1990b) Population replication and ethical poverty measurement. Mathematical Social Sciences 20.
Bossert W, Chakravarty SR, D'Ambrosio C (2008) Poverty and time. ECINEQ Working Paper No. 2008-87.
Bossert W, D'Ambrosio C (2007) Dynamic measures of individual deprivation. Social Choice and Welfare 28.
Bossert W, D'Ambrosio C, Peragine V (2007) Deprivation and social exclusion. Economica 74.
Bossert W, Pfingsten A (1990) Intermediate inequality: concepts, indices and welfare implication. Mathematical Social Sciences 19.
Bossert W, Schworm W (2006) Measures of polarization. University of Montreal, QC, Canada.
Bourguignon F (1979) Decomposable income inequality measures. Econometrica 47.
Bourguignon F (1989) Family size and social utility: income distribution dominance criteria. Journal of Econometrics 43.
Bourguignon F (1999) Comment on Maasoumi. In: Silber J (ed.) Handbook on income inequality measurement. Kluwer, MA.
Bourguignon F (2005) Comment on Deaton. Review of Economics and Statistics 87.
Bourguignon F, Chakravarty SR (1999) A family of multidimensional poverty measures. In: Slottje DJ (ed.) Advances in econometrics, income distribution and methodology of Science: essays in honor of C. Dagum, Springer-Verlag, London.
Bourguignon F, Chakravarty SR (2003) The measurement of multidimensional poverty. Journal of Economic Inequality 1.
Bourguignon F, Chakravarty SR (2008) Multidimensional poverty orderings: theory and applications. In: Basu K, Kanbur R (eds.) Welfare, development, philosophy and social science: essays for Amartya Sen's 75th birthday (Vol. 2: Development economics and policy). Clarendon Press, Oxford.
Bourguignon F, Fields GS (1990) Poverty measures and poverty policy. Recherches economiques de Louvain 56.
Bourguignon F, Fields GS (1997) Discontinuous losses from poverty, generalized measures and optimal transfers to the poor. Journal of Public Economics 63.
Bourguignon F, Morrisson C (2002) Inequality among world citizens. American Economic Review 92.
Bresson F, Labar K (2007) Leftist, rightist and intermediate decompositions of poverty: variations with an application to China from 1990 to 2003. ECINEQ Working Paper No. 2007-76.
Broome J (1996) The welfare economics of population. Oxford Economic Papers 48.
Burk R, Gehrig W (1978) Indices of income inequality and societal income, an axiomatic approach. In: Eichhorn W, Henn R, Opitz O, Shephard RW (eds.) Theory and applications of economic indices. Physica-Verlag, Wurzburg.

Calvo S, Dercon S (2007) Chronic poverty and all that: the measurement of poverty over time. CPRC Working Paper No. 89. University of Oxford, London.

Carter MR, Barrett CB (2004) The economics of poverty traps and persistent poverty: an asset based approach. BASIS background paper, Combating persistence poverty in Africa conference. University of Wisconsin, Madison.

Cerioli A, Zani S (1990) A fuzzy approach to measurement of poverty. In: Dagum C, Zenga M (eds.) Income and wealth distribution, inequality and poverty. Studies in contemporary economics. Springer Verlag, Berlin.

Chakraborty A, Pattanaik P, Xu Y (2008) On the mean of squared deprivation gaps. Economic Theory 34.

Chakravarty SR (1983a) Ethically flexible measures of poverty. Canadian Journal of Economics 16.

Chakravarty SR (1983b) Measures of poverty based on representative income gap. Sankhya, The Indian Journal of Statistics B 45.

Chakravarty SR (1983c) A new index of poverty. Mathematical Social Sciences 6.

Chakravarty SR (1988a) On quasi-ordering of income profiles. Methods of Operations Research 60.

Chakravarty SR (1988b) Extended Gini indices of inequality. International Economic Review 29.

Chakravarty SR (1990) Ethical social index numbers. Springer-Verlag, New York.

Chakravarty SR (1997a) On Shorrocks' reinvestigation of the Sen poverty index. Econometrica 65.

Chakravarty SR (1997b) Relative deprivation and satisfaction orderings. Keio Economic Studies 34.

Chakravarty SR (1999) Measuring inequality: the axiomatic approach. In: Silber J (ed.) Handbook on income inequality measurement. Kluwer, Boston, MA.

Chakravarty SR (2006) An axiomatic approach to multidimensional poverty measurement via fuzzy sets. In: Lemmi A, Betti G (eds.) Fuzzy set approach to multidimensional poverty measurement. Springer-Verlag, New York.

Chakravarty SR (2007) A deprivation-based axiomatic characterization of the absolute Bonferroni index of inequality. Journal of Economic Inequality 5.

Chakravarty SR (2008a) Equity and efficiency as components of a social welfare function. International Journal of Economic Theory, forthcoming.

Chakravarty SR (2008b) Inequality, deprivation and welfare. Japanese Economic Review, forthcoming.

Chakravarty SR, Chattopadhyay N, Majumder A (1995) Income inequality and relative deprivation. Keio Economic Studies 32.

Chakravarty SR, D'Ambrosio C, Muliere P (2003) Target shortfall ordering and indices. DIW, Berlin.

Chakravarty SR, Deutsch J, Silber J (2008) On the Watts multidimensional poverty index and its decomposition. World Development 36.

Chakravarty SR, Dutta B (1987) A note on measures of distance between income distributions. Journal of Economic Theory 41.

Chakravarty SR, Eichhorn W (1994) Measurement of income inequality: true versus observed data. In: Eichhorn (ed.) Models and measurement of welfare and inequality. Springer-Verlag, Heidelberg, Germany.

Chakravarty SR, Kanbur R, Mukherjee D (2006) Population growth and poverty measurement. Social Choice and Welfare 26.

Chakravarty SR, Majumder A (2001) Inequality, polarization and welfare: theory and applications. Australian Economic Papers 40.

Chakravarty SR, Majumder A, Roy R (2007) A treatment of absolute indices of polarization. Japanese Economic Review 58.

Charavarty SR, Moyes P (2003) Individual welfare, social deprivation and income taxation. Economic Theory 21.

Chakravarty SR, Mukherjee D (1999) Measures of deprivation and their meaning in terms of social satisfaction. Theory and Decision 47.

Chakravarty SR, Mukherjee D, Ranade R (1998) The family of subgroup and factor decomposable measures of multidimensional poverty. Research on Economic Inequality 8.

Chakravarty SR, Muliere P (2003) Welfare indicators: a review and new perspectives I. Measurement of inequality. Metron-International Journal of Statistics 61.

Chakravarty SR, Muliere P (2004) Welfare indicators: a review and new perspectives II. Measurement of poverty. Metron-International Journal of Statistics 62.

Chakravarty SR, Silber J (2007) A generalized index of employment segregation. Mathematical Social Sciences 53.

Chakravarty SR, Silber J (2008) Measuring multidimensional poverty: the axiomatic approach. In: Kakwani N, Silber J (eds.) Palgrave-Macmillan.

Chakravarty SR, Tyagarupananda S (2008) The subgroup decomposable intermediate indices of inequality. Spanish Economic Review, forthcoming.

Chambaz C, Maurin E (1998) Atkinson and Bourguignon's dominance criteria: extended and applied to the measurement of poverty in France. Review of Income and Wealth 44.

Champernowne DG (1974) A comparison of measures of inequality of income distribution. Economic Journal 84.

Champernowne DG, Cowell FA (1998) Economic inequality and income redistribution. Cambridge University Press, Cambridge.

Chateauneuf A, Gajdos T, Wilthien P-H (2002) The principle of strong diminishing transfer. Journal of Economic Theory 103.

Chateauneuf A, Moyes P (2004) Lorenz non-consistent welfare and inequality. Journal of Economic Inequality 2.

Chateauneuf A, Moyes P (2006) A non-welfarist approach to inequality measurement. In: McGillivray M (ed.) Inequality, poverty and well-being. Palgrave-Macmillan, London.

Cheli B, Lemmi A (1995) A 'totally' fuzzy and relative approach to the multidimensional analysis of poverty. Economic Notes 24.

Chiappero Martinetti E (1996) Standard of living evaluation based on Sen's approach: some methodological suggestions. Politeia 12.

Chiappero Martinetti E (2006) Capability approach and fuzzy set theory: description, aggregation and inference issues. In: Lemmi A, Betti G Fuzzy set approach to multidimensional poverty measurement. Springer-Verlag, New York.

Chipman JS (1974) The welfare ranking of Pareto distributions. Journal of Economic Theory 9.

Chronic Poverty Report (2004–2005) Chronic Poverty Research Center. University of Manchester, UK.

Chotikapanich D (1994) Techniques for measuring income inequality. Avebury, Aldershot.

Chotikapanich D, Griffiths WE (2005) Averaging Lorenz curves. Journal of Economic Inequality 3.

Clark D, Hulme D (2005) Towards a unified framework for understanding the depth, breadth and duration of poverty. University of Manchester, UK.

Clark S, Hemming R, Ulph D (1981) On indices for the measurement of poverty. Economic Journal 91.

Collier P, Hoeffler A (2001) Greed and grievances in civil war. World Bank.

Cowell FA (1980) On the structure of additive inequality measures. Review of Economic Studies 47.

Cowell FA (1984) The structure of American income inequality. Review of Income and Wealth 30.

Cowell FA (1985a) A fair suck of the sauce bottle? Or, what do you mean by inequality. Economic Record 61.

Cowell FA (1985b) Multidimensional decomposition of Theil's index of inequality. Review of Income and Wealth 31.

Cowell FA (1988a) Poverty measures, inequality and decomposability. In: Bos D, Rose M, Seidl C (eds.) Welfare and efficiency in public economics. Springer–Verlag, New York.

Cowell FA (1988b) Inequality decomposition: three bad measures. Bulletin of Economic Research 40.

Cowell FA (1995) Measuring inequality, 2nd edition. Wheatsheaf, New York.

Cowell FA (1998) Measurement of inequality. In: Atkinson AB, Bourguignon F (eds.) Handbook of income distribution. North-Holland, Amsterdam.
Cowell FA (2003) The economics of poverty and inequality. Edward Elgar, Cheltenham.
Cowell FA (2008) Gini, deprivation and complaints. In: Betti G, Lemmi A (eds.) Advances in income inequality and concentration measures. Routledge, London.
Cowell FA, Ebert U (2004) Complaints and inequality. Social Choice and Welfare 23.
Cowell FA, Ebert U (2008) Inequality and envy. Research on Economic Inequality, 16.
Cowell FA, Kuga K (1981a) Additivity and the entropy concept: an axiomatic approach to inequality measurement. Journal of Economic Theory 25.
Cowell FA, Kuga K (1981b) Inequality measurement: an axiomatic approach. European Economic Review 15.
Cowell FA,Victoria-Feser M-P (2002) Welfare rankings in the presence of contaminated data. Econometrica 70.
Creedy J (1977) The principle of transfers and the variance of logarithms. Oxford Bulletin of Economics and Statistics 39.
Dagum C (1980) Inequality measures between income distributions with applications. Econometrica 48.
Dagum C (1990) On the relationship between income inequality measures and social welfare functions. Journal of Econometrics 43.
Dagum C (1997) A new approach to the decomposition of the Gini income inequality ratio. Empirical Economics 22.
Dagum C, Zenga M (eds.) (1990) Income and wealth distribution, inequality and poverty. Springer-Verlag, New York.
D'Ambrosio C (2001) Household characteristics and the distribution of income in Italy: an application of a social distance measure. Review of Income and Wealth 47.
Dalton H (1920) The measurement of the inequality of incomes. Economic Journal 30.
Dardanoni V (1995) On multidimensional inequality. Research on Economic Inequality 6.
Dasgupta P (1993) An inquiry into well-being and destitution. Carendon Press, Oxford.
Dasgupta P, Sen AK, Starrett D (1973) Notes on the measurement of inequality. Journal of Economic Theory 6.
Datt G, Ravallion M (1992) Growth and redistribution components of changes in poverty measures: a decomposition with application to Brazil and India in the 1980s. Journal of Development Economics 38.
Davidson R, Duclos J-Y (2000) Statistical inference for stochastic dominance and for the measurement of poverty and inequality. Econometrica 68.
Davies JB, Hoy M (1994) The normative significance of using third degree stochastic dominance in comparing income distributions. Journal of Economic Theory 64.
Davies JB, Hoy M (1995) Making inequality comparisons when Lorenz curves cross. American Economic Review 85.
Deaton A (2001) Inequalities in income and inequalities in health. In: Welch F (ed.) The causes and consequences of increasing inequality. University of Chicago Press, Chicago.
Deaton A (2005) Measuring poverty in a growing world (or measuring poverty in a poor world). Review of Economics and Statistics 87.
Deaton A (2008) Price trends in India and their implications for measuring poverty. NBER, Princeton University, New Jersey.
Deaton A, Muellbauer J (1980) Economics and consumer behavior. Cambridge University Press, Cambridge.
Del Rio C, Alonso-Villar O (2007) New unit-consistent intermediate inequality indices. ECINEQ Working Paper No. 2007-63.
Del Rio C, Alonso-Villar O (2008) Rankings of income distributions: a case of intermediate inequality indices. Research on Economic Inequality 16.
Del Rio C, Ruiz-Castillo J (2000) Intermediate inequality and welfare. Social Choice and Welfare 17.
Desai M, Sen AK, Boltvinik J (1992) Social progress index: a proposal. UNDP, Bogota.

Deutsch J, Silber J (2005) Measuring multidimensional poverty: an empirical comparison of various approaches. Review of Income and Wealth 51.
Diez H, Lasso de la Vega MC, de Sarachu A, Urrutia AM (2007) A consistent multidimensional generalization of the Pigou-Dalton transfer principle: an analysis. BE Journal of Theoretical Economics 7.
Diez H, Lasso de la Vega MC, Urrutia AM (2007) Unit consistent aggregative multidimensional inequality measures: a characterization. ECIEEQ Working Paper No. 2007-66.
Doksum K (1969) Star-shaped transformations and the power of rank tests. Annals of Mathematical Statistics 40.
Dominguez J, Velazquez J (2007) A proposal of a synthetic indicator to measure poverty intensity, with an application to EU-15 countries. ECINEQ Working Paper No. 2007-81.
Donaldson D, Weymark JA (1980) A single parameter generalization of the Gini indices of inequality. Journal of Economic Theory 22.
Donaldson D, Weymark JA (1983) Ethically flexible Gini indices of inequality for income distributions in the continuum. Journal of EconomicTheory 29.
Donaldson D, Weymark JA (1986) Properties of fixed-population poverty indices. International Economic Review 27.
Dorfman R (1979) A formula for the Gini coefficient. Review of Economics and Statistics 61.
Duclos J-Y, Echevin D (2005) Bipolarization comparisons. Economics Letters 87.
Duclos J-Y, Gregoire P (2002) Absolute and relative deprivation and the measurement of poverty. Review of Income and Wealth 48.
Duclos J-Y, Makdissi P (2005) Sequential stochastic dominance and the robustness of poverty orderings. Review of Income and Wealth 51.
Duclos J-Y, Esteban J, Ray D (2004) Polarization: concepts, measurement, estimation. Econometrica 72.
Duclos J-Y, Araar A, Giles J (2006) Chronic and transient poverty: measurement and estimation, with evidence from China. IZA DP No. 2078.
Duclos J-Y, Sahn D, Younger SD (2006a) Robust multidimensional poverty comparisons. Economic Journal 116.
Duclos J-Y, Sahn D, Younger SD (2006b) Robust multidimensional spatial poverty comparisons in Ghana, Madagascar, and Uganda. World Bank Economic Review 20.
Duncan OD, Duncan B (1955) A methodological analysis of segregation indices. American Sociological Review 20.
Dutta B (2002) Inequality, poverty and welfare. In: Arrow KJ, Sen AK, Suzumura K (eds.) Handbook of social choice, Vol. 1. North Holland, Amsterdam.
Dutta B, Esteban JM (1992) Social welfare and equality. Social Choice and Welfare 9.
Ebert U (1984) Measures of distance between income distributions. Journal of Economic Theory 32.
Ebert U (1987) Size and distributions of income as determinants of social welfare. Journal of Economic Theory 41.
Ebert U (1988a) Measurement of inequality: an attempt at unification and generalization. Social Choice and Welfare 5.
Ebert U (1988b) On the decomposition of inequality: partition into non-overlapping subgroups. In: Eichhorn W (ed.) Measurement in economics. Physica-Verlag, Heidelberg.
Ebert U (1988c) On a family of aggregate compromise inequality measures. International Economic Review 29.
Ebert U (1995) Income inequality and differences in household size. Mathematical Social Sciences 30.
Ebert U (1997) Social welfare when needs differ: an axiomatic approach. Economica 64.
Ebert U (1999a) Dual decomposable inequality measures. Canadian Journal of Economics 32.
Ebert U (1999b) Using equivalent income of equivalent adults to rank income distributions. Social Choice and Welfare 16.
Ebert U (2000) Sequential generalized Lorenz dominance and transfer principles. Bulletin of Economic Research 52.

Ebert U (2003) Inequality measurement for homogeneous groups. Research on Economic Inequality 9.
Ebert U (2004a) Coherent inequality views: linear invariant measures reconsidered. Mathematical Social Sciences 47.
Ebert U (2004b) Social welfare, inequality and poverty when needs differ. Social Choice and Welfare 23.
Ebert U (2007) Ethical inequality measures and the redistribution of income when needs differ. Journal of Economic Inequality 5.
Ebert U, Moyes P (2000) An axiomatic characterization of the Yitzhaki index of individual deprivation. Economics Letters 68.
Ebert U, Moyes P (2002) A simple axiomatization of the Foster, Greer and Thorbecke poverty orderings. Journal of Public Economic Theory 4.
Eichhorn W (1988) On a class of inequality measures. Social Choice and Welfare 5.
Eichhorn W (ed.) (1988) Measurement in economics. Physica-Verlag, Heidelberg.
Eichhorn W (ed.) (1994) Models and Measurement of Welfare and Inequality. Springer-Verlag, New York.
Eichhorn W, Gehrig W (1982) Measurement of inequality in economics. In: Korte B (ed.) Modern applied mathematics. North-Holland, Amsterdam.
Elbers C, Lanjouw P, Mistiaen J, Ozler B (2008) Reinterpreting subgroup inequality decompositions. Journal of Economic Inequality 6.
Elteto O, Frigyes E (1968) New income inequality measures as efficient tools for causal analysis and planning. Econometrica 36.
Esteban JM, Ray D (1994) On the measurement of polarization. Econometrica 62.
Esteban JM, Ray D (1999) Conflict and distribution. Journal of Economic Theory 87.
Esteban JM, Ray D (2005) A comparison of polarization measures. CSIC, Barcelona.
Esteban JM, Gradin C, Ray D (2007) Extensions of a measure of polarization, with an application to income distribution of five OECD countries. Journal of Economic Inequality 5.
European Foundation (1995) Public welfare services and social exclusion: the development of consumer oriented initiatives in the European Union. The European Foundation for the Living and Working Conditions, Dublin.
Farina F, Savaglio G (eds.) (2006) Inequality and economic integration. Routledge, London.
Fei JCH (1981) Equity oriented fiscal programs. Econometrica 49.
Fei JCH, Ranis G, Kuo SWY (1978) Growth and the family distribution of income by factor components. Quarterly Journal of Economics 92.
Fei JCH, Ranis G, Kuo SWY (1979) Growth with equity: the Taiwan case. Oxford University Press, London.
Fields GS (1979) Income inequality in urban Columbia: a decomposition analysis. Review of Income and Weralth 25.
Fields GS (1980) Poverty, inequality and development. Cambridge University Press, Cambridge.
Fields GS (2001) Distribution and development: a new look at the developing world. MIT Press, Cambridge.
Fields GS, Fei JCH (1978) On inequality comparisons. Econometrica 46.
Fishburn PC, Willig RD (1984) Transfer principles in income distribution. Journal of Public Economics 25.
Fleurbaey M, Trannoy A (2003) The impossibility of a Paretian egalitarian. Social Choice and Welfare 21.
Fleurbaey M, Hagnere C, Trannoy A (2003) Welfare comparisons with bounded equivalence scales. Journal of EconomicTheory 110.
Fluckiger Y, Silber J (1994) The Gini index and the measurement of multidimensional inequality. Oxford Bulletin of Economics and Statistics 56.
Formby JP, Smith JW, Zheng B (1997) The coefficient of variation, stochastic dominance and inequality: a new interpretation. Economics Letters 62.
Foster JE (1983) An axiomatic characterization of the Theil measure of inequality. Journal of Economic Theory 31.

Foster JE (1984) On economic poverty: a survey of aggregate measures. Advances in econometrics 3.
Foster JE (1985) Inequality measurement. In: Young HP (ed.) Fair allocation. American Mathematical Society, Providence.
Foster JE (1994) Normative economics: is theory relevant? American Economic Review 84.
Foster JE (1998) Absolute versus relative poverty. American Economic Review 88.
Foster JE (2005) Poverty indices. In: de Janvry A, Kanbur R (eds.) Poverty, inequality and development, essays in honor of E. Thorbecke. Springer-Verlag, New York.
Foster JE (2008) A class of chronic poverty measures. In: Addison A, Hulme D, Kanbur R (eds.) Poverty dynamics: towards inter-disciplinary approaches. Oxford University Press, Oxford.
Foster JE, Jin Y (1998) Poverty orderings for the Dalton utility-gap measures. In: Jenkins SP, Kaptyn A, van Praag B (eds.) The distributions of welfare and household production: international perspective. Cambridge University Press, Cambridge.
Foster JE, Ok E (1999) Lorenz dominance and variance of logarithms. Econometrica 67.
Foster JE, Sen AK (1997) On economic inequality: after a quarter century, annex to enlarged edition of On economic inequality by AK Sen. Clarendon Press, Oxford.
Foster JE, Shneyerov A (1999) A general class of additively decomposable inequality measures. Economic Theory 14.
Foster JE, Shneyerov A (2000) Path independent inequality measures. Journal of Economic Theory 91.
Foster JE, Shorrocks AF (1988a) Poverty orderings. Econometrica 56.
Foster JE, Shorrocks AF (1988b) Poverty orderings and welfare dominance. Social Choice and Welfare 5.
Foster JE, Shorrocks AF (1990) Poverty indices and decomposability. In: Myles G (ed.) Measurement and modeling in economics. North-Holland, Amsterdam.
Foster JE, Shorrocks AF (1991) Subgroup consistent poverty indices. Econometrica 59.
Foster JE, Wolfson MC (1992) Polarization and the decline of the middle class: Canada and the US. Vanderbilt University, Nashville, TN.
Foster JE, Greer J, Thorbecke E (1984) A class of decomposable poverty measures. Econometrica 42.
Fuchs V (1976) Redefining poverty and redistributing income. The Public Interest 8.
Gaertner W, Namezie C (2003) Income inequality, risk and the transfer principle: a questionnaire experimental investigation. Mathematical Social Sciences 45.
Gaiha R (1989) Are the chronically poor also the poorest in rural India? Development and Change 20.
Gaiha R (1992) On the chronically poor in rural India. Journal of International Development 4.
Gaiha R, Deolikar AB (1993) Persistent, expected and innate poverty: estimates for semi arid rural south India. Cambridge Journal of Economics 17.
Gajdos T, Weymark JA (2005) Multidimensional generalized Gini indices. Economic Theory 26.
Garcia -Montalvo J, Reynal-Querol M (2002) Why ethnic fractionalization? Polarization, ethnic conflict and growth. Mimeograph.
Garcia -Montalvo J, Reynal-Querol M (2005) Ethnic polarization, potential conflict and civil war. American Economic Review 95.
Gastwirth JL (1971) A general definition of the Lorenz curve. Econometrica 39.
Gigliarano C (2006) Polarization measurement in one or more dimensions. Ph.D. Thesis, Bocconi University, Milan.
Gilboa I, Schmeidler D (1994) Additive representations of non-additive measures and the Choquet integral. Annual of Operations Research 52.
Gini C (1936) On the measure of concentration with especial reference to income and wealth. Cowles Commission.
Giorgi GM, Crescenzi M (2001) A proposal of poverty measures based on the Bonferroni inequality index. Metron-International Journal of Statistics 59.
Gordon D, Nandy S, Pantazis C, Pemberton S, Townsend P (2003) Child poverty in the developing world. Policy Press, Bristol.

Graaff JDV (1977) Equity and efficiency as components of the general welfare. South African Journal of Economics 45.
Gradin C (2000) Polarization by sub-populations in Spain, 1973–1991. Review of Income and Wealth 46.
Gradin C (2002) Polarization and inequality in Spain, 1973–1991. Journal of Income Distribution 11.
Gravel N, Mukhopadhyay A (2007) Is India better off today than 15 years ago? A robust multidimensional answer. CSH, New Delhi.
Grootaert C (1996) Analyzing poverty and policy reform: the experience of Cote d'Ivoire. Avebury, Brookfield.
Hadar J, Russell W (1969) Rules for ordering uncertain prospects. American Economic Review 59.
Hagenaars A (1986) Perception of poverty. North-Holland, Amsterdam.
Hagenaars A (1987) A class of poverty indices. International Economic Review 28.
Hamada K, Takayama N (1977) Censored income distributions and the measurement of poverty. Bulletin of the International Statistical Institute 47.
Hammond PJ (1975) A note on extreme inequality aversion. Journal of Economic Theory 11.
Hammond PJ (1976a) Equity, Arrow's conditions and Rawls' difference principle. Econometrica 44.
Hammond PJ (1976b) Why ethical measures of inequality need interpersonal comparisons. Theory and Decision 7.
Hammond PJ (1977) Dual interpersonal comparisons of utility and the welfare of income distribution. Journal of Public Economics 6.
Hardy GH, Littlewood J, Polya G (1934) Inequalities. Cambridge University Press, Cambridge.
Harrison E, Siedl C (1994) Perceptional inequality and preference judgments: an empirical examination of distributional axioms. Public Choice 79.
Hey JD, Lambert PJ (1980) Relative deprivation and the Gini coefficient: comment. Quarterly Journal of Economics 95.
Horrigan MW, Haugen SE (1988) The declining middle class: a sensitivity analysis. Monthly Labour Review 111.
Howes S (1993) Mixed dominance: a new criterion for analysis. London School of Economics.
Hoy M, Zheng B (2006) Measuring lifetime poverty. Mimeograph.
Hulme D, McKay A (2005) Identifying and measuring chronic poverty: beyond monetary measures. University of Bath, UK.
Hulme D, Shepherd A (2003a) Conceptualizing chronic poverty. World Development 31.
Hulme D, Shepherd A (eds.) (2003b) Special issue: chronic poverty and development policy. World Development 31.
Hutchens R (1991) Segregation curves, Lorenz curves, and inequality in the distribution of people across occupations. Mathematical Social Sciences 21.
Hutchens R (2004) On a measure of segregation. International Economic Review 45.
Ilg RE, Haugen SE (2000) Earnings and employment trends in the 1990s. Monthly Labour Review 123.
Jalan J, Ravallion M (1998) Transient poverty in post-reform rural China. Journal of Comparative Economics 26.
Jalan J, Ravallion M (2000) Determinants of transient and chronic poverty: evidence from rural China. Journal of Development Studies 36.
Jenkins SP (1991) The measurement of income inequality. In: Osbeg L (ed.) Economic inequality and poverty: international perspective. Sharpe, New York.
Jenkins SP (1995) Did the middle class shrink during the 1980s? UK evidence from kernel density estimates. Economics Letters 49.
Jenkins SP, Lambert PJ (1993) Ranking income distributions when needs differ. Review of Income and Wealth 39.
Jenkins SP, Lambert PJ (1997) Three 'I's of poverty curves, with an analysis of UK poverty trends. Oxford Economic Papers 49.

Jenkins SP, Lambert PJ (1998a) Three 'I's of poverty curves and poverty dominance: TIP for poverty analysis. Research on Economic Inequality 8.

Jenkins SP, Lambert PJ (1998b) Ranking poverty gap distributions: further TIPs for poverty analysis. Research on Economic Inequality 8.

Jenkins SP, Kapteyn A, van Praag B (eds.) (1998) The distributions of welfare and household production: international perspective. Cambridge University Press, Cambridge.

Jewitt I (1989) Choosing between risky prospects: the characterization of comparative statics results, and location independent risk. Management Science 35.

Johnson DT (1996) Poverty, inequality and social welfare in Australia. Physica-Verlag, Heidelberg.

Jorgenson D, Slesnick D (1984) Inequality in the distribution of individual welfare. Advances in econometrics 3.

Kakwani NC (1977a) Applications of Lorenz curves in economic analysis. Econometrica 45.

Kakwani NC (1977b) Measurement of Poverty and negative income tax. Australian Economic Papers 16.

Kakwani NC (1980a) Income inequality and poverty: methods of estimation and policy applications. Oxford University Press, Oxford.

Kakwani NC (1980b) On a class of poverty measures. Econometrica 48.

Kakwani NC (1981a) Welfare measures: an international comparison. Journal of Development Economics 8.

Kakwani NC (1981b) Note on a new measure of poverty. Econometrica 49.

Kakwani NC (1984a) The relative deprivation curve and its applications. Journal of Business and Economic Statistics 2.

Kakwani NC (1984b) Welfare ranking of income distributions. Advances in econometrics 3.

Kakwani NC (1984c) Issues in measuring poverty. Advances in econometrics 3.

Kakwani NC (1985) Measurement of welfare with applications to Australia. Journal of Development Economics 18.

Kakwani NC (1986) Analyzing redistribution policies. Cambridge University Press, Cambridge.

Kakwani NC (1993) Statistical inference in the measurement of poverty. Review of Economics and Statistics 75.

Kakwani NC (1999) Inequality, welfare and poverty: three interrelated phenomena. In: Silber J (ed.) Handbook of income inequality measurement. Kluwer Academic, Boston.

Kakwani NC, Silber J (eds.) (2008) Quantitative approaches to multidimensional poverty measurement. Palgrave MacMillan, London.

Kanbur R (1984) The measurement and decomposition of inequality and poverty. In: van der Ploeg F (ed.) Mathematical methods in economics. Wiley, New York.

Kanbur R (1987) Transfer, targeting and poverty. Economic Policy 4.

Kanbur R (2001) Economic policy, distribution and poverty: the nature of disagreements. World Development 30.

Kats A (1972) On the social welfare function and the parameters of income distribution. Journal of Economic Theory 5.

Klassen S (2008) Poverty, under-nutrition and child mortality: some inter-regional puzzles and their implications for research and policy. Journal of Economic Inequality 6.

Knack S, Keefer P (2001) Polarization, politics and property rights: links between inequality and growth. World Bank.

Kolm SC (1969) The optimal production of social justice. In: Margolis J, Guitton H (eds.) Public economics. Macmillan, London.

Kolm SC (1976a) Unequal inequalities I. Journal of Economic Theory 12.

Kolm SC (1976b) Unequal inequalities II. Journal of Economic Theory 13.

Kolm SC (1977) Multidimensional egalitarianism. Quarterly Journal of Economics 91.

Kondor Y (1971) An old-new measure of income inequality. Econometrica 39.

Kondor Y (1975a) Value judgment implied by the use of various measures of income inequality. Review of Income and Wealth 21.

Kondor Y (1975b) The Gini coefficient of concentration and the Kuznets measure of inequality: a note. Review of Income and Wealth 21.

Koshevoy G (1995) Multivariate Lorenz majorization. Social Choice and Welfare 12.

Koshevoy G (1998) The Lorenz zonotope and multivariate majorizations. Social Choice and Welfare 15.

Koshevoy G, Mosler K (1996) The Lorenz zonoid of a multivariate distribution. Journal of the American Statistical Association 60.

Kosters M, Ross M (1988) A shrinking middle class? The Public Interest 90.

Kovacevic M, Binder D (1997) Variance estimation for measures of income inequality and polarization: the estimating equations approach. Journal of Official Statistics 13.

Krtscha M (1994) A new compromise measure of inequality. In: Eichhorn W (ed.) Models and measurement of welfare and inequality. Springer, Berlin Heidelberg.

Kuga K (1980) Gini index and the generalized entropy class: further results and a vindication. Economic Studies Quarterly 31.

Kundu A, Smith TE (1983) An impossibility theorem on poverty indices. International Economic Review 24.

Kurbayashi Y, Yatsuka A (1977) Redistribution of income and measures of income inequality. In: Fuji T, Sato R (eds.) Resource allocation and division of space. Springer-Verlag, New York.

Kurosaki T (2006) The measurement of transient poverty: theory and application to Pakistan. Journal of Economic Inequality 4.

Kuznets S (1963) Quantitative aspects of economic growth of nations: VIII, distribution of income by size. Economic Development and Cultural Change 11.

Lambert PJ (1985) Social welfare and the Gini coefficient revisited. Mathematical Social Sciences 9.

Lambert PJ (1992) Rich-to-poor income transfers: a generalization. Research on Economic Inequality 2.

Lambert PJ (2001) The distribution and redistribution of income. Manchester University Press, Manchester.

Lambert PJ, Aronson JR (1993) Inequality decomposition analysis and the Gini coefficient revisited. Economic Journal 103.

Lambert PJ, Lanza G (2006) The effect on inequality of changing one or two incomes. Journal of Economic Inequality 4.

Lambert PJ, Ramos X (2002) Welfare comparisons: sequential procedures for heterogeneous populations. Economica 69.

Lambert PJ, Yitzhaki S (1995) Equity, equality and welfare. European Economic Review 39.

Lambert PJ, Millimet DL, Slottje D (2003) Inequality aversion and the natural rate of subjective inequality. Journal of Public Economics 87.

Landsberger M, Meilijson I (1994) Comonotone allocations, Bickel-Lehmann dispersion and the Arrow-Pratt measure of risk aversion. Annals of Operation Research 52.

Lanzouw P, Ravallion M (1995) Poverty and household size. Economic Journal 105.

Lasso de la Vega MC, Urrutia AM (2006). An alternative formulation of the Esteban-Gradin-Ray extended measure of polarization. Journal of Income Distribution 15.

Lasso de la Vega MC, Urrutia AM (2008) The extended Atkinson family: the class of multiplicatively decomposable inequality measures and some new graphical procedures for analysis. Journal of Economic Inequality 6.

Lebreton M, Trannoy A (1987) Measures of inequality as an aggregation of individual preferences about income distribution: the Arrowian case. Journal of Economic Theory 41.

Lemmi A, Betti G (eds.) (2006) Fuzzy set approach to multidimensional poverty measurement. Springer-Verlag, New York.

Lerman RI, Yitzhaki S (1979) Income inequality effects by income source: a new approach and applications to the USA. Review of Economics and Statistics 67.

Lerman RI, Yitzhaki S (1985) A note on the calculation and interpretation of the Gini index. Review of Economics and Statistics 15.

Levy F, Murname RJ (1992) U.S. earnings levels and earnings inequality: a review of recent trends and proposed explanations. Journal of Economic Literature 30.
Lewis WG, Ulph D (1988) Poverty, inequality and welfare. Economic Journal 98.
Lipton M (1985) A problem in poverty measurement. Mathematical Social Sciences 10.
Lipton M, Ravallion M (1995) Poverty and policy. In: Behrman J, Srinivasan TN (eds.) Handbook of development economics, Vol. 3. North-Holland, Amsterdam.
List C (1999) Multidimensional inequality measurement. Nuffield College, Oxford.
Lokshin M, Ravallion M (2006) On the consistency of poverty lines. In: de Janvry A, Kanbur R (eds.) Poverty, inequality and development: essays in Honor of Erik Thorbecke. Springer, New York.
Love R, Wolfson MC (1976) Income inequality: statistical methodology and Canadian illustrations. Statistics Canada, Ottawa.
Lugo AM (2005) Comparing multidimensional indices of inequality. ECINEQ Working Paper No. 2005-14.
Lugo AM, Maasoumi E (2008a) The information basis of multivariate poverty assessments. In: Kakwani NC, Silber J (eds.) Quantitative approaches to multidimensional poverty measurement. Palgrave MacMillan, London.
Lugo AM, Maasoumi E (2008b) Multidimensional poverty measures from an information theory perspective. ECINEQ Working Paper No. 2008-85.
Maasoumi E (1986) The measurement and decomposition of multidimensional inequality. Econometrica 54.
Maasoumi E (1989a) Composite indices of income and other developmental indicators: a general approach. Research on Economic Inequality 1.
Maasoumi E (1989b) Continuously distributed attributes and measures of multivariate inequality. Journal of Econometrics 42.
Maasoumi E (1999) Multidimensional approaches to welfare analysis. In: Silber J (ed.) Handbook of income inequality measurement. Kluwer Academic, Boston.
Maasoumi E, Nickelsburg G (1988) Multivariate measures of well-being and an analysis of inequality in the Michigan data. Journal of Business and Economic Statistics 6.
Mack J, Lindsay S (1985) Poor Britain. George Allen and Unwin, London.
Maiti P (1998) Studies on absolute level of living and poverty in India. In: Chakravarty SR, Coondoo D, Mukherjee R (eds.) Quantitative economics: theory and practice, essays in honor of N. Bhattacharya. Allied, New Delhi.
Marshall AW, Olkin I (1979) Inequalities: theory of majorization and its applications. Academic Press, New York.
Marshall AW, Olkin I, Proschan P (1967) Monotonicity of ratios of means and other applications of majorizations. In: Shisha O (ed.) Inequalities. Academic Press, New York.
McKay A, Lawson D (2003) Assessing the extent and nature of chronic poverty in low income countries: issues and evidence. World Development 31.
McMahon PJ, Tsechetter JH (1986) The declining middle class: a further analysis. Monthly Labour Review 109.
Mehran F (1975) A statistical analysis of income inequality based on a decomposition of the Gini index. Bulletin of the International Statistical Institute 46.
Mehran F (1976) Linear measures of income inequality. Econometrica 44.
Mehta AK, Shah A (2003) Chronic poverty in India: incidence, causes and policies. World Development 31.
Mehta AK, Shepherd A (eds.) (2006) Chronic poverty and development policy in India. Sage, New Delhi.
Milanovic B (2000) A new polarization measure and some applications. World Bank.
Mookherjee D, Shorrocks AF (1982) A decomposition analysis of the trend in UK income inequality. Economic Journal 92.
Moore RE (1996) Ranking income distributions using the geometric mean and a related general measure. Southern Economic Journal 63.
Morduch J (1994) Poverty and vulnerability. American Economic Review 84.

Morris M, Bernhart A, Handcock MS (1994) Economic inequality: new methods for new trends. American Sociological Review 59.

Mosler K (2004) Restricted Lorenz dominance of economic inequality in one or many dimensions. Journal of Economic Inequality 2.

Mosler K, Muliere P (1996) Inequality indices and the star shaped principle of transfers. Statistical Papers 37.

Moyes P (1987) A new concept of Lorenz domination. Economics Letters 23.

Moyes P (1988) A note on minimally progressive taxation and absolute income inequality. Social Choice and Welfare 5.

Moyes P (1989) Some classes of functions that preserve the inequality and welfare orderings of income distributions. Journal of Economic Theory 49.

Moyes P (1994) Inequality reducing and inequality preserving transformations of incomes: symmetric and individualistic transformations. Journal of Economic Theory 63.

Moyes P (1999) Stochastic Dominance and the Lorenz Curve. In: Silber J (ed.) Handbook of income inequality measurement. Kluwer, Boston.

Moyes P (2007) An extended Gini approach to inequality measurement. Journal of Economic Inequality 5.

Muellbauer J (1974) Inequality measures, prices and household composition. Review of Economic Studies 41.

Muirhead RF (1903) Some methods applicable to identities and inequalities of symmetric algebraic functions of n letters. Proceedings of Edinburgh Mathematical Society 21.

Muliere P, Scarsini NM (1989) A note on stochastic dominance and inequality measures. Journal of Economic Theory 49.

Naga RHA, Geoffard P-Y (2006) Decomposition of bivariate inequality indices by attributes. Economics Letters 90.

Newbery DMG (1970) A theorem on the measurement of inequality. Journal of Economic Theory 2.

Nygard F, Sandstrom A (1981) Measuring income inequality. Almqvist and Wicksell International, Stockholm.

Ok E (1995) Fuzzy measurement and income inequality: a class of fuzzy inequality measures. Social Choice and Welfare 12.

Ok E (1996) Fuzzy measurement of income inequality: some possibility results on the fuzzification of the Lorenz ordering. Economic Theory 7.

Ok E, Lambert PJ (1999) On evaluating social welfare by sequential generalized Lorenz dominance. Economics Letters 63.

Osberg L (2000) Poverty in Canada and the United States: measurement, trends, and implications. Canadian Journal of Economics 33.

Osmani SR (1982) Economic inequality and group welfare: a theory of comparison with application to Bangladesh. Clarendon Press, Oxford.

Paglin M (1975) The measurement and trend of inequality: a basic revision. American Economic Review 65.

Parfit D (1984) Reasons and persons. Oxford University Press, Oxford.

Pattanaik P, Sengupta M (1995) An alternative axiomatization of Sen's poverty measure. Review of Income and Wealth 41.

Paul S (1989) A model of constructing the poverty line. Journal of Development Economics 30.

Paul S (2004) Income sources effects on inequality. Journal of Development Economics 73.

Pigou AC (1912) Wealth and welfare. Macmillan, London.

Pollak RA (1971) Additive utility functions and linear Engel curves. Review of Economic Studies 38.

Pradhan M, Ravallion M (2000) Measuring poverty using qualitative perceptions of consumption adequacy. Review of Economics and Statistics 82.

Pratt JW (1964) Risk aversion in small and large. Econometrica 32.

Pressman S (2001) The decline of the middle class: an international perspective. Luxembourg Income Study Working Paper Series No. 280, Economics and Finance Faculty, Monmouth University.
Preston I (1990) Ratios, differences and inequality indices. IFS Working Paper No. W 90–99.
Pyatt G (1976) On the interpretation and disaggregation of Gini coefficients. Economic Journal 68.
Pyatt G (1987) Measuring welfare, poverty and inequality. Economic Journal 97.
Pyatt G (1990) Social evaluation criteria. In: Dagum C, Zenga M (eds.) Income and. wealth distribution, inequality and poverty. Springer, Berlin, Heidelberg.
Pyatt G, Chen C, Fei JCH (1980) The distribution of income by factor components. Quarterly Journal of Economics 95.
Qizilbash M (2003) Vague language and precise measurement: the case of poverty. Journal of Economic Methodology 10.
Qizilbash M (2006) Philosophical accounts of vagueness, fuzzy poverty measures and multidimensionality. In Lemmi A, Betti G (eds.) Fuzzy set approach to multidimensional poverty measurement. Springer-Verlag, New York.
Quah D (1997) Empirics for growth and distribution: stratification, polarization and convergence clubs. Journal of Economic Growth 2.
Quiggin J (1993) Generalized expected utility theory: the rank-dependent model. Kluwer, Boston.
Ramos HM, Ollero J, Sordo MA (2000) A sufficient condition for generalized Lorenz order. Journal of Economic Theory 90.
Ravallion M (1988) Expected poverty under risk-induced welfare variability. Economic Journal 98.
Ravallion M (1990) Income effects on nutrition. Economic Development and Cultural Change 38.
Ravallion M (1992) On 'Hunger and public action': a review article on the book by J. Dreze and A. K. Sen. World Bank Research Observer 7.
Ravallion M (1994a) Poverty comparisons. Routledge, London.
Ravallion M (1994b) Measuring social welfare with and wiyhout poverty lines. American Economic Review 84.
Ravallion M (1996) Issues in measuring and modeling poverty. Economic Journal 106.
Ravallion M (2005) A poverty-inequality trade off. Journal of Economic Inequality 3.
Ravallion M (2007) Poverty lines. In: Blume L, Durlauf S (eds.) The new Palgrave dictionary of economics. Palgrave Macmillan, London.
Rawls J (1971) A theory of justice. Harvard University Press, Cambridge.
Reynal-Querol M (2002) Ethnicity, political systems and civil wars. Journal of Conflict Resolution 46.
Rodgers JR, Rodgers JL (2006) Chronic and transitory poverty in Australia. University of Wollongong, Australia.
Rodriguez J, Salas R (2003) Extended bipolarization and inequality measures. Research on Economic Inequality 9.
Roemer JE (1985) Equality of talent. Economics and Philosophy 1.
Roemer JE (1996) Theories of distributive justice. Harvard University Press, Cambridge.
Rosenbluth G (1951) Note on Mr. Schutz's measure of inequality. American Economic Review 41.
Rosenthal NH (1985) The shrinking middle class: myth or reality? Monthly Labour Review 108.
Rothschild M, Stiglitz JE (1970) Increasing risk I: a definition. Journal of Economic Theory 2.
Rothschild M, Stiglitz JE (1973) Some further results on the measurement of inequality. Journal of Economic Theory 6.
Rudin W (1976) Principles of mathematical analysis. McGraw Hill, London.
Runciman WG (1966) Relative deprivation and social justice. Routledge, London.
Russell RR (1985) Decomposable inequality measures. Review of Economic Studies 52.
Salas R (1997) Welfare-consistent inequality indices in changing populations: the marginal population replication axiom, a note. Journal of Public Economics 67.
Saposnik R (1981) Rank dominance in income distribution. Public Choice 36.
Saposnik R (1983) On evaluating income distributions: the Suppes–Sen grading principle of justice and Pareto optimality. Public Choice 40.
Sastre M, Trannoy A (2001) Shapley inequality decomposition by factor components: some methodological issues. Journal of Economics (Suppl. 9).

Sastry DVS, Kelkar UR (1994) Note on the decomposition of Gini inequality. Review of Economics and Statistics 76.
Satchell SE (1987) Source and subgroup decomposition inequalities for the Lorenz curve. International Economic Review 28.
Satt E (1996) Relative deprivation in the kibbutz economy: an exploration of the concepts of equality and equity. Economica 63.
Savaglio E (2006a) Three approaches to the analysis of multidimensional inequality. In: Farina F, Savaglio G (eds.) Inequality and economic integration. Routledge, London.
Savaglio E (2006b) Multidimensional inequality with variable population size. Economic Theory 28.
Schluter C, Trede M (2002) Statistical inference for inequality and poverty measurement with dependent data. International Economic Review 43.
Schutz RR (1951) On the measurement of income inequality. American Economic Review 41.
Seidl C (1988) Poverty measurement: a survey. In: Bos D, Rose M, Seidl C (eds.) Welfare and efficiency in public economics. Springer-Verlag, New York.
Seidl C, Pfingsten A (1997) Ray invariant inequality measures. Research on Economic Inequality 7.
Sen AK (1973) On economic inequality. Clarendon Press, Oxford.
Sen AK (1974) Informational basis of alternative welfare approaches: aggregation and income distribution. Journal of Public Economics 3.
Sen AK (1976a) Poverty: an ordinal approach to measurement. Econometrica 44.
Sen AK (1976b) Real national income. Review of Economic Studies 43.
Sen AK (1978) Ethical measurement of inequality: some difficulties. In: Krelle W, Shorrocks AF (eds.) Personal income distribution. North-Holland, Amsterdam.
Sen AK (1979) Issues in the measurement of poverty. Scandinavian Journal of Economics 81.
Sen AK (1981) Poverty and famines. Clarendon Press, Oxford.
Sen AK (1982) Choice, welfare and measurement. Blackwell, Oxford.
Sen AK (1983) Poor, relatively speaking. Oxford Economic Papers 35.
Sen AK (1985a) Commodities and capabilities. North Holland, Amsterdam.
Sen AK (1985b) A sociological approach to the measurement of poverty: a reply to Professor Peter Townsend. Oxford Economic Papers 37.
Sen AK (1987) On ethics and economics. Blackwell, Oxford.
Sen AK (1992) Inequality re-examined. Harvard University Press, Cambridge.
Sen AK (1999) Development as freedom. Oxford University Press, Oxford.
Sen AK (2000) Social exclusion: concept, application, and security. Asian Development Bank, Manila.
Sen AK (2002) Rationality and freedom. Harvard University Press, Cambridge.
Sharma S (2004) Poverty estimates in India: some key issues. Asian Development Bank, Manila.
Sheshinski E (1972) Relation between a social welfare and the Gini index of inequality. Journal of Economic Theory 4.
Sheshinski E, Weiss Y (1982) Inequality within and between families. Journal of Political Economy 90.
Shorrocks AF (1980) The class of additively decomposable inequality measures. Econometrica 48.
Shorrocks AF (1982a) On the distance between income distributions. Econometrica 50.
Shorrocks AF (1982b) Inequality decomposition by factor components. Econometrica 50.
Shorrocks AF (1983a) Ranking income distributions. Economica 50.
Shorrocks AF (1983b) The impact of income components on the distribution of family incomes. Quarterly Journal of Economics 98.
Shorrocks AF (1984) Inequality decomposition by population subgroups. Ecomometrica 52.
Shorrocks AF (1988) Aggregation issues in inequality. In: Eichhorn W (ed.) Measurement in economics. Springer-Verlag, New York.
Shorrocks AF (1995) Revisiting the Sen poverty index. Econometrica 63.
Shorrocks AF (1998) Deprivation profiles and deprivation indices. In: Jenkins SP, Kapteyn A, van Praag BMS (eds.) The distributions of welfare and household production: international perspective. Cambridge University Press, Cambridge.

Shorrocks AF (2004) Inequality and welfare evaluation of heterogeneous income distribution. Journal of Economic Inequality 2.

Shorrocks AF, Foster JE (1987) Transfer sensitive inequality measures. Review of Economic Studies 54.

Silber J (1989) Factor components, population subgroups and the computation of the Gini index of inequality. Review of Economics and Statistics 71.

Silber J (1993) Inequality decomposition by income. Review of Economics and Statistics 75.

Silber J (ed.) (1999) Handbook of income inequality measurement. Kluwer, Boston.

Silber J (2004) Inequalities: theory, experiments and applications. European Journal of Political Economy 20.

Silber J, Deutsch J, Hanoka M (2007) On the link between the concepts of kurtosis and bipolarization. Economics Bulletin 4.

Slesnick DJ (1989) Specific egalitarianism and total welfare inequality: a decomposition analysis. Review of Economics and Statistics 71.

Slesnick DJ (1993) Gaining ground: poverty in the postwar United States. Journal of Political Economy 101.

Slesnick DJ (1994) Consumption, needs and inequality. International Economic Review 35.

Slottje DJ (1989) The structure of earnings and the measurement of income inequality in the US. Elsevier Science, New York.

Son HH (2003) A new poverty decomposition. Journal of Economic Inequality 1.

Spencer B, Fisher S (1992) On comparing distributions of poverty gaps. Sankhya, The Indian Journal of Statistics B 54.

Squire L (1993) Fighting poverty. American Economic Review 83.

Stark O, Yitzhaki S (1988) Labor migration as a response to relative deprivation. Journal of Population Economics 1.

Streeten P (1981) First things first: meeting basic human needs in developing countries. Oxford University Press, Oxford.

Subramanian S (1987) A simple transfer sensitive index of inequality. Economics letters 23.

Subramanian S (2002) Counting the poor: an elementary difficulty in the measurement of poverty. Economics and Philosophy 18.

Subramanian S (2006) Rights, deprivation, and disparity: essays in concepts and measurement. Oxford University press, New Delhi.

Suppes P (1977) The distributive justice of income inequality. Erkenntnis 11.

Suppes P (1988) Lorenz curves for various processes: a pluralistic approach. Social Choice and Welfare 5.

Szal R, Robinson S (1977) Measuring income inequality. In: Frank CR, Webb RC (eds.) Income distribution in less developed countries. Brookings Institution, Washington, DC.

Takayama N (1979) Poverty, income inequality and their measures: Professor Sen's axiomatic approach reconsidered. Econometrica 47.

Tam M-YS, Zhang R (1996) Ranking income distributions: the trade off between efficiency and equality. Economica 63.

Temkin L (1986) Inequality. Philosophy and Public Affairs 15.

Temkin L (1993) Inequality. Oxford University Press, Oxford.

Theil H (1967) Economics and information theory. North-Holland, Amsterdam.

Theil H (1972) Statistical decomposition analysis. North-Holland, Amsterdam.

Thistle PD (1989) Ranking distributions with generalized Lorenz curves. Southern Economic Journal 56.

Thistle PD (1994) On Atkinson's index and consensus in rankings of income distributions. In: Eichhorn W (ed.) Models and measurement of welfare and inequality. Springer-Verlag, Heidelberg.

Thon D (1979) On measuring poverty. Review of Income and Wealth 25.

Thon D (1981) Income inequality and poverty: some problems. Review of Income and Wealth 27.

Thon D (1982) An axiomatization of the Gini coefficient. Mathematical Social Sciences 2.

Thon D (1983a) A poverty measure. Indian Economic Journal 30.

Thon D (1983b) A note on a troublesome axiom for poverty indices. Economic Journal 93.
Thon D, Wallace S (2004) Dalton transfers, inequality and altruism. Social Choice and Welfare 22.
Thorbecke E (2006) Multidimensional poverty: concepts and measures. Paper presented at Many Dimensions of Poverty conference, Brasilia.
Thurow L (1984, February 5) The disappearance of the middle class. New York Times.
Tobin J (1971) On limiting the domain of inequality. Journal of Law and Economics 13.
Townsend P (1979) Poverty in the United Kingdom. Penguin, Harmondsworth.
Townsend P (1985) A sociological approach to the measurement of poverty: a rejoinder to Professor Amartya Sen. Oxford Economic Papers 3.
Toyoda T (1980) Decomposability of inequality measures. Economic Studies Quarterly 31.
Trannoy A (1986) On Thon's axiomatization of the Gini index. Mathematical Social Sciences 11.
Trannoy A (2003) About the right weights of the social welfare function when needs differ. Economics letters 81.
Tsakloglou P (1993) Aspects of inequality in Greece: measurement, decomposition and intertemporal change: 1974, 1982. Journal of Development Economics 40.
Tsui K-Y (1995) Multidimensional generalizations of the relative and absolute inequality indices: the Atkinson–Kolm–Sen approach. Journal of Economic Theory 67.
Tsui K-Y (1996) Growth-equity decomposition of a change in poverty: an axiomatic approach. Economics Letters 50.
Tsui K-Y (1999) Multidimensional inequality and multidimensional generalized entropy measures: an axiomatic derivation. Social Choice and Welfare 16.
Tsui K-Y (2002) Multidimensional poverty indices. Social Choice and Welfare 19.
Tsui K-Y, Wang Y-Q (2000) A new class of deprivation- based generalized Gini indices. Economic Theory 16.
Tungodden B (2005) Poverty measurement: the critical comparison value. Social Choice and Welfare 25.
UNDP (1990, 1997) Human development report. Oxford University Press, Oxford.
Varian HR (1974) Equity, envy and efficiency. Journal of Economic Theory 9.
Vaughan R (1987) Welfare approaches to the measurement of poverty. Economic Journal 98.
Wang Y-Q, Tsui K-Y (2000) Polarization orderings and new classes of polarization indices. Journal of Public Economic Theory 2.
Watts H (1968) An economic definition of poverty. In: Moynihan DP (ed.) On understanding poverty. Basic Books, New York.
Weiss Y, Fershatman C (1998) Social status and economic performance. European Economic Review 42.
Weymark JA (1981) Generalized Gini inequality indices. Mathematical Social Sciences 1.
Weymark JA (1995) An alternative proof of Ben Porath and Gilboa's proof of generalized Gini characterization theorem. Journal of Economic Theory 66.
Weymark JA (1999) Comment on Blackorby et al. (1999). In: Silber J (ed.) Handbook on income inequality measurement. Kluwer, Boston.
Weymark JA (2006) The normative approaches to the measurement of multidimensional inequality. In: Farina F, Savaglio E (eds.) Inequality and economic integration. Routledge, London.
Whitmore GA (1970) Third degree stochastic dominance. American Economic Review 24.
Wolfson MC (1994) When inequalities diverge. American Economic Review 84.
Wolfson MC (1997) Divergent inequalities: theory and empirical results. Review of Income and Wealth 43.
Xu K, Osberg L (1998) A distribution-free test for deprivation dominance. Econometric Reviews 17.
Xu K, Osberg L (2001) How to decompose the Sen–Shorrocks–Thon poverty index? A practitioner's guide. Journal of Income Distribution 10.
Xu K, Osberg L (2002) The social welfare implications, decomposability and geometry of the Sen family of poverty indices. Canadian Journal of Economics 35.
Yaari M (1987) The dual theory of choice under risk. Econometrica 55.
Yaari M (1988) A controversial proposal concerning inequality measurement. Journal of Economic Theory 44.

Yaqub S (2000a) Intertemporal welfare dynamics: extent and causes. In: Globalization, new opportunities, new vulnerabilities workshop. Brookings Institute.

Yaqub S (2000b) Chronic poverty: scrutinizing estimates, patterns, correlates and explanations. University of Manchester, UK.

Yitzhaki S (1979) Relative deprivation and the Gini coefficient. Quarterly Journal of Economics 93.

Yitzhaki S (1982a) Relative deprivation and economic welfare. European Economic Review 17.

Yitzhaki S (1982b) Stochastic dominance, mean variance and Gini's mean difference. American Economic Review 72.

Yitzhaki S (1983) On an extension of the Gini inequality index. International Economic Review 24.

Yitzhaki S (1998) More than a dozen alternative ways of spelling Gini. Research on Economic Inequality 8.

Yitzhaki S (1999) Necessary and sufficient conditions for dominance using generalized Lorenz curves. In: Slottje DJ (ed.) Advances in econometrics, income distribution and scientific methodology: essays in honor of Camilo Dagum. Physica-Verlag, Heidelberg.

Yitzhaki S (2002) Do we need a separate poverty measurement? European Journal of Political Economy 18.

Yntema DB (1933) Measures of inequality in the personal distribution of wealth and income. Journal of the American Statistical Association 28.

Yoshida T (2005) Social welfare rankings of income distributions: a new parametric concept of intermediate inequality. Social Choice and Welfare 24.

Young HP (1994) Equity in theory and practice. Princeton University Press, New Jersey.

Zagier D (1983) Inequalities for the Gini coefficient of the composite population. Journal of Mathematical Economics 12.

Zhang X, Kanbur R (2001) What differences do polarization measures make? An application to China. Journal of Development Studies 37.

Zheng B (1993) An axiomatic characterization of the Watts poverty measure. Economics Letters 42.

Zheng B (1994) Can a poverty index be both relative and absolute ? Econometrica 62.

Zheng B (1997) Aggregate poverty measures. Journal of Economic Surveys 11.

Zheng B (1999) On the power of poverty orderings. Social Choice and Welfare 16.

Zheng B (2000a) Minimum distribution-sensitivity, poverty aversion and poverty orderings. Journal of Economic Theory 95.

Zheng B (2000b) Poverty orderings: a review. Journal of Economic Surveys 14.

Zheng B (2001) Poverty orderings: a graphical illustration. Social Choice and Welfare 18.

Zheng B (2002) Testing Lorenz curves with non-simple random samples. Econometrica 70.

Zheng B (2004) On intermediate measures of inequality. Research on Economic Inequality 12.

Zheng B (2007a) Unit- consistent decomposable inequality measures. Economica 74.

Zheng B (2007b) Utility-gap dominances and inequality orderings. Social Choice and Welfare 28.

Zheng B (2007c) Unit-consistent poverty indices. Economic Theory 31.

Zheng B (2007d) Inequality orderings and unit consistency. Social Choice and Welfare 29.

Zoli C (1999a) A generalized version of the inequality invariance criterion: a surplus sharing characterization, complete and partial orderings. In: Swart H De (ed.) Logic, game theory and social choice. Tilburg University Press, Tilburg.

Zoli C (1999b) Intersecting generalized Lorenz curves and the Gini index. Social Choice and Welfare 16.

Zoli C (2000) Inverse sequential stochastic dominance, rank-dependent welfare, deprivation and poverty measurement. University of Nottingham, UK.

Zoli C (2002) Inverse stochastic dominance, inequality measurement and Gini indices. Journal of Economics (Suppl. 9).

Zoli C (2003) Characterizing inequality equivalence criteria. Presented at the conference on inequality, poverty and human well Being, WIDER, Helsinki.

Zoli C, Lambert PJ (2005) Sequential procedures for poverty gap dominance. University of Oregon, Eugene, OR.

Glossary of Notation

N: Set of positive integers/natural numbers

1^n: n-coordinated vector of ones

R^n_+: Nonnegative orthant of the n-dimensional Euclidean space R^n

$\hat{R}^n_+$: $\{x \in R^n_+ : x_1 \le x_2 \le \ldots \le x_n\}$

Γ^n: R^n_+ with the origin deleted

D^n: $\{x \in \Gamma^n : x_1 \le x_2 \le \ldots \le x_n\}$

Γ^n_+, D^n_+: Positive parts of Γ^n and D^n respectively

$\hat{R}_+$: $\bigcup_{n \in N} \hat{R}^n_+$, Γ : $\bigcup_{n \in N} \Gamma^n$, D : $\bigcup_{n \in N} D^n$, Γ_+ : $\bigcup_{n \in N} \Gamma^n_+$, D_+ : $\bigcup_{n \in N} D^n_+$, R_+ : $\bigcup_{n \in N} R^n_+$

λ: Mean income, m: Median income

W: Social welfare function, Ξ: Abbreviated or reduced form welfare function

$E(x)$: Atkinson-Kolm-Sen representative income corresponding to the income distribution x

z: Poverty line, $\underline{z} = (z_1, z_2, .., z_d)$: Vector of poverty thresholds

x^*: Censored income distribution corresponding to the distribution x

$\ge_{\mathrm{LC}}$: Lorenz dominance, $\ge_{\mathrm{GL}}$: Generalized Lorenz dominance

$\ge_{\mathrm{PG}}$: Poverty gap profile dominance

$\ge_{\mathrm{AD}}$: Absolute deprivation dominance, $\ge_{\mathrm{RD}}$: Relative deprivation dominance

$\ge_{\mathrm{RS}}$: Relative satisfaction dominance, $\ge_{\mathrm{GS}}$: Generalized satisfaction dominance

$\ge_{\mathrm{AC}}$: Absolute contentment dominance, $\ge_{\mathrm{RC}}$: Relative contentment dominance

$\ge_{\mathrm{ADI}}$: Absolute differentials dominance, $\ge_{\mathrm{RDI}}$: Ratio differentials dominance

$\geq_{LU}$: Look-up dominance, $\geq_{LD}$: Look-down dominance

$\geq_{CC}$: Complaint dominance

$\geq_{RB}$: Relative bipolarization dominance

Index

MIX
Papier aus verantwortungsvollen Quellen
Paper from responsible sources
FSC® C105338

If you have any concerns about our products,
you can contact us on
ProductSafety@springernature.com

In case Publisher is established outside the EU,
the EU authorized representative is:
Springer Nature Customer Service Center GmbH
Europaplatz 3, 69115 Heidelberg, Germany

Printed by Libri Plureos GmbH
in Hamburg, Germany